CW01329464

FRANK TYSON
THE CRICKET COACHING MANUAL

PELHAM BOOKS
London

First published in Great Britain by
Pelham Books Ltd
44 Bedford Square
London WC1B 3DP
1986

First published in Australia by
Thomas Nelson Australia
480 La Trobe Street Melbourne Victoria 3000
1985
Copyright © The Victorian Cricket Association 1985

Some parts of this work originally
appeared in Frank Tyson's *Complete
Cricket Coaching Illustrated* (Nelson,
1976 and Pelham, 1977)

ISBN 0 7207 1653 5

Typeset in Plantin by Abb-typesetting Pty Ltd, Melbourne
Printed in Australia by Impact Printing

Contents

Foreword by Keith Andrew	v
Acknowledgements	vi
Introduction	vii
The coach	1
The elementary skills	6
BATTING	**9**
Preparations for batting	10
The front-foot drive	14
Variations on the front-foot drive	17
The forward defensive stroke	22
The leg glance off the front foot	24
The sweep	26
Detection and correction of faults in front-foot strokes	28
The back-foot drive	38
Variations on the back-foot drive	40
The back-foot defensive shot	43
The leg glance off the back foot	45
The square cut	47
The late cut	49
The pull	51
The hook	53
Detection and correction of faults in back-foot strokes	55
Running between the wickets	67
BOWLING	**71**
Bowling: the run-up	72
The basic action	75
The outswinger	79
The off cutter	82
The off spinner and its variations	84
The right-handed wrist-spun leg spinner and its variations	89
The inswinger	94

The leg cutter	97
Bowling tactics	100
Detection and correction of faults in the run-up and basic bowling action	102
Wicketkeeping	107
FIELDING	115
Basic principles of fielding	116
The attacking outfielder	124
The defending outfielder	127
The close-to-the-wicket fielder	129
Detection and correction of faults in fielding	132
Physical fitness for cricket	136
Captaincy	157
Modified cricket	163
The Laws of Cricket and their interpretation	167
Index	205

Foreword

Both Lancastrians, Frank Tyson and I first played cricket together in the 1940s for Middleton and Werneth in the Central Lancashire League. I think we were both sixteen. Just after the war, league cricket was at its strongest, supported by large crowds and with a high calibre Test player in nearly every team. Winning cricket matches was the most important thing in our young lives.

My clearest memory of Frank in those days was not so much his fast bowling, but his Middleton Grammar School cap. It was the brightest scarlet I had ever seen and no matter at what angle, or how carefully it was initially set, the peak always finished up pointing over his left ear! Cricket in the league was a hard game, but fair, and a marvellous apprenticeship for any young player.

We learned well and in the early 1950s, through the combined efforts of Ken Turner, Jock Livingston and Jack Mercer, we joined the staff of Northamptonshire C.C.C., England's smallest first-class county. In 1954 we became the first ever professionals from the county to be selected to tour Australia with the M.C.C. This was Len Hutton's tour, but Frank had phenomenal success, as he became 'Typhoon Tyson', one of, if not, the fastest bowlers ever. It was a tour of destiny in more ways than one, as he married an Australian girl and raised a family in the sun.

Thirty-plus years on, Frank and I are still the best of pals. Of all the people most deeply involved in cricket, and coaching in particular, what a coincidence it is that we two share a similar role, Frank in Australia, myself in England. Those 'discussions' we had in countless cricketing hideaways must have been more potent than we thought! Maybe they have contributed in some small way to this marvellous book. I should like to think so, but really it is all Tyson — erudite, thorough and, like his bowling, something special to make you sit up and take notice.

As I expected, this new edition up-dates many aspects of coaching that I know are near to Frank's heart and, in fact, are becoming increasingly significant in successful performance. I think particularly of the way in which Frank has linked physical fitness with skill, and as an academic himself, he has presented both text and diagrams in a way that the educationalist will appreciate. This is not a book for skimming through; it needs to be studied thoroughly, just as it has been written. Only then will it give of its best — and its best is very, very good for cricketers everywhere.

What happy memories I have as I read Frank's writings and listen to his incisive commentaries from across the world. On some summer days, I can still see his splay-footed run-up and the ball rocketing towards me ... even his scarlet cap!

K.V. Andrew
Director of Coaching
National Cricket Association
Lord's Cricket Ground

Acknowledgements

The author, the publisher and the Victorian Cricket Association gratefully thank all those who contributed ideas and assistance for the previous book on which this one is based, *Complete Cricket Coaching*, and express particular gratitude to the following people who have lent their expertise, technical support and physical help to the production of this new manual: Peter Burke (Victoria College, Rusden Campus), Gerard Cramer (Carey Baptist Grammar School), Simon Davis (Victoria), Ken Davis (Deakin University), Michael Dimattina (Victoria), John Emburey (Middlesex and England), John Harmer (Victoria College, Burwood Campus), John Harris (Bendigo College of Advanced Education), Bronwyn Jones (Victorian Women's Cricket Association), Dean Jones (Australia and Victoria), Dr John Lill (Melbourne Cricket Club), Dr Lewis McGill (Tasmanian College of Advanced Education), Simon O'Donnell (Australia and Victoria), Abdul Qadir (Pakistan), Bill Smyth (VCA Umpires' Adviser) and Philip Tyson (photographer). Our special thanks to John Harris and to Peter Burke for their help with the fielding, activities and physical fitness sections and with checking the book at every stage.

The Laws of Cricket are reproduced by permission of the Marylebone Cricket Club, Lord's Ground, London.

The author, the publisher and the Victorian Cricket Association also gratefully acknowledge the sponsorship of the Shell Company of Australia Limited in the production of this manual.

Introduction

Since my book COMPLETE CRICKET COACHING was first published in 1976, the teaching and learning of cricket competence has undergone a minor revolution. There is now, for instance, a far greater appreciation amongst coaches and players at all levels of the importance of pre-season fitness training, physical preparation for competition and pre-match warm-up procedures. Coaches have come to the realisation that in order to trace faults in technique and to cure them, they must acquire a working knowledge of scientific reasons behind skills and develop an analytical method of stroke or delivery. Cricketers and coaches alike are now fully aware of the importance of going into a game in a positive frame of mind and consciously cultivate psychological ploys such as goal-setting, positive imagery and mental rehearsal. Coaches now know that it is of great significance to the athletes — in terms of player rehabilitation — and to him or herself — in terms of exploiting potential to the fullest — to acquire a working knowledge of sports medicine and emergency first-aid procedures. The whole spectrum of skill acquisition has been transformed — not only because of modern methods of instruction: vide the National Cricket Association's instructional video tape 'This Game of Cricket'. One could go on *ad infinitum* cataloguing areas of learning and coaching in which the ten years have seen a greater acceptance amongst cricketers of the work of the sports scientists. It is this augmentation of our cricketing knowledge which convinced me that the time was ripe to revise COMPLETE CRICKET COACHING incorporating the advances in learning and coaching which have occurred in the last decade.

My major goals are to teach coaches of cricket how to coach, and to explain the skills of cricket in terms which are understandable to the expert player and the beginner alike. The CRICKET COACHING MANUAL is a coaching book for advanced coaches and at the same time is still oriented towards youngsters who can pick it up to learn from simple instructions why, when and how to perform cricket skills.

The manual is based on modern coaching methods and the practical cricket skills which have evolved from the experience of generations of cricketers past. The sections dealing with the detection and correction of faults are greatly expanded in comparison with those in COMPLETE CRICKET COACHING. I have explored the scientific reasons behind an individual's performance, so that both the player and the coach may systematically analyse the desirable and the actual performances, compare them, and remedy faults which occur in the skills. Coaching methods, physical preparation for practice and competition, fielding techniques and motivational activities have also been more thoroughly covered than before with the inclusion of a wider range of group activities for practice, fitness procedures more specific to cricket, more detailed descriptions of the fielding skills, and a greater selection of modified games for both seniors and juniors. Theoretical and practical aspects of cricket are blended in a harmonious mix of description of skills, the reasons behind them, and a programme of practice drills.

Each lesson is devoted to a single cricket skill, and is presented in such a way as to help the coach motivate the player by first explaining the reason behind the performance. After the 'why' and 'wherefore' comes the 'when' and 'how' of carrying out the skill. Describing the appropriate time to execute a particular stroke, bowl a specific ball or carry out a fielding or wicketkeeping skill may not enable players to overcome a lack of ball sense, but it provides them with a livelier appreciation of when to perform a skill, an appreciation which will eventually increase their capacity to match the skill with the right moment. A greater knowledge of how a skill is performed will, with a commensurate amount of practice, help players improve their motor performance. Every skill is carefully illustrated by photographs of contemporary players, and the range of pictorial descriptions has been greatly expanded from the previous book. The photographs also reflect the greater interest and increased participation of ladies in cricket, an interest and participation which has moved me to write this manual in terms applicable to both sexes. Thus 'batsmen' and 'fieldsmen' are referred to in this manual as 'batters' and 'fielders'.

The skill section of each lesson is immediately followed by practice activities, which enables coach and player to treat each segment as a complete learning, teaching and practice unit, whether for a club or an individual. Exact specifications for the lay-out of group activities are given, together with the space and equipment needed to carry out the drills. At the end of each skill segment is a checklist of the component parts of the performance set out in chronological order and reduced to abbreviated, simple and general terms. These checklists are intended to help younger players understand the general descriptions of the skill and to act as an aide-mémoire for coach and player alike. They have been tabulated to correspond with the more detailed descriptions of the segments of the skill given in the preceding text. I have emphasised throughout the importance of balance, of keeping one's eye on the ball and of presenting the hitting surface to the ball as effectively as possible.

To sum up, I have tried to systematise and simplify the learning of cricket skills, and to synthesise all the elements of the art of coaching. Above all, I have tried to promote the concept that the coaching and learning of cricket skills is fun.

Frank Tyson
Director of Coaching
Victorian Cricket Association

The coach

The cricket coach's primary goal is to improve the player's technical skills and tactical knowledge of the game and, through this increased proficiency, to increase enjoyment and the ability to participate. So the coach requires, beyond a knowledge about the game, an ability to communicate both that knowledge and enthusiasm for cricket. The coach's functions could be summed up as:
- Encouraging the players to enjoy the game
- Giving players knowledge about the game
- Enabling players to win
- Improving individuals' performances.

Coaching styles may differ. Some coaches may be authoritarian ('Play the forward defensive stroke as I show you'); some may teach by setting tasks ('Bowl eight balls short of a length outside the off stump. See how well you do'). Some coach by partner involvement (one partner informs the other during a drill that the stroke being practised is across the line of the ball); some by individual programmes (each batter plays eight cover drives, then eight leg glances). Some teach by guided discovery (asking the players to find out how to perform a certain skill), others by problem solving (asking the question, 'How would you deal with a bowler pitching short outside the off stump?'). These styles move from an authoritarian approach through to an individually centred coaching method. The coach has to decide the method best suited to the teacher and the player. The needs of the particular player may require any one of these approaches, so the coach has to be adaptable and observant.

Cricketers enjoy the game for many different reasons. Some get physical satisfaction from it, so the coach needs to make sure that even in the worst weather there is an outlet for their energy. They may enjoy the activity for its own sake or the pleasure of feeling that they are performing well – that their co-ordination in a particular stroke is smooth, that they beat a ball to the boundary, that they produced an ounce of extra speed in a fast delivery – or they may simply enjoy being out in the fresh air. Some cricketers get mental satisfaction from the game. They may become fascinated by the complexities of the game or by its unpredictability, or they may want to understand the physical reasons for the ball's movements in the air or off the pitch. The coach needs to know how to stimulate their curiosity and requires an armoury of knowledge to answer their questions. Some cricketers like to gain a sense of achievement, whether simply by not getting out before tea, by taking a record number of wickets or by getting their names in the newspapers. The coach should praise them when possible and try to prevent their becoming discouraged with themselves and with the game. Some cricketers play for the companionship being part of a team provides. Some cricketers want to be leaders; others are content to be part of a team. Some play because they are aggressive and want to beat their opponents or even hurt them. Their aggression may grow if they are in a frustrating position. Some players like to be independent. They may thrive in a formal competitive atmosphere whilst they may get very little out of a routine practice.

In every case the coach should understand why each member of the team plays in order to put them, as far as is practicable, in a situation where each will get most enjoyment out of the game. The coach must understand his or her own motives and avoid letting personal likes or dislikes affect important decisions. Much of the conflict in coaching comes from a lack of understanding between the coach and the athlete, a lack of knowledge that the coach has about his or her standing within the team or an inability to communicate because of personality differences or failure to understand the player's problems.

The coach needs to organise the requisite coaching material and to have a clear idea of long- and short-term aims. For example, in the short term, the coach may aim to teach the simple skill of the forward defensive stroke, but the logical extension of that skill and the long-term goal would be all of the shots which might develop from it. Coaching also hinges on the ability to modify instructional approaches according to the player's responses as a practice session progresses. Each skill lesson should fit an overall scheme of coaching. Beyond this the coach must be able to organise equipment, timetables, practices and to make the best use of the players' time.

This book advocates the introduction into cricket coaching of as much constructive learning, interaction and communication between athletes and coach as possible. Problems and policy should be discussed and a collective solution sought. Coaching is a two-way process between coach and player, athlete and athlete. The coach is in a communication-interaction situation with individuals and with groups. Adaptation to any situation which may arise is therefore imperative. One of the most effective methods of encouraging communication and interaction is the group activity. Players are grouped with their peers and friends and the competitive atmosphere of more formal coaching approaches, which may discourage the less confident cricketer, is played down.

Communication is the key to success in coaching. The coach's statements should be to the point, simple, clear and well timed. Instructions should not be too technical and specific issues should be discussed directly with the person concerned. Avoid giving players a general instruction and leaving them to make their own inferences. Since communication is a two-way process, the cricketer must also be able to communicate with the coach. The coach should always be willing to listen and be approachable and available. Ask if your players understand an instruction. Hold regular meetings for discussion between player and player. Ask the player for an opinion about how he or she is performing. Involve yourself with the side.

If the coach gives support, advice and opinion to a cricketer about a performance, this will encourage the cricketer to repeat and improve on that performance. Encouragement and advice should be given immediately after the performance, and the cricketer should know exactly what is being praised or criticised.

A coach can also correct a bad performance with punishment. This method works quickly to prevent a repetition of that bad performance but it does not eradicate its cause. If a punishment routine is to be successful, it should be used every time a lapse occurs and no lapse overlooked. Moreover, it should increase in intensity. Two punishment laps of the oval for a fielding error will have no effect if the cricketer can run them comfortably. Punishment gives the coach a sense of power but it also causes resentment. Punishment routines should be carried out, if at all, unemotionally and a demonstration of the correct skill performance given immediately. As a general principle the coach should minimise failure.

The coach helps the athlete to see information in its proper perspective. Within a well-designed coaching programme, it is possible to help players plan their own activities and skills practices. The coach also helps to cement relationships between the members of the side by sharing in discussions with the cricketers, planning well ahead, outlining goals and aims, planning and giving reasons for practice routines, emphasising quality not quantity in skills practice, initiating new practice ideas and refusing to halt the flow of practice activities.

The post of coach should always be held with the agreement and support of the players. The status of the coach as a leader depends upon this premise. The coach's position as leader hinges on:
- the coach's personality
- the needs, attitudes, problems and interests of the team members
- the relationships between the coach and the individual members of the team (can the coach afford to be a leader to some players and a tyrant to others?)
- the exact nature of the sport and the cricketers' tasks (the batters will demand individual and personal leadership in order to master their complex skills, whilst the fielders will need a co-ordinator of their activities)
- the needs of the situation (each team will have particular needs to make it more productive – encouragement, instruction, discipline, etc).

The coach's advice to the athletes must be constructive, unguarded and genuine. Sensitivity to the cricketer's problems is essential and advice must be given unconditionally. Like any other confidence, a team member's trust should be respected so that the player feels secure and free to come to the coach at any time.

To communicate how to perform a particular cricket skill, the coach should be able to say not only, 'Do as I say', but 'Do as I show you'. The theory behind the front-foot drive should be reinforced by the ability to demonstrate it for imitation by the players. Demonstration is a *sine qua non* if a learner is to identify and reproduce a skill. It should be one of the first steps in coaching a stroke or delivery.

When demonstrating a cricket skill, always bear in mind that the demonstration should be pitched at the ability level of the learner. Children can only master a limited number of movements at a time and only remember these movements for a short period. With young cricketers, it is better to make one important point about a stroke, which may lead to other correct movements, than to risk confusing them with less important points or more complicated movements.

Demonstrate the skill at normal speed, since this is how the shot or bowling action will be executed under match conditions and will be remembered by the cricketer. If you analyse the skill in slow motion at one stage, remember to finish the demonstration at normal speed. Give brief descriptive comments before and during the demonstration, but do not theorise about the stroke or action. Before you start the demonstration, decide upon its focal point. This will determine the relative positions of the coach and the athletes. For instance, a straight back lift and proximity of the bat to the pad is more easily seen with the coach and the cricketers facing one another. The length of a delivery is more easily discernible with the learners watching from a side-on position. Bear in mind such considerations as the ability of the players to hear and see the demonstration when the wind is blowing and the sun is shining.

Always repeat the demonstration until the player has absorbed its main points, even if this means repeating the demonstration many times. It is a constructive and time-saving ploy to tell the learners to try the stroke or skill after they have watched it for a while and are clear about what to do.

Always encourage the players. Tell them what they are doing right. While you should not reinforce a negative skill by allowing it to go uncorrected, minimise the fault and underline the good aspects of the performance.

In each skill unit of this manual, the necessary movements are listed in numerical and chronological sequence and described in detail. The coach is also provided with a checklist of the main points of the skill to facilitate communication with the player. The unit concludes with group activities to practise the skills in the game situation.

The elementary skills

A mastery of the elementary skills of hitting, stopping, catching and throwing is fundamental to the game of cricket. Such skills provide an introduction to the game components of batting, bowling, fielding and wicketkeeping.

REMEMBER: BE BALANCED. WATCH THE BALL.

Hitting

1 Just before the ball is delivered, swing the bat back. This back swing initiates the bat movement and determines the power of the stroke.
2 Watch the ball before delivery, during its flight and on to the hitting surface.
3 In most hitting skills your body should be side-on to the direction in which you will hit the ball.
4 In most hitting skills transfer your weight either forward or back in the direction in which you will hit the ball. At the same time you will make a corresponding foot movement.
5 In all hitting skills follow through in the direction of the hit.

Stopping

1 When stopping a ball which has been struck or thrown along the ground, you must watch the ball right up to the time that it comes to rest in your hands.
2 After the ball has been struck, move quickly into the path of the ball.
3 Place your body behind the line of the ball and use it as a second line of defence.
4 Place your hands close together with the fingers pointing towards the ground behind the line of the ball.
5 Allow the ball to come into your hands, watching it all the way. Let your hands give with the ball to absorb its force. Never grab at it.

Catching

1 When catching a ball which has been struck or thrown into the air, watch the ball at all times, right up to the time that it comes to rest in your hands. The most effective catching is done above and just below eye level.
2 After the ball has been struck into the air, position yourself quickly in line with the flight of the ball, and beneath it.
3 Stretch out your arms, slightly bent, to receive the ball. Above and at eye level the ball can be sighted through the fingers.

4 The palms of your hands should face the ball. Your fingers should point up, down or to the side but never towards the ball. Your hands should be cupped together and work in unison.
5 Let your hands give with the ball to absorb the force.

Close catching requires a crouched and stationary position which can be likened to sitting on the edge of a chair watching a detective movie on TV. You must be comfortable, relaxed and your weight evenly distributed, but mentally alert. Catching from this position is generally carried out close to the ground with the fingers pointing downwards or to the side. Movement into the path of the ball is easier if the feet are not too far apart.

Catches can generally be classified into the three categories: above eye level (high outfield catches); at eye level (mid-field skimmers); and below eye level (catches which travel only a short distance quickly).

Throwing

1 Hold the ball in your fingers away from the palm of the hand.
2 Grip the ball with the first and second fingers across the seam, thumb and third finger directly underneath.
3 Stand side-on to the throwing target.
4 Step towards the throwing target with your front leg.
5 Point your front arm at the throwing target.
6 During the 'cocking' action of the throw, your elbow must go as high as your shoulder, making an 'L' sign between the forearm and shoulder.
7 As the throw is made, lead with the elbow of the throwing arm.
8 After the throw, bring your arm down and across your body.
9 Follow through towards the target.

Simplified hints and checklist

HITTING
1 Swing the bat back
2 Eyes on the ball
3 Point your front shoulder at the ball
4 Step towards the ball
5 Throw your hands after the ball.

STOPPING
1 Eyes on the ball
2 Move towards the ball
3 Put up the barricades
4 Hands together, fingers towards 6 o'clock
5 Imagine you are stopping a raw egg.

CATCHING
1 Eyes on the ball
2 Get underneath the ball
3 Arms stretched towards the ball – relax
4 Point your fingers at 12, 6, 3 or 9 o'clock
5 Soft hands.

THROWING
1 Watch the target
2 Finger the ball
3 Start side-on to target and step towards it
4 Make an 'L' shape
5 Follow through with the arm and the body.

REMEMBER: BE BALANCED. WATCH THE BALL.

Group activity

1 HITTING
- Batter B uses a 'rounders' bat
- Bowler A bounces a tennis ball to the batter
- Batter tries to hit the ball
- Players rotate positions after 5 deliveries.

2 STOPPING
- The players are in pairs
- Each player defends a goal 2 metres wide
- Players try to roll the ball through their opponent's goal
- Highest number of goals is the winner.

3 CATCHING
- Player A throws a tennis ball to rebound off a wall in the air and moves to the end of the line
- Player B tries to take the catch
- Player B then throws a rebound catch for player C
- Highest number of catches is the winner.

4 THROWING
- Draw a target on a wall, approximately 2 metres in diameter
- Players standing back an appropriate distance throw at the target in turn
- Points are scored as indicated on the target
- Highest score wins.

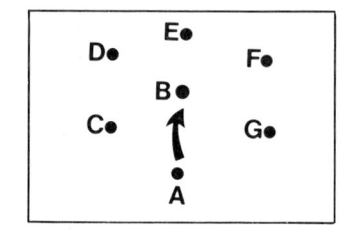

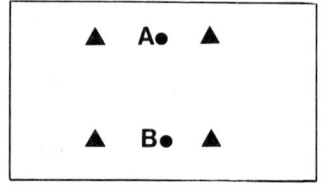

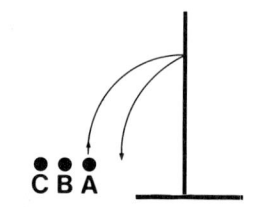

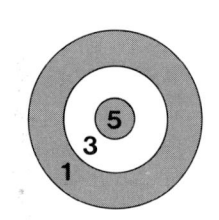

Batting

Preparations for batting

Before going in to bat

1 Always ensure that you are wearing adequate protective gear so that you are not anxious about being hurt. Your equipment should include: pads, batting gloves, a protector, a thigh pad and a helmet.
2 Equipment should always be comfortable and of the right size. Your bat should not be too big and should rest on the inside of your front thigh when you take up your stance. The knee joint of your pads should coincide with your knee. Your batting gloves should fit snugly and enable you to grip the bat efficiently.
3 Make sure you are ready to bat before going in. Practise and warm up to prevent muscle injury and to reinforce your batting skills. Make a note of the tactics and field positions which the bowlers are using. Accustom your eyes to the light conditions which you will encounter at the crease. Sit on the boundary behind the bowler's arm to find out what his stock ball is and how the wicket is behaving.
4 Prepare yourself mentally for your batting task. Think positively. Remember your last big innings and how pleased you felt after it. Think of how happy you will feel after you have played another big innings. Seg-

ment your goals, striving initially to survive the first ball, then the first over, then to score one run, five runs and so on. These goals are more easily attainable and once attained provide the motivating force to go on to bigger things.

At the crease

1 TAKING GUARD You take guard after arriving at the crease so that when you take up your stance and place your bat in the position indicated by the umpire, you are aware of where you are standing in relation to your stumps and are better able to defend them. You ask the umpire for guard by holding the bat perpendicularly in front of the wicket you are protecting. The umpire aligns the bat with the middle stump at the bowler's end and the line of the stump which you request.

Leg stump   Middle-and-leg   Middle

If you want 'leg-stump', or 'one-leg', guard, place your bat in front of the leg stump. For 'middle-and-leg', or 'two-leg', guard, position your upright bat between the middle and leg stumps on the popping crease. For 'middle', or 'centre', your bat should be in line with your middle stump. Mark the guard on the batting or popping crease by drawing a mark with the spikes of your boot or with your bat. This is your block mark, which gives you a guide about where you are standing in relation to your stumps. You place your bat on this mark when you take up your stance. Your guard may vary according to the bowler's tactics. If a bowler attacks your leg stump, you may ask for guard on the leg stump so that you can play more strokes on the off side and avoid the fielders which your opponent has positioned on the leg-side of the wicket.

2 THE GRIP You hold the bat and stand in an orthodox way so that you will be ready to face the bowler's delivery in a relaxed comfortable position with the best chance of making quick, correct movements and originating strokes.

Assume your stance as the bowler turns at the end of his run-up and moves in to deliver the ball.

You grip the bat:
- With both hands
- With the hands together near the middle of the bat handle
- With the V's formed by the forefinger and thumb of each hand aligned with the spine of the bat and the open end of the V's pointing up their respective arms
- Firmly but not too tightly.

3 THE STANCE Wait to receive the ball in a comfortable, relaxed and still position with:
- Your front shoulder, side and leading leg pointing up the wicket towards the bowler and your chest towards point. The toes of your feet are aligned
- Your weight evenly distributed between your front and back feet, which are usually slightly apart and straddle the batting crease
- Your head upright and motionless, facing the bowler and your eyes steady and level
- The toe of your bat resting in the block hole and the top of its handle leaning against the top of the inside of your front thigh
- Knees slightly bent and the trunk of your body upright.

Simplified hints and checklist

THE GRIP Place the bat on the ground, face downwards with its handle towards you, and pick it up as though it were an axe:
1 In both hands
2 With both hands together in the middle of the bat handle.

THE STANCE
1 Side-on
2 You are a boxer ready to move forward or back
3 Head and eyes steady and level
4 Don't lean on your bat; let it lean on your thigh
5 Stand up and be comfortable. Knees slightly bent.

REMEMBER: WATCH THE BALL. BE BALANCED.

Group activity

1 GRIP
• Wind two strips of tape around the handle of the bat as indicated in the diagram. Batters should grip the handle between the two lines made
• To remind players of where the V's formed by the first finger and thumb should point, place or draw an arrow on the back of the bat.

2 STANCE
• To ensure players assume a side-on position in their stance, draw a line 20 cm long at right angles to the batting crease along the imaginary line joining the two middle stumps
• The batter's toes in the stance should either be on this line or an equal distance from it.

3 BACKLIFT
• Players work in pairs
• One player designated the striker assumes normal batting stance
• Partner stands behind with one arm outstretched horizontally, palm down in line with off stump
• Batter plays imaginary drives
• If backlift is straight, contact will be made between the partner's palm and the bat during the backlift phase of the stroke.

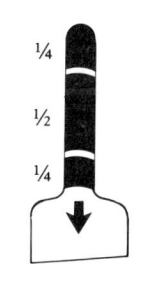

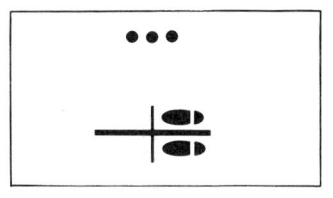

The front-foot drive

The front-foot drive is played to punish an overpitched ball – that is, a bad ball which does not bounce or bounces within reach of the batter stepping forward from the batting crease. At the same time, hitting an overpitched delivery has to be carried out in the safest way. The front-foot drive is played to an overpitched delivery or full toss which is in line with or just outside the line of the stumps. The overpitched delivery which bounces within reach of the batter stepping forward is called a half volley.

REMEMBER: WATCH THE BALL. BE BALANCED.

How to play the front-foot (off) drive

1 BACKLIFT Lift the bat in its preparatory backswing as the bowler is about to deliver the ball. Your backlift should be in line with the middle and off stumps and, since you will hit this shot hard, is high. The top hand controls the bat.

2 FOOT MOVEMENT As the ball arrives on the full toss, or bounces within reach, move your front foot towards the line of the ball and alongside the bounce or the ball on the full, transferring your weight to the front foot. Your toe should point in the direction of the intended stroke. Strike the ball when it is level with the instep of your front foot. Your weight should be over the ball on contact so that you can keep it on the ground.

3 HEAD AND EYES As you push your front foot forward alongside the line of the ball, move your head and eyes over the point of contact between bat and ball.

4 WEIGHT TRANSFERENCE AND BODY POSITION Your front shoulder should point towards the line of the ball. Your front elbow should be bent and pointing in the same direction. Bend your front knee slightly for balance. It should also point alongside the line of the ball.

5 BATSWING AND FOLLOW-THROUGH By this stage you will have swung the bat down from the top of the backlift. It should be perpendicular. Your bent front elbow will enable you to swing it close to the front pad, leaving no gap between the bat and pad. Tuck your rear elbow into your side on the downswing. This will ensure a straight downswing so that you will swing the bat in the same line as the approaching ball.

Your bent front elbow and front shoulder will push the top of the bat blade ahead of the bottom at the point of contact with the ball.

Follow through on the stroke. Swing your arms and shoulders vertically in the direction of the shot. Let your bat travel through and high after the point of contact, finishing over your front shoulder, which points in the

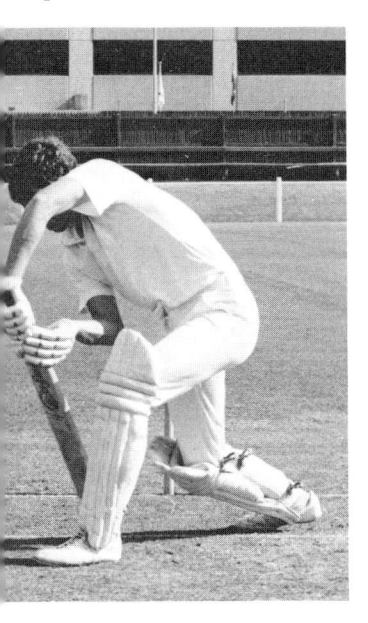

direction of the stroke. Your weight is now over the front knee. Keep your head down with your eyes still on the point of contact between bat and ball. A straight follow-through indicates that you have swung the bat through in a straight plane. The follow-through shows that your weight has been transferred and that the bat is moving quickly at the point of contact.

Make sure your back foot stays grounded behind the front foot.

Simplified hints and checklist
1 Lift your bat back straight and high
2 Step forward with your front foot alongside the line of the ball
3 Smell the ball
4 Lean into the ball with your front shoulder, side, elbow and knee
5 Almost brush your front pad with your bat as you hit the ball
6 Keep the figure 9 formed by your shoulders, arms and bat; throw your top then your bottom hand at the ball
7 Let the bat swing through
8 Your back foot is pegged to the ground.

REMEMBER: BE BALANCED. WATCH THE BALL.

Group activity
1 THE FRONT-FOOT DRIVE
- Feeder A throws 10 balls to batsman B from a distance of 5-8 m on the half volley
- The striker attempts to drive the ball between two goal posts 15 m apart on the off side
- Fielders D, E and F attempt to stop the ball passing through the goal
- Players rotate positions after 10 deliveries
- Score 4 runs for each ball successfully driven through the goal. A 2-run penalty is incurred if the ball is caught.

Number of players: 6
Equipment: 1 bat, 1 ball, 1 set of stumps, 2 markers for goalposts.

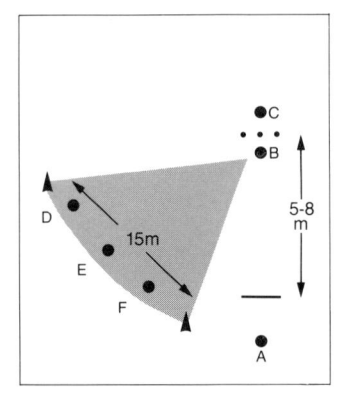

2 VARIATION ONE (for beginners)
- Batter B attempts to drive the ball off a tee through the goal
- Goalposts 1-2 m apart and 8-10 m from the batter
- Fielder A stops the ball after it passes through the goal
- Players change positions after 10 attempts
- Highest number of goals is the winner.

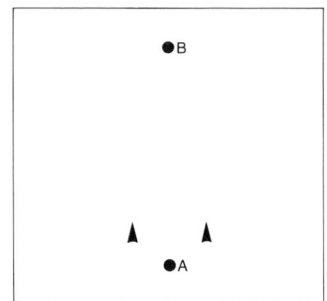

3 VARIATION TWO
- As above except that a third player stands one step in front of the batter on the off side
- The ball is dropped vertically to bounce in front of the batter
- Batter drives the ball towards the goal.

Variations on the front-foot drive

The front-foot cover drive

Play the cover drive to punish a delivery which bounces within reach or arrives on the full toss wide of the stumps on the off side.

The first movements of the cover drive are identical to those of the front-foot drive, but the movement of the front foot, head and eyes, and the front shoulder, elbow and knee will be more towards the cover position, and the ball will be struck far squarer, towards cover. The toe of your front foot should point towards cover point. This shot can be risky since the direction of the stroke is across the line of the ball in an off-side direction.

The front-foot straight drive

The front-foot straight drive returns a straight overpitched ball back past the bowler. It is played when an overpitched delivery bounces within reach of the batter or arrives on the full toss in line with the stumps.

In the straight drive the movement of the front foot, head and eyes, and

The front-foot on-drive

The on-drive is played to hit an overpitched ball bouncing around the line of leg stump through the area between mid-wicket and the bowler. It is played to a delivery bouncing within reach of the batter or arriving on the full toss in line with or just outside the leg stump.

In the on-drive the front foot, head and eyes, and the front shoulder, elbow and knee move more towards the mid-wicket/mid-on area and the

the front shoulder, elbow and knee is back towards the bowler. The toe of your front foot points towards mid-off. This shot can be used to loft the ball back over the bowler's head if you strike the ball with the bottom of the bat ahead of the top at the point of contact.

ball is struck in that area. Your front hip and foot have to adopt a far more open position, so that they do not obstruct the stroke. Your toe should now point towards mid-on and your chest should be square-on to the bowler. The right hand plays a more important part in this drive than in the others, providing the power at the end of the stroke to swing the ball away on the leg side.

Moving out to drive
(on, off, straight and cover drive)

Move out to drive in order to make a slow good-length ball into a delivery which can be punished. In this way you can dictate terms to the bowler and seize the initiative. You move out to resolve uncertainty in your mind about the length of the ball and the problems of flight. Thus you can be sure of reaching the ball on the half volley or full toss before it can turn off the wicket or even bounce.

It is possible to move out when the flight of the ball allows enough time to move out of your crease to meet it on the half volley or full toss. Moving out of the crease means you must take one, two or three skipping paces down the wicket before you can go through the movements of the drive. First take a long step down the wicket with your front foot. Your head should be steady, eyes on the ball and your front shoulder pointing at the line of the ball. Then draw your back foot up to and behind the front in a sideways-skipping crab-like motion and transfer your weight to the back foot once more. Now move the front foot forward towards and alongside the bounce of the ball and continue the movements of the forward drive. The movement out of the crease should be definite and pronounced: once out of your ground you can be stumped by a centimetre or a metre – degree is of no importance once your decision has been taken.

Group activity

VARIATIONS ON THE FRONT-FOOT DRIVE
- Feeder A throws 10 balls to batter B from a distance of 8 m on the half volley
- Batter attempts to drive the ball between one of the goalposts
- The keeper C and fielders D, E and F retrieve the ball
- Players rotate positions after 10 deliveries
- Score 1 point for each shot which passes through the goalposts.

Number of players: 6
Equipment: 1 bat, 1 ball, 1 set of stumps, 3 sets of goalposts.

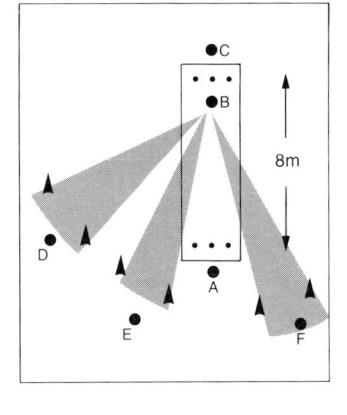

The forward defensive stroke

The forward defensive stroke is played to defend the wicket, without giving a catch, against a good-length ball which bounces in line with or just outside the line of the stumps. This delivery is termed 'a good-length ball' because it makes the batter unsure whether to play forward or back. The ball bounces just outside the reach of the batter stepping and stretching forward from the crease.

To build an innings you must be at the wicket to score runs. If you are out, you cannot contribute to the score. The basis of a good innings is therefore a sound defence.

REMEMBER: WATCH THE BALL. BE BALANCED.

How to play a forward defensive stroke

1 BACKLIFT Lift your bat in its preparatory backswing as the bowler is about to deliver the ball. The backlift should be in line with the middle and off stumps and stump-high. Control the bat with your top hand. A straight backlift ensures that these straight-batted shots are played with a greater chance of success.

2 FOOT MOVEMENT As the ball bounces on a spot just outside your reach, put your front foot forward towards and alongside the line of the ball and as close as possible to its bounce. Transfer your weight to your front foot with your front toe pointing approximately in the direction of the stroke. This is the movement which takes the head and eyes behind the line of the ball.

3 HEAD AND EYES As you push your front foot towards the bounce of the ball, move your head and eyes towards the spot where the ball will bounce.

4 WEIGHT TRANSFERENCE AND BODY POSITION In transferring your weight to the front foot, point your front shoulder towards the line of the ball. Your front elbow should be bent and pointing in the same direction. Bend your front knee slightly to maintain balance and point it towards a position just inside the line of the ball.

5 BATSWING AND FOLLOW-THROUGH As the bat swings down from the top of the backlift, keep it perpendicular. Your bent front elbow will bring the bat alongside your front leg or pad leaving no gap between the two for the ball to pass through. The bat contacts the ball level with the instep of the front foot and stops with the top of the blade ahead of the bottom.

Simplified hints and checklist

1 Imagine the wicketkeeper has tied a piece of string to the bottom of your bat and is pulling it back towards him
2 Step forward alongside the line of the ball
3 Smell the ball
4 Lean into the ball with your front shoulder, side, elbow and knee. Maintain the figure 9 formed by your shoulders, arms and the bat
5 Almost brush your front pad with the bat and play the ball alongside your front foot.
6 Push the ball into the ground.

REMEMBER: BE BALANCED. WATCH THE BALL.

Group activity

THE FORWARD DEFENSIVE STROKE
• Feeder A throws 10 balls to batter B from a distance of 5 m
• The batter attempts to survive each delivery by playing a forward defensive shot
• The keeper C and fielders D, E and F attempt to catch the ball
• Players rotate positions after 10 deliveries
• Score 1 run for each ball successfully defended. A 1-run penalty is incurred if the ball is missed, caught or driven past the feeder.

Number of players: 6
Equipment: 1 bat, 1 ball, 1 set of stumps.

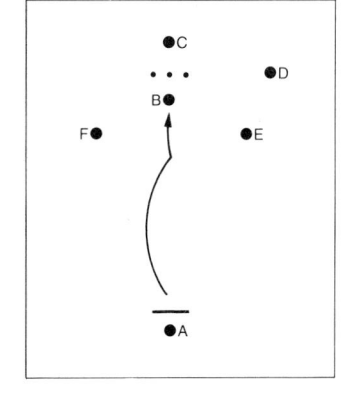

The leg glance off the front foot

The leg glance off the front foot is played in order to deflect a good-length or overpitched ball, when it bounces on or outside the line of the leg stump, going further down the leg side in the direction of fine leg.

REMEMBER: WATCH THE BALL. BE BALANCED.

How to play the leg glance off the front foot

1 BACKLIFT Lift your bat in its preparatory backswing as the bowler is about to deliver the ball. Your backlift should be in line with the middle and off stumps, stump-high, and controlled by the top hand.

2 FOOT MOVEMENT As the ball bounces just outside leg stump or on the leg stump going further down the on side and on a good length or overpitched, move your front foot alongside and inside the line of the ball and as close as possible to its bounce. Your front toe should point to mid-on with your weight on the front foot.

3 HEAD AND EYES As you push your front foot towards the bounce of the ball, move your head and eyes to a position as close as possible to the bounce of the ball and behind its line.

4 WEIGHT TRANSFERENCE In transferring the weight to the front foot, your front shoulder should point towards the line of the ball. Your front elbow should be bent and pointing in the same direction. Your hips should be square-on to the bowler and the front knee bent slightly to maintain balance and pointing towards a line inside that of the ball.

5 BATSWING AND FOLLOW-THROUGH By this stage you will have swung the bat down from the top of the backlift. The blade should be perpendicular: as your front elbow is bent, it will pass alongside the front pad leaving no gap. The bat will contact the ball just in front of your front leg. It is important to swing the bat along the line of the ball as this gives a better chance of contact.

At the point of contact your bent front elbow and front shoulder push the top of the blade ahead of the bottom. With your top hand turn the blade from a full-face position to the ball to a full-face position towards mid-wicket.

Maintain your balance with a bent front knee and make sure that your back foot remains behind the popping crease.

Simplified hints and checklist

1 Lift the bat straight back with the top hand in control
2 Stride forward with the front leg to a position just inside the line of the ball
3 Sniff the ball
4 Lean into the ball with your front shoulder, side, elbow and knee. Maintain the figure 9 formed by the shoulders, arms and the bat
5 Almost brush your front pad with your bat. Angle the face of the bat to mid-wicket
6 Help the ball on its way to fine leg along the ground
7 Keep your back foot pegged behind the batting crease.

REMEMBER: BE BALANCED. WATCH THE BALL.

Group activity

THE LEG GLANCE OFF THE FRONT FOOT
• Feeder A throws 10 balls firmly to batter B from a distance of 8 m on the half volley in line with or just outside the leg stump
• Batter B attempts to deflect the ball to pass through the goals in the direction of fine leg
• Keeper C and fielder D retrieve the ball
• Players rotate positions after 10 deliveries
• Score 1 point for each shot which passes through the goalposts.

Number of players: 4
Equipment: 1 bat, 1 ball, 1 set of stumps, 1 set of goalposts.

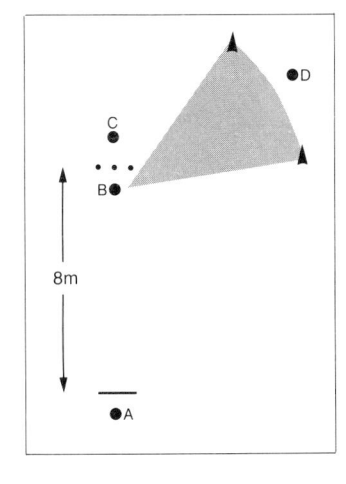

The sweep

The sweep is played to punish an overpitched delivery which bounces or arrives on the full toss outside the line of the leg stump at slow pace. It is struck in the direction of square leg.

REMEMBER: WATCH THE BALL. BE BALANCED.

How to play the sweep

1 BACKLIFT Just before the bowler releases the ball lift the bat back in its preparatory backswing. In its initial stages the backlift should be in line with the middle and off stumps and controlled by the top hand. Make sure your backlift is high since this stroke requires power. At the end of the backlift your bottom hand should take control, swinging the bat slightly behind your back shoulder ready to execute a cross-bat stroke parallel to the ground.

2 FOOT MOVEMENT As the ball arrives on the full pitch or half volley, move your front foot towards and inside its line. Your front leg is slightly bent and straightens as the rear knee is lowered to the ground. Your front foot points to mid-off and the rear foot remains grounded behind the batting crease. Your weight should be evenly distributed between front foot and back knee.

3 HEAD AND EYES At the same time as the foot movement move your head and eyes towards and inside the line of flight of the ball and as close as possible to its bounce. Keep your eyes fixed on the ball and your head steady and low behind the bounce as your rear knee makes contact with the ground.

4 BATSWING After you have positioned your feet, begin the downswing. Keep your rear elbow tucked into your side and your leading shoulder above your bent front knee as your bottom hand takes control. Swing the bat horizontally in a scything motion from outside the off stump to the leg side, almost brushing the ground, until it makes contact with the ball level with and to the leg side of your front leg. At the point of contact with the ball your arms are extended and your bottom hand rolls above the top, turning the face of the bat towards the ground, thus keeping the ball down.

Simplified hints and checklist
1 Swing your bat back like a golf club
2 Step forward with your front foot until it is almost straight and just inside the line of the ball. Lower your back knee to the ground
3 Sniff the ball
4 Scythe the ball away on the leg side, rolling your wrists over the ball.

REMEMBER: BE BALANCED. WATCH THE BALL.

Group activity
THE SWEEP
- Feeder A gently throws 10 balls to batter B, overpitched and slightly outside the line of leg stump
- Batter attempts to sweep the ball in the direction of the fielders at square leg
- Keeper C and fielders D, E and F attempt to catch the ball
- Players rotate positions after 10 deliveries
- Score 1 run for each shot successfully hit along the ground. No score if the ball is caught.

Number of players: 5
Equipment: 1 bat, 1 ball, 1 set of stumps.

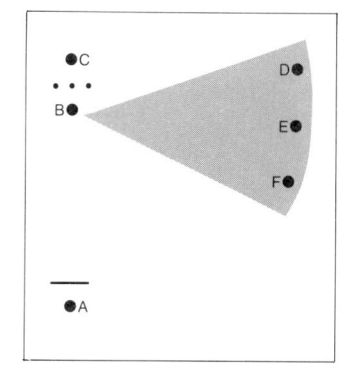

Detection and correction of faults in front-foot strokes

The detection and correction of faults in cricket skills revolves around the coach's ability to:
- Have in his or her mind's eye a correct model of the skill to be performed
- Isolate the critical phases of the skill at which faults occur (e.g. grip, backlift, movement of the feet, etc.)
- Observe repeatedly, from different vantage points, the performance of the skill
- Mentally replay to him or herself the cricketer's performance
- Compare mentally the cricketer's performance with the ideal correct model
- Trace backwards from an unsatisfactory result of the skill, or forwards in chronological order, the evolution or development of a fault and its consequences at each critical phase of the skill
- Identify the fundamental cause of a fault and its consequences at each phase of the skill
- Have a knowledge of specific strategies to correct the cause of faults and their consequences
- Implement those strategies so that the player receives feedback about self-improvement in a meaningful and active practice situation.

The coach is therefore faced with a complex task which demands a thorough knowledge of technique, a good grasp of the reasons behind techniques, the ability to 'eyeball' a player's performance and analyse it logically and scientifically, and a practitioner's expertise to correct faults in the field. It is sometimes impossible to analyse complex skills with the naked eye because of the speed at which they are performed; in this context a video-replay facility is an invaluable coaching aid. The coach must be careful not to identify obvious faults in too categorical a manner and attempt to correct them prematurely; they may have their origins in less noticeable and more individualistic performance areas of the skill.

In order to facilitate the identification and correction of faults in the skills, a checklist of the correct performance in the specific skills is provided in the left-hand column; in the right-hand column, the consequences of deviating from the recommended methods are enumerated and commented on. The critical phases of each skill are listed in the chronological order in which they occur. A recommended correction technique follows each critical phase of the skills and the faults which occur in them.

1 Front-foot straight-bat strokes

Correct model

Comments on the reasons behind the skill and possible faults

● GRIP

1 The batter's hands should be behind the bat handle
2 The batter's hands should not be too far apart on the handle
3 The batter's hands should not be too high on the handle
4 The batter's hands should not be too low on the handle.

The most efficient way of putting power into a stroke is to transfer the weight, strength and forward momentum of the body through the hands. This moves the bat quickly, but only if the power is directly behind the bat handle. If a batter's hands are too far apart on the handle they do not work in unison. If the batter's hands are too high on the bat handle, it is difficult to control the bat. If they are too low, it reduces the swing of the bat, 'choking' the stroke and minimising its power. A low grip on the bat handle indicates the dominance of the natural hand in playing strokes, a characteristic which generally causes the batter to hit across the line of the ball.

CORRECTION STRATEGIES

Place the bat on the ground face downwards, handle towards the batter, and ask the player to pick it up as though picking up an axe, with the hands in the middle of the handle. Establish the span of the hands by placing an elastic band just above the top hand and another just below the bottom. The bat should be held with the hands between the elastic bands until the practice becomes automatic. To ensure that the hands are behind the bat, place a strip of coloured sticky tape at the top of the back of the bat blade, just to the left of its spine. The open end of the V's formed by the thumb and forefinger of each hand should point directly towards this tape.

● STANCE

1 The head and eyes should be level and steady
2 The feet should not be too far apart
3 The feet should not be too close together
4 The feet should be parallel and their toes point towards point
5 The batter's weight should be firmly on the balls of the feet
6 The batter's front shoulder, hip and side should point down the wicket towards the bowler
7 The batter's knees should be slightly bent
8 The top of the bat handle should rest lightly on the top and inside of the batter's front thigh

The batter should be ideally balanced and perfectly still in the stance, ready to execute strokes correctly. Movement of the head and eyes demands the continual refocusing of the eyes and slows down reaction time. A wide stance increases the stability of the batter but reduces the ability to move quickly. A narrow stance reduces balance and stability but enables the batter to move quickly. The positioning of the front shoulder, hip, side and feet enables the batter to swing the bat back straight and bring it through in line with the flight path of the ball. Any deviation from the side-on position usually causes the batter to lift the bat back towards first slip or fine leg and hit across the line of the ball.

Distribution of the batter's weight on the toes or heels will cause overbalancing towards the off or leg side and prevent quick and firm movement behind the line of the ball. If a batter overbalances towards the off side, leg-side shots will be lofted. The movement of the batter's weight towards the leg side will produce a tendency to edge balls outside the off stump. Balance, with the knees slightly bent, is therefore of paramount importance. If the batter leans on the bat rather than allowing it to rest on the top and inside of the front thigh, a

9 The batter's stance should be comfortable and balanced.

redistribution of weight will be necessary before a stroke can be executed. There may also be a tendency to overbalance towards the off side as the weight is taken off the bat, a fault which will again cause the lofting of leg-side strokes. The correct positioning of the bat also ensures that a batter uses the right-size bat. Leaning on the bat will also cause the head and eyes to deviate from a level position.

CORRECTION STRATEGIES

Manipulate the player physically into the correct position in the stance. Use verbal cues, such as 'side-on!', to ensure that the position is maintained. Use a squash ball wedged between the batter's chin and front shoulder to ensure that the head and eyes remain steady in the execution of the stroke. The same effect may be obtained by placing a piece of coloured sticky tape on the inside of the batter's front shoulder and ensuring that it is visible as the batter takes up the stance and plays a stroke.

● BACKLIFT

1 The backlift is not too high before the bat descends
2 The backlift is not too low
3 The backlift is not towards the slips
4 The backlift is not towards fine leg.

A high backlift is used to obtain power in a stroke since it enables the batter to swing the bat quicker. It also requires more time to execute and could lead to vulnerability against fast bowlers if the batter is not able to get the bat down in time. A low backlift reduces the power in a stroke and may prevent the batter from driving the ball. It could also denote that the bottom hand is controlling the stroke and this in turn could cause the batter to lift the bat back towards slip. This fault means that the bat is not lifted back straight and will not therefore descend in the same line as the approaching ball, causing the shot to be executed across the line of the ball with a proportionate reduction in the chances of making contact. The backlift towards fine leg usually indicates a 'closed' stance in which the batter's front foot is advanced more towards the off side than the back foot. This makes the batter vulnerable against the ball pitching on the leg side of the front pad, since the bat will have to describe a semicircle around the front pad to make contact with it – an operation which takes unnecessary time and causes the batter to hit across the line of the ball. The backlift towards fine leg may also cause the batter to hit across the line of the ball towards the off side because the swing of the bat will be from fine leg to cover.

CORRECTION STRATEGIES

The height and straightness of the batter's backlift can be corrected by an activity using two players. One is a batter who assumes the stance. The partner kneels a bat's length behind the batter, holding out a hand, palm downwards, at the correct height and in the correct line for the backlift. When the batter lifts the bat back correctly, contact is made with the palm of the partner's hand. A batter can correct a backlift fault by standing in front of a full-length mirror and practising lifting the bat back correctly, at the same time observing the performance in the mirror. The straightness of the backlift can be checked by a batter standing alongside and flush with a wall, which prevents the bat deviating from a straight line. Another method of ensuring the straightness of the backlift is to practise it using only the top hand on the bat.

- FRONT-FOOT MOVEMENT

1 The front foot moves alongside the line of the ball
2 The front foot moves far enough forward
3 The front foot movement is quick and decisive
4 The front foot stabilises
5 The front knee bends for balance and stability.

The front foot's movement alongside the line of the ball takes the batter's head and eyes behind its line, from which vantage point it is possible to observe swing and spin. If the front foot is not alongside the line of the ball, the bat has to swing wide of the front leg to make contact with the ball, leaving a gap between bat and pad through which the ball may pass and hit the stumps if there is any movement off the pitch. If the front foot does not advance as close as possible to the bounce of the ball, it allows more time for it to deviate from its original path. A hesitant forward movement of the front foot may involve more than one movement and occupy unnecessary time. It may also prevent the front foot from stabilising quickly. The bat will not descend in the execution of a stroke until such time as the front foot stabilises and establishes a firm base for the summation of the force in the shot. The flexing of the leading knee in front-foot strokes lowers the batter's centre of gravity and prevents the transfer of weight beyond the front leg. This in turn prevents the batter overbalancing and stumbling forward – an involuntary movement which causes the back leg to swing around the front foot, dragging the shoulders and bat with it across the line of the ball.

CORRECTION STRATEGIES

To establish the correct motor skill of the front foot moving to a position alongside the line of the ball, place a cardboard cone one pace in front of the batter and ask the player to drive the cone, whilst ensuring that the front foot is placed alongside it. The extension of this practice leads to the batter striking a ball off an appropriately placed batting tee, then to driving a ball dropped by a partner from a position alongside and on the off side of the batter, and finally to hitting a ball fed by a partner standing a few yards in front of the batter. The feeder may throw the ball from a short distance before bowling it over a longer distance, but the ball must be delivered on a drivable length and the feeder must position him or herself in such a way as to avoid being hit by a return drive.

Indecisive and inadequate movement of the front foot usually stems from the batter's hesitancy about whether to play forward or back. This hesitancy can be resolved in the practice nets by:

- Drawing a line approximately 1.5 metres (4 ft) in front of the batting crease and instructing the batter to play forward to any delivery which bounces on the side of the line closer to the batter
- Cueing a batter verbally or visually to play forward as you feed a ball on an appropriate length
- Using a bowling machine or accurate bowler to pitch the ball consistently on a length appropriate to a front-foot stroke.

The bending of the front knee and stabilisation of the front foot in front-foot strokes depends on the batter lowering his or her centre of gravity whilst playing the shot. Therefore you should use verbal cues to ensure that the batter keeps his or her head low over the point of contact with the ball and does not allow the head to go beyond the front knee. Appropriate cues would be: 'Sniff the ball'; 'Lean into the ball'; 'Push your front knee at the ball'.

- POSITIONING OF THE HEAD AND EYES

1 The head and eyes are positioned behind the line of the ball
2 The head is stable in the execution of the stroke
3 The eyes are level in the execution of the stroke
4 The batter's head does not lift when the bat contacts the ball.

The batter's head is taken into a position behind the line of the ball by the movement of the front leg alongside the line of the ball. From this position the batter is able to discern the behaviour of the ball through the air and off the wicket. Continual movement of the head and eyes during the execution of the stroke necessitates constant refocusing of the eyes, with a proportionate increase in the reaction and movement times of the batter. If the eyes are not level in the playing of the stroke, more eye muscles are required to focus the batter's vision and, again, this increases reaction and movement time, making the batter slower in the execution of the shot. If the batter lifts the head during the execution of the stroke, a corresponding shift of weight occurs backwards away from the point of contact between bat and ball. This causes the ball to be lofted as well as making the batter take his or her eyes off the ball.

CORRECTION STRATEGIES

Strategies should be linked to both the execution of the stroke and the phases of the stroke which occur before movement is initiated. For instance, the head and eyes may not be stable and level in the execution of the stroke because the batter is leaning on the bat in the stance or because the batter is moving whilst awaiting the delivery of the ball; the head and eyes may not be behind the line of the ball because the batter's front foot does not move to a position alongside the line of the ball. Use the correct strategies enumerated from these phases of the skill.

Employ verbal cues to ensure the stability and levelness of the head and eyes, e.g. 'Sniff the ball'. To ensure that the head does not lift at the point of contact between bat and ball, ask the batter to bend the front knee so that the centre of gravity is lowered and the head is kept low and maintains its forward movement, looking at the spot where the bat hits the ball.

- BODY MOVEMENT

1 The body moves forward in the line of the intended stroke
2 The body maintains a sideways posture with the front shoulder, bent elbow, hip and the leading side of the front leg pointing to a position just inside the line of the ball.

The forward movement of the body enables the batter to impart force into the stroke along the line of the approaching ball and the intended direction of the stroke. The maintenance of a sideways posture facilitates the swing of the bat and shoulders along the line of the ball, avoiding the fault of hitting across the line and thus increasing the efficiency of the transfer of forces from the bat into the stroke.

CORRECTION STRATEGIES

Use verbal cues: 'Point your front shoulder at the line of the ball'; 'Lean into the ball with your front shoulder, elbow, side and leg'; 'Step towards the ball, sideways leaning into it'.

- MOVEMENT OF THE SHOULDERS AND ARMS

1 The shoulders rotate vertically around the axis of the head towards the line of the approaching ball

The vertical rotation of the shoulders around the axis of the head along the line of the ball maintains the batswing on the same plane, avoiding the error of hitting across the line of the delivery and

2 The configuration of the shoulders, arms and the bat maintain a figure 9 shape: the hollow of the 9 is formed by the straight line of the shoulders and the bent arms, and the tail of the numeral by the bat
3 The elbows of both arms are kept close to the body
4 Just before contact with the ball, the wrists move quickly through a wide flat arc as the 'hands are thrown at the ball'.
NB: this wrist action does not occur in the front-foot defensive stroke. In this case the batswing is arrested with the bat alongside the front pad and level with the instep.

imparting power from the shoulder girdle. The maintenance of the figure 9 ensures that the top of the bat blade is advanced ahead of the bottom at the point of contact with the ball, thus keeping it on the ground. The elbows are kept close to the body to keep the bat vertical and to avoid the fault of the bat straying too far from the front leg, leaving a gap through which the ball can pass. The wrists 'break' just before the bat makes contact with the ball, moving through a wide arc very quickly and flattening the swing of the bat. This represents the final phase in the summation of forces, at which stage force is transmitted to the bat by the rapid motion of the wrists. After the wrist movement, the shoulders and arms lose their figure 9 configuration.

CORRECTION STRATEGIES
Use verbal cues: 'Point your front shoulder at the ball'; 'Keep the figure 9'; 'Elbows in'; 'Throw your hands at the ball'.

● BATSWING
1 Throughout the stroke the bat remains vertical
2 Throughout the stroke the bat swings consistently on the same line as the approaching ball
3 Just before and at the point of contact with the ball the vertical bat is in close proximity to the front leg
4 At the point of contact the top of the bat blade is ahead of the bottom
5 In the final stages of the batswing, its arc flattens as the movement of the wrists accelerates for attacking strokes
6 At the point of contact the bat is moving quickly.
NB: This does not apply to the front-foot defensive stroke, at the conclusion of which the bat is stationary.

The vertical rotation of the shoulders and the closeness of the batter's elbow to the body keep the bat vertical. The vertical rotation of the shoulders around the axis of the head also maintains the swing of the bat along the same line as the approaching ball, provided that the front shoulder is pointing towards that line and the front leg has been advanced to a position just inside the line. The closeness of the elbows to the body throughout the batswing ensures that the bat is swung close to the front leg. The retention of the figure 9 configuration of shoulders and arms until the point of contact guarantees that the top of the bat blade is advanced ahead of the bottom at that juncture. Just before the point of contact, the power of the body, shoulders, and arms is transferred to the wrists, causing them to move quickly. From a laid-back position, they move through an angle of almost 180 degrees if the stroke is an aggressive one. They stop at the 60-degree position if the stroke is defensive.

CORRECTION STRATEGIES
Many of the errors which occur at this stage of the skill must be remedied in its earlier stages. Use verbal cues to reinforce previous remedial measures, e.g. 'Point your front shoulder, elbow and side at the ball' (use coloured tape on the inside of the leading shoulder and ensure that it remains visible throughout the execution of the stroke as the front shoulder maintains its forward movement towards the line of the

ball). Use other cues: 'Brush the side of your leading leg with your bat'; 'Throw your hands at the ball, hitting first with the top and then the bottom hand'; 'Grind the ball into the ground' (to ensure that the top of the bat blade is ahead of the bottom at the point of contact and that the correct amount of force is imparted to the stroke).

- FOLLOW-THROUGH

1 The follow-through is in the direction of the line of the intended stroke
2 The follow-through is full for attacking strokes
3 There is no follow-through for defensive strokes.

The follow-through is an indication of the correctness or otherwise of the stroke. If it is in the same line as the intended direction of the stroke, the batswing has been true and straight. A full follow-through indicates that at the moment of contact between bat and ball the bat was accelerating (correct for attacking strokes). If there is little or no follow-through, the bat was decelerating at the point of contact (correct for defensive strokes).

CORRECTION STRATEGIES
There can be no correction of the follow-through, since it is merely a reflection of the preceding phases of the skill. If these are correct, the follow-through gives the correct feedback.

- RESULT OF THE STROKE

The stroke has been performed a) correctly, b) incorrectly.

The desired result from the stroke usually indicates its correctness; an incorrect performance indicates the necessity for remedial procedures previously outlined.

- NOTES ON THE FRONT-FOOT STRAIGHT-BAT STROKES PLAYED ON THE LEG SIDE

The playing of the front-foot on-drive, the front-foot defensive stroke to a ball on the leg stump, and the leg glance, demands a technique which varies from the usual 'side-on' method of executing front-foot straight-bat shots. Because of the line of the ball to be played, the batter's front shoulder and leading hip fall away slightly to the on side, producing a slightly 'chest-on' or open posture as the striker moves forward to hit the ball. The opening of the body position enables the batter to place the front foot alongside the line of the ball and slightly to its leg side and maintains the batswing directly towards the approaching delivery. If the batter maintains a closed, side-on position in playing these strokes, the front foot is placed on the off side of the line of the ball and to make contact with it the bat has to move in an arc around the leading pad, a movement which will cause the striker to play across the line. To play front-foot straight-bat strokes on the leg side effectively it is sometimes necessary in the backswing to lift the bat slightly towards slip to ensure that the stroke will be on the same plane as the approaching delivery.

2 The front-foot cross-bat stroke — the sweep

Correct model

Comments on the reasons behind the skill and possible faults

- BACKLIFT

1 The bat is in a horizontal position at the top of the backlift
2 The bat is lifted high and above the possible bounce of the ball in the backlift.

The backlift brings the bat into a horizontal plane, ready to execute a batswing which will be parallel to the ground. The backlift is high to ensure that the stroke hits down on the ball, keeping it along the ground. One of the main faults in this stroke is the failure to hit down on the ball.

CORRECTION STRATEGIES
Use similar strategies to those used to correct the straight-back backlift, with the batter employing the services of a partner who stands behind the striker and holds out a hand with which the bat makes contact when it is lifted correctly. Use verbal cues to ensure that the bat is lifted high and above the bounce of the ball.

- FRONT-FOOT MOVEMENT

1 The front foot moves down the wicket to a position on the off side of the ball and as close as possible to its bounce
2 The front knee remains fairly straight as the back knee is lowered to the ground.

The front leg should be advanced as close as possible to the bounce of the ball so that it does not lift off the pitch and prevent the batter from hitting it along the ground. The leg remains straight so that the batter can lower the stroke's centre of gravity over the ball by bending the back knee. The positioning of the front leg places it between the ball and the stumps so that if the bat misses the ball, the pad acts as a second line of defence and prevents the striker from being bowled around the leg.

CORRECTION STRATEGIES
Use a 'footprint' (the insole of a shoe) to indicate where the batter should place the front foot. Employ verbal cues to ensure that the batter 'gets down on the ball' to play the stroke: 'Sniff the ball'.

- POSITIONING OF THE HEAD AND EYES

1 The head is low but above the bounce of the ball
2 The head moves forward into the stroke and remains down
3 The head and eyes are just inside the line of the ball.

The head and eyes must be low enough to guarantee a low centre of gravity for a stable base to the stroke but high enough to be above the bounce of the ball, making sure that the bounce of the ball is gauged correctly and that the stroke is executed down on the ball. The forward movement of the head indicates that maximum force is being imparted to the stroke by the forward momentum of the body. It also brings the head and eyes as close as possible to the bounce of the ball and over it ensuring that it will be kept on the ground. If the batter throws the head up and back in the execution of this stroke, the weight of the body will also be moved backwards and away from the bounce of the ball, which will cause the lofting of the ball. The positioning of the head and eyes just inside the line of the ball enables the batter to discern any movement of the ball back in towards the stumps from outside the leg stump.

CORRECTION STRATEGIES
Use motor-skill practices without a ball, practising keeping the head and eyes down, forward and just inside the line of an imaginary ball. Use verbal cues: 'Sniff just inside the line of the ball.'

• MOVEMENT OF THE SHOULDERS AND ARMS

1 The shoulders move horizontally around the axis of the head and slightly downwards
2 The arms are fully extended at the point of contact between bat and ball.

The horizontal downward swing of the shoulders ensures that the arms will move in the same direction and bring the bat down on the ball.

The sweep cannot be executed if the ball is too close to the body of the batter. A full swing of the bat with the arms extended and with the point of contact well in front of the batter's body is necessary for the successful execution of the stroke. A batter being cramped in the unsuccessful execution of the stroke usually arises from the batter choosing the wrong delivery – generally a ball of too full a length – to sweep.

CORRECTION STRATEGIES
With players operating in pairs, practise the sweep stroke. One player bats whilst the other feeds the ball, throwing from a distance of a few metres, on to a designated target area, from which the shot may be played. Balls not landing on the target area should not be swept but should evince another batting response.

• BATSWING

1 The bat swings horizontally down on the ball
2 The bat face is closed at the point of contact.

The horizontal, downward swing of the closed bat face ensures that the ball is kept along the ground. To close the face of the bat, the batter rolls the wrists over the ball at the point of contact. Note that whilst this procedure is not the most efficient way of transmitting force to the stroke, it is the safest method of preventing a lofted stroke.

CORRECTION STRATEGIES
Use the same correction strategies as for faults in the swing of the shoulders and arms. An additional refinement to the group activity may be added by the provision of a (20-metre) target area in the square-leg region (indicated by stumps in the ground). The ball should pass through the target area along the ground.

• FOLLOW-THROUGH

1 The follow-through is horizontal and close and parallel to the ground
2 The follow-through is initially in direction of the stroke before swinging behind the batter's body on the leg side
3 The follow-through is full
4 The bat face is closed and angled towards the ground in the follow-through.

The horizontal bat indicates the correct execution of a cross-bat shot whilst the closeness of the blade to the ground shows that contact with the ball has been made shortly after it bounced, thus ensuring that it is kept on the ground.

The initial movement of the follow-through in the direction of the stroke is an indication that the power of the shot is in that direction, whilst its subsequent movement behind the batter's body absorbs the force in the swing of the shoulders and arms.

The fullness of the follow-through is another indicator of the power of the stroke whilst the closed face of the bat demonstrates that the ball has been hit into the ground, avoiding the common fault of lofting a catch to deep square leg.

CORRECTION STRATEGIES
The follow-through reflects the correct execution of the previous phases of the stroke. Strategies to ensure a correct follow-through should therefore have been carried out in the earlier stages of the stroke.

● RESULT OF THE STROKE

| The stroke has been performed a) correctly, b) incorrectly. | The desired result from the stroke usually indicates its correctness; an incorrect result shows the necessity for the remedial procedures previously outlined. |

The back-foot drive

The back-foot drive is played to punish a ball which bounces short of a good length, usually just outside the line of the stumps, in such a way as to prevent a batter being dismissed. This stroke may be made against balls pitching in line with the stumps if you are well set.

REMEMBER: WATCH THE BALL. BE BALANCED.

How to execute the back-foot (off) drive

1 BACKLIFT As the bowler is about to deliver the ball, lift the bat back in its preparatory backswing. The backlift is straight and in line with the middle and off stumps. Your top hand controls this action. The backlift for a back-foot drive is high for power.

2 FOOT MOVEMENT When you have decided that the ball will bounce short of a length, move your back foot back towards the stumps and the off side, bringing your legs and body into a position just inside the line of the ball. Pull your front foot back to your rear foot. The foot movement will take you close to the stumps, giving you more time to sight the ball. The toes of your back foot should point towards point. Your front foot will act as a balancing agent with the toes resting lightly on the ground.

3 HEAD AND EYES In moving back to the stumps, bring your head and eyes into position directly behind the line of the ball and slightly to the off side of the back leg. Keep your head steady and alongside the leading shoulder. Your eyes should be level and fixed on the ball.

4 WEIGHT TRANSFERENCE AND BODY POSITION Your weight is firmly on the ball of the back foot with the front foot acting as a counterbalance. Your leading shoulder, side and front elbow should point towards the ball's flight. Your chest should face the general direction of point and you should be side-on to the bowler.

5 BATSWING AND FOLLOW-THROUGH From the top of the backlift, bring the bat down, bend and raise your front elbow and tuck your rear elbow into your side. This brings the bat into the perpendicular as it almost brushes the side of the back pad. Your front shoulder, elbow and top hand on the bat push the top of the blade ahead of the bottom of the point of contact with the ball. In the follow-through the bottom hand and back shoulder push the bat through, giving power to the stroke and carrying the bat high above your head after contact with the ball.

Simplified hints and checklist

1 Lift the bat back straight and high with the top hand in control
2 Back and across to a position inside the line of the ball
3 Sniff the ball
4 Plant yourself on the ball of your back foot. Point your front shoulder, elbow and leg at the line of the ball
5 Maintain the figure 9 formed by your shoulders, arms and bat. Swing it sideways towards the ball
6 Throw your hands at the ball and let the bat swing through.

REMEMBER: BE BALANCED. WATCH THE BALL.

Group activity

THE BACK-FOOT DRIVE
• Feeder A throws 10 balls short of a length to batter B
• The batter attempts to drive the ball off the back foot between 2 goalposts 10 m apart on the off side
• Fielders D, E and F attempt to stop the ball passing through the goalposts
• Players rotate positions after 10 deliveries
• Score 1 run for each ball successfully driven and 4 runs if it passes through the goal. A 2-run penalty is incurred if the ball is caught.

Number of players: 6
Equipment: 1 bat, 1 ball, 1 set of stumps, 2 markers for goalposts.

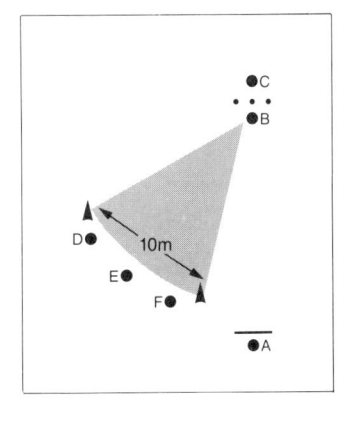

Variations on the back-foot drive

The back-foot cover drive

The back-foot cover drive is played to hit a ball bouncing short of a length and wide on the off side of the wicket, through the cover area without risk of dismissal.

To hit a back-foot cover drive move as if you were hitting the back-foot drive, except that the movements of your back foot, head and eyes will be more towards the off side. The movement of your front foot to the rear foot will bring that foot and the front shoulder to the off side of the rear foot and shoulder. The front shoulder, elbow and side point towards cover in the execution of the stroke. This shot incurs greater risk since the direction of the stroke is across the line of the ball in an off side direction.

The back-foot straight drive

The back-foot straight drive is played in order to hit a short, straight ball back past the bowler without risk of dismissal.

To hit the back-foot straight drive follow the movements of the back-foot drive, except that your back foot, head and eyes move towards middle stump and your front shoulder should point straight back towards the bowler. The movement of your front foot to the rear foot will bring it and the front shoulder into direct line with both the back foot and shoulder. Your front shoulder will point up the wicket, towards the line of the ball. Strike the ball back past the bowler either to the off or leg side.

This shot can be used to loft the ball back over the bowler's head if you move the bottom of the bat ahead of the top of the blade at the point of contact with the ball.

The back-foot on-drive

The back-foot on-drive is played in order to hit a short delivery bouncing on or outside the line of leg stump through the area between mid-wicket and the bowler without risk of dismissal.

For the back-foot on-drive follow the movements of the back-foot drive, except that your back foot should move back nearer leg stump and your front shoulder, elbow and hip fall away to the leg side and point in the direction of the stroke. As your front foot moves back near the back foot it stops just in front of it, pointing towards mid-on, and acts as a balancing agent. In the back-foot on-drive make sure your front foot and side are removed from the striking area towards the leg side, or they may obstruct the stroke. Your chest should face the bowler. The bottom hand plays a far more important part in this drive than in the others; indeed, it provides the power in all leg-side shots.

Group activity

VARIATIONS ON THE BACK-FOOT DRIVE
- Feeder A throws 10 balls short of a length from 5 m
- Goalposts 5 m apart are placed 10 m from the batter in the direction of mid-off and mid-on
- Batter B attempts to drive the ball off the back foot through either goal
- Fielders D and E attempt to prevent the ball passing through the goals
- Players rotate positions after 10 deliveries
- Score 1 run if the ball is stopped between the goalposts and 4 runs if it passes through.

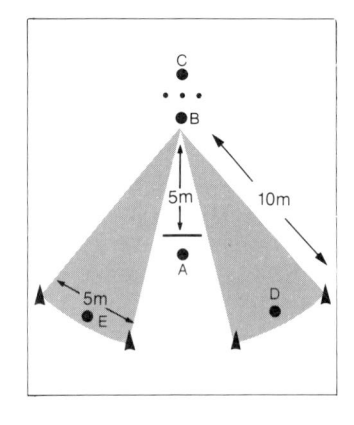

Number of players: 5
Equipment: 1 bat, 1 ball, 1 set of stumps, 4 markers for goalposts.

The back-foot defensive shot

The back-foot defensive stroke is played to protect the wicket against a ball which bounces just short of a good length and in line with or just outside the line of the stumps, and in such a way as to prevent the batter being dismissed.

REMEMBER: WATCH THE BALL. BE BALANCED.

How to play the back-foot defensive shot

1 BACKLIFT As the bowler is about to deliver the ball, lift your bat back in its preparatory backswing. Your backlift should be straight, in line with middle and off stumps and stump-high. Your top hand should govern this action.

2 FOOT MOVEMENT As soon as you decide that the ball will bounce just short of a length, move your back foot into the stumps and across towards the off side, bringing your body and legs into a position just inside the line of the ball. Now draw your front foot towards your back. This foot movement will take you back close to the stumps to give you extra time in which to sight the ball. The toes of your back foot should point towards point. Your front foot will act as a balancing agent with the toes resting lightly on the ground.

3 HEAD AND EYES In moving back to the stumps, bring your head and eyes into a position directly behind the line of the ball and slightly to the off side of the back leg. Keep your head steady and alongside the leading shoulder. Your eyes should be level and fixed on the ball.

4 WEIGHT TRANSFERENCE AND BODY POSITION Your weight should be firmly on the back foot with the front foot acting as a counterbalance. The leading shoulder, side and bent front elbow should point in the direction of the ball's flight. Your chest faces the general direction of point and you should be side-on to the bowler.

5 BATSWING AND FOLLOW-THROUGH From the top of the backlift, bring the bat down as you bend and raise your front elbow and tuck your rear elbow into your side. This will bring the bat down in perpendicular fashion almost brushing the top side of the back pad. With your front shoulder, elbow and top hand on the bat, push the top of the blade ahead of the bottom. Slacken the grip of the bottom hand at point of contact and stop the bottom of the bat level with the rear pad and at the point of contact with the ball.

Simplified hints and checklist

1 The wicketkeeper has tied a piece of string to the bottom of your bat and is pulling it back towards him
2 Step back and across to the off side to a position just inside the line of the ball
3 Sniff the ball
4 Plant yourself on the back foot, side-on
5 Maintain the figure 9 formed by your shoulders, arms and bat. Almost brush the top of your back pad with your bat and push the ball into the ground.

REMEMBER: BE BALANCED. WATCH THE BALL.

Group activity

THE BACK-FOOT DEFENSIVE SHOT
- Feeder A throws 10 balls short of a length to batter B from a distance of 5 m
- The batter attempts to survive each delivery by playing a back-foot defensive shot
- The keeper C, the fielders D, E and F attempt to catch the ball
- Players rotate positions after 10 deliveries
- Score 1 run for each ball successfully defended. A 1-run penalty is incurred if the ball is caught or driven past the feeder.

Number of players: 6
Equipment: 1 bat, 1 ball, 1 set of stumps.

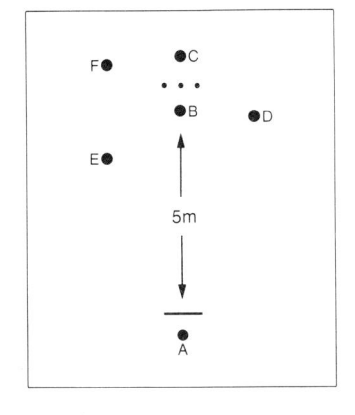

The leg glance off the back foot

The leg glance off the back foot is played in order to deflect the ball which is short of a good length and bounces on or outside the line of the leg stump and is going further down the leg side towards fine leg, in such a way as to prevent the batter being dismissed.

REMEMBER: WATCH THE BALL. BE BALANCED.

How to play the leg glance off the back foot

1 BACKLIFT As the bowler is about to deliver the ball, lift your bat in its preparatory backswing. The backlift is in line with the middle and off stumps and governed by the top hand.

2 FOOT MOVEMENT As the ball bounces short of a length and just outside or on the leg stump going further down the leg side, move your back foot well back to a position just inside the line of the ball. The toes of your back foot should point down towards mid-off. Move your front foot back to a position just in front and slightly to the leg side of the front leg. Your front hip points to mid-on or mid-wicket.

3 HEAD AND EYES In moving back towards your stumps, bring your head and eyes into a position just inside the line of flight of the ball. Your head should be steady and tucked alongside the leading shoulder. Keep your eyes level and fixed on the ball.

4 WEIGHT TRANSFERENCE AND BODY POSITION Your weight should be firmly on the back foot with the front foot acting as a counter-balance. Your leading shoulder, side and bent front elbow should point at the line of the ball. Since this is a leg-side stroke your chest is in an open position pointing approximately at mid-off.

5 BATSWING AND FOLLOW-THROUGH From the top of the back-lift, bring the bat down as you bend your front elbow and tuck your rear elbow into your side. This will keep the bat perpendicular almost brushing the back pad. Swing the bat towards the line of the ball. Your front shoulder, elbow and top hand on the bat push the top of the blade ahead of the bottom at the point of contact. As the bat makes contact with the ball just in front of your back leg, angle its face towards mid-wicket. The bat follows through towards mid-wicket.

Simplified hints and checklist

1 Straight back with the bat stump-high
2 Step back and across your wicket to the off side, just inside the line of the ball
3 Sniff the ball
4 Stand firm and point your front side and elbow at the ball
5 Swing your bat like a pendulum, deflecting the ball away towards fine leg.

REMEMBER: BE BALANCED. WATCH THE BALL.

Group activity

THE LEG GLANCE OFF THE BACK FOOT
• Feeder A throws ball quickly and short of a length on the leg stump from 5 m
• Batter B attempts to leg glance off the back foot
• Wicketkeeper C and fielders D, E and F attempt to catch the ball
• Players rotate positions after 10 deliveries
• Score 1 run for each ball successfully leg glanced in the direction of fine leg. A 1-run penalty is incurred if the ball is caught.

Number of players: 6
Equipment: 1 bat, 1 ball, 1 set of stumps.

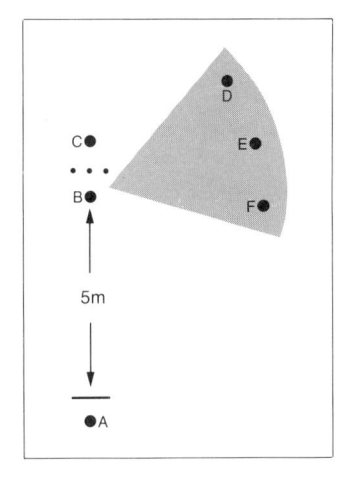

The square cut

A square cut is played to score off a delivery which is very short and at least 30 cm (12 in) wide of the off stump. The ball has to be struck past point on the ground with the least risk of dismissal.

REMEMBER: WATCH THE BALL. BE BALANCED.

How to play a square cut

1 BACKLIFT Just before the bowler delivers the ball, lift the bat back in the early stages with the top hand, over the middle and off stumps. At the end of the backswing your bottom hand takes control, pulling the bat behind the rear shoulder ready to execute a cross-bat shot.

2 FOOT MOVEMENT As the backlift is executed, move your back foot back and across the stumps to a position just in front of or outside the off stump. The toes of your back foot should point towards point. Your weight should be on the back foot, leaving your front foot resting on the ground, level with the popping crease, to act as a balance.

3 HEAD AND EYES As you transfer your weight, move your head and eyes to a position just above the bent back knee to ensure the bat meets the ball at arm's length. Hold your head steady and keep your eyes on the ball. In previous strokes the head and eyes have been behind the point of contact with the ball. In the square cut, if the head and eyes are too close to the line of the ball, the stroke will be cramped; if they are too far away you won't hit the ball with the centre of the blade or you may not even be able to reach it.

4 BATSWING AND BODY POSITION Swing the bat down into a horizontal position from behind the back shoulder. Straighten your arms and strike the ball downwards in the middle of the bat, with both arms extended at a point level with the back hip.

Let the ball do the work rather than hitting it hard. At the point of contact close the face of the bat and roll your bottom hand on the bat handle over the top hand thus hitting the ball into the ground.

5 FOLLOW-THROUGH In the follow-through bring the bat down and across the front of your body at arm's length, finishing over the front shoulder. The face of the bat should point downwards and your eyes should still be fixed on the point of contact with the ball.

Simplified hints and checklist

1 Swing the bat back like a baseball bat
2 Step back with your back foot as though you are doing a feet astride jump towards cover
3 Sight the ball along your extended arms and rear shoulder
4 Imagine you have an axe and are chopping down a tree at hip level
5 Your axe has missed its mark, let it swing through.

REMEMBER: BE BALANCED. WATCH THE BALL.

Group activity

THE SQUARE CUT
• Feeder A throws 10 balls to batter B, short of a length and wide of the off stump
• The batter attempts to cut the ball in the direction of fielders D, E and F
• The fielders attempt to stop the ball or catch it
• Players rotate positions after 10 deliveries
• Score 4 runs for each hit which penetrates the field and 1 run for any shot hit in the direction of the fielders. No score is recorded if the batter is dismissed or fails to hit the ball.

Number of players: 6
Equipment: 1 set of stumps, 1 bat, 1 ball.

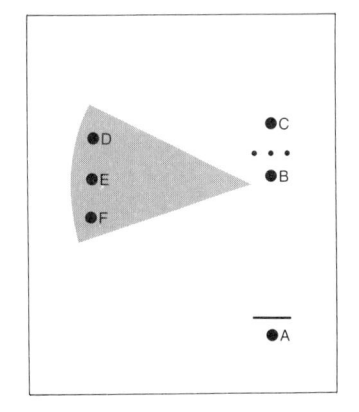

The late cut

The late cut is played in order to punish a ball bouncing short of a length just outside or wide of the off stump, with the least risk of dismissal. The ball must be wide enough to allow room for the stroke, and not involve any danger of the batter being bowled or hitting the ball in the air. Strike the ball along the ground in the area between gully and the wicketkeeper and between the fielders.

REMEMBER: WATCH THE BALL. BE BALANCED.

How to play the late cut

1 BACKLIFT Just before the bowler delivers the ball, lift the bat, first with the top hand, over the middle and off stumps. Then allow your bottom hand to take control at the end of the backswing, pulling the bat slightly behind the rear shoulder, ready to execute a cross-bat shot.

2 FOOT MOVEMENT As the backlift is executed, move your back foot back and across the stumps to a position just in front of or outside the off stump. The toes of your back foot should point slightly behind point and your weight should be on your back foot. Bend your rear knee slightly leaving your front foot towards mid-on or mid-wicket with the toes resting lightly on the ground to maintain balance.

3 HEAD AND EYES Move your head and eyes to the off side above the rear knee and just inside and above the point of contact with the ball. Keep your head steady and your eyes on the ball. At the point of contact look towards the direction of the stroke and along your arms.

4 WEIGHT TRANSFERENCE AND BODY POSITION Your weight should be on the back foot from the first foot movement. Your rear shoulder, hip and leg should point in the direction of the shot and your front side, shoulder and leg should be angled towards mid-wicket or mid-on. Your weight should be above the shot. Don't crouch.

5 BATSWING AND FOLLOW-THROUGH From behind the rear shoulder, swing the bat down on the ball until your arms are fully extended at the point of contact with it. At this stage the bat is almost horizontal and pointing towards slip with its face closed. The wrists roll the bat down on the ball. The follow-through takes it down and across the front of your body. Control the stroke with your bottom hand.

Simplified hints and checklist

1 Swing the bat back like a golf club in a short flat arc
2 Back and across with the back foot towards first slip
3 Sight the ball along your arms
4 Point your rear side towards the direction of the stroke
5 Guide the ball past the slip fielder and let the bat swing through.

REMEMBER: BE BALANCED. WATCH THE BALL.

Group activity

THE LATE CUT
- Feeder A throws 10 deliveries to batter B, short of a length outside the off stump
- The batter attempts to late-cut the ball through the goals in the direction of slips
- Fielder D standing between the goals attempts to catch or stop the ball
- Players rotate positions after 10 deliveries
- Score 4 runs for each shot which passes through the goals (2 runs if it is stopped by the fielders in front of the goals, but would have passed through). No score if the batter is dismissed or fails to hit the ball.

Number of players: 4
Equipment: 1 bat, 1 ball, 1 set of stumps, 1 set of goals.

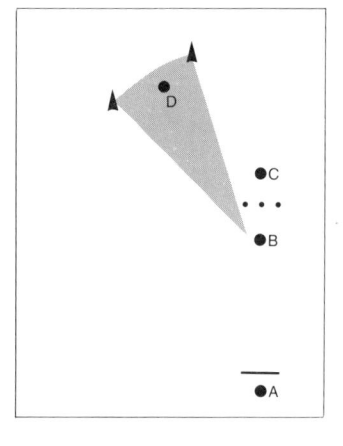

The pull

Play the pull stroke to punish a long hop or half-pitcher which bounces in line with the stumps or just outside off or leg stump and hit it into the area between square leg and the bowler. The stroke must be carried out in such a way as to prevent dismissal. It may also be used against a full toss in line with the stumps or outside leg stump.

A long hop or half-pitcher is a bad ball which pitches very short and rises as high as the batter's midriff. The shortness of the ball means that the batter has a lot of time to play the shot. This stroke should only be played when the batter has been at the crease for some time and is accustomed to the pace of the wicket, the light, the bowling, etc.

REMEMBER: WATCH THE BALL. BE BALANCED.

How to play the pull stroke

1 BACKLIFT As the bowler is about to deliver the ball, lift the bat back in a flat arc, in the early stages with your top hand; then, at the end of the backswing, let your bottom hand take control, pulling the bat high behind your rear shoulder ready to execute a cross-bat stroke.

2 FOOT MOVEMENT As you lift the bat back, move the back foot back and across to the off side to a position close to the stumps or bowling crease. The toes of your back foot take your weight and point towards mid-off or the bowler. Swing the front foot back in an arc until it points in the intended direction of the stroke and ground it lightly.

3 HEAD AND EYES Move your head and eyes until they are slightly to the off or leg side of the line of the ball or behind it. Keep them steady and your eyes on the ball.

4 BATSWING As you begin to swing the bat down from behind your rear shoulder, straighten your arms, swinging the bat downwards and horizontally in front of your body at midriff height. Make contact with the ball at arm's length on the leg side, in front, and sometimes on the off side of your body. Angle the bat face downwards at point of contact to keep the ball on the ground.

5 WEIGHT TRANSFERENCE AND FOLLOW-THROUGH At the beginning of the stroke move your weight onto the toes of the back foot. As you begin to swing the bat, transfer your weight onto the front foot, which is thrust forward in the intended direction of the stroke between square leg and mid-on. Thus your weight adds power to your stroke. The follow-through should be full, causing your body to pivot on the toes of the back foot. You will pivot less if you hit the ball early and towards mid-on and more if you hit the ball late and towards square leg. Your follow-through takes the bat across your body over your original front shoulder.

Simplified hints and checklist

1 Swing the bat back as though you are playing baseball
2 Feet astride toward mid-off
3 Line the ball up with the mid-off/mid-on fielder or bowler
4 Scythe the ball away on the leg side at waist height down onto the ground
5 Retreat to line up the ball and advance to hit it.

REMEMBER: WATCH THE BALL. BE BALANCED.

Group activity

THE PULL
- Feeder A throws 10 deliveries to batter B short of a length in line with the stumps
- The batter attempts to pull the ball between the goalposts which have been set up on the leg side, square with the wicket and some 20 m distant from the batter
- Fielders D, E, F and G attempt to stop the ball passing through the goals
- Players rotate positions after 10 deliveries
- Score 4 runs for each shot which passes through the goals along the ground and 1 run for each shot which is successfully hit into the ground on the leg side. No score if the batter is dismissed or fails to hit the ball.

Number of players: 6–8
Equipment: 1 bat, 1 ball, 1 set of stumps, 1 set of goals.

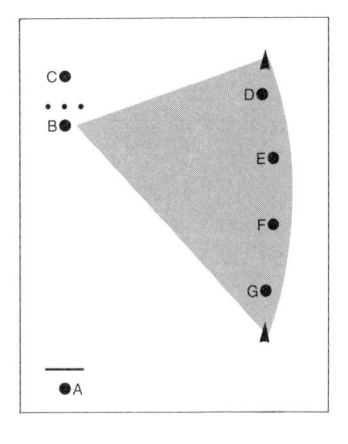

The hook

The hook stroke is played to punish a ball which pitches very short of a length in line with, or outside, the leg stump and rises to a height between the batter's chest and head. The ball should be hit between square and fine leg in such a way as to avoid giving a catch. The difference between the pull and the hook shots is that the pull drags the ball off its original course into the area between square leg and mid-on, whereas the hook helps the ball on its way into the area between fine leg and square leg.

The stroke is generally made against a fast bowler's 'bouncer' or 'bumper': a very short, quick ball directed just over the stumps or in line with the batter's body and continuing on an upward path as it arrives at the batting crease. You should only play the hook when you have been at the crease for some time.

REMEMBER: WATCH THE BALL. BE BALANCED.

How to play the hook stroke

1 BACKLIFT As the bowler is about to deliver the ball, lift the bat back in a flat arc, in the early stages by the top hand; then, at the end of the backswing, let the bottom hand take control, pulling the bat high behind the rear shoulder ready to execute a cross-bat stroke.

2 FOOT MOVEMENT As you lift the bat back, move the back foot back and across towards the off side and to a position close to the stumps or bowling crease. Take the weight on the toes of your back foot which should point towards mid-off or the bowler as they act as a pivot. As the stroke is executed, swing your front foot back in an arc past the back foot, continuing towards the leg stump, and behind the back foot.

3 HEAD AND EYES Move your head and eyes with the feet until they are inside the line of the ball, but keep them steady and your eyes fixed on the ball.

4 BATSWING As you begin to bring the bat down from behind the rear shoulder, straighten your arms, swinging the bat horizontally in front of your body or head. Make contact with the ball at arm's length and on the leg side of your body, level with the shoulders or head. At the point of contact with the ball, angle the face of the bat towards the ground.

5 WEIGHT TRANSFERENCE AND FOLLOW-THROUGH At the beginning of the stroke move your weight onto the toes of your back foot, which acts as a pivot for the shot. Your front foot should swing in an arc from the batting crease to a position in line with or outside and very close to the leg stump, then in front of the stumps to complete a semicircle,

finishing outside the off stump. Carry the shoulders and bat in a horizontal circular movement, finishing up with the bat over your original front shoulder and your rear shoulder pointing to square leg.

Simplified hints and checklist
1 Swing the bat back like a golf club
2 Step back until your head is inside the line of the ball. Your feet are astride and your chest faces point
3 Sniff the ball as it is about to pass over your front shoulder
4 Chop down at a tree on your leg side, shoulder-high
5 Swivel on the toes of back foot.

REMEMBER: BE BALANCED. WATCH THE BALL.

Group activity
THE HOOK
- Feeder A throws 10 deliveries short of a length in line with or just outside the leg stump to batter B
- The batter attempts to hook the ball in the direction of fine leg
- Fielders D, E and F attempt to catch the ball
- Players rotate positions after 10 deliveries
- Score 4 runs for each successful shot. A 2-run penalty is incurred if the ball is caught by a fielder. No score if the batter fails to hit the ball.

Number of players: 6–8
Equipment: 1 bat, 1 rubber ball or tennis ball, 1 set of stumps.

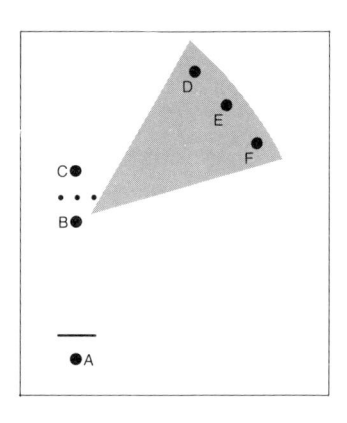

Detection and correction of faults in back-foot strokes

For the procedure to be followed in order to detect faults see *Detection and correction of faults in front-foot strokes* (page 28).

1 Back-foot straight-bat strokes

Correct model

Comments on the reasons behind the skill and possible faults.

- GRIP
- STANCE
- BACKLIFT

See *Detection and correction of faults in front foot strokes* (page 29).

- BACK-FOOT MOVEMENT

1 The back foot moves back and across towards the off side, to a position inside and alongside the line of the ball
2 The back foot moves far enough back and across
3 The back-foot movement is quick and decisive
4 The back foot stabilises
5 The front foot moves backwards towards the rear foot and rests lightly on the ground.

The movement of the back foot back and across towards the off side brings the head and eyes into a position just to the off side of the back leg and behind the line of the ball, from which position the batter is able to discern the swing and spin of the ball. The backward step also affords the batter more time in which to track the ball, make decisions about the stroke to play, and execute the stroke. Inadequate movement back and across will prevent the batter sighting the ball properly and making the appropriate decisions and executing the stroke correctly. Research indicates that the backward step should not be too pronounced since this will occupy too much time and make the batter late in playing the shot. A hesitant backward movement will also involve more than one movement and occupy unnecessary time, as well as prevent the back foot from stabilising quickly. The stabilisation of the back foot provides a firm base from which to transmit the force of the stroke. This is of paramount importance in the back-foot strokes because, since the rear foot moves back, many of the shots produced are hit in front of the wicket. This means that the batter must launch the body weight forward into the stroke off the firm foundation of the back foot. Back-foot strokes should be played off the ball or flat of the rear foot, since this provides a wider and more stable centre of gravity. Many players express their determination to get behind the line of the ball by exaggerating their movement across the wicket towards the off side. Often this action causes the batter's head and centre of gravity to move too far across to the off side beyond the rear leg, making the striker overbalance in that direction. This loss of balance will cause the batter to hit any delivery on the leg side of his body into the air on the on side.

The front leg also has a role to play in the execution of back-foot strokes. After the back foot is firmly planted and stabilised, the front leg is drawn backwards towards it, with the front foot resting lightly on the ground. This assists the batter's balance. It is also important that the front of the leading leg should point in the direction of the line of the ball and the intended stroke. The falling away of the front leg towards the leg side during the execution of a back-foot stroke causes the batter's weight to move in the same direction and away from the line of the approaching ball. This will often cause the batter to edge the ball outside the off stump as a catch to the wicketkeeper or slips. Quite a common fault amongst youngsters playing this stroke is a tendency to back away towards the leg side because of a fear of the hard ball.

CORRECTION STRATEGIES
From a distance of about 10 metres, throw balls to the batter, so that they bounce in front of a line 2 metres from the popping crease and in line with the stumps. The player then has to step back to play a back-foot stroke with the rear foot planted just inside the line of the ball. You may use a soft, bouncy ball and the batter may dispense with the bat; in this instance the striker should catch the ball with the natural hand as it arrives alongside the thigh of the back leg. Use verbal cues: 'Back and across'; 'Get behind the ball', etc. 'Footprints' (shoe insoles) may be used to indicate to the batter the correct placement of the rear foot for a delivery on a predetermined line. To prevent players backing away, position a cardboard cone behind the batter's legs halfway between the bowling and batting creases. When the batter plays back, the rear foot must not kick the cone, but move inside it and towards the off side. As with the front-foot strokes, use a bowling machine, pitching the ball in front of a line 2 metres in front of the popping crease so that the batter has to play back.

● POSITIONING OF THE HEAD AND EYES
See *Detection and correction of faults in front-foot strokes* (page 32).

● BODY MOVEMENT
1 The body moves back towards the off side and the stumps as the batter executes a short, decisive and quick step backwards
2 The weight of the body is then transferred forward in the direction of the ball's line as shots in front of the wicket are executed

It is important to establish the body on a solid stabilised base before back-foot shots can be played. The movement of the body backwards also provides the batter with more time to play the stroke since it increases the distance the ball must travel. In order to hit the ball in front of the wicket, however, the weight of the body must then be transferred forward into the stroke. The force of this forward transfer of weight will depend on the power with which the shot is played. Thus a back-foot defensive stroke will have little forward movement of weight, whilst the back-foot drive will cause the shoulders and body to move towards the line of the ball quite forcibly. It is important to maintain the side-on

3 The body maintains a side-on position during the playing of the stroke with the front shoulder, elbow, side, hip and leg pointing in the direction of the intended shot. position during the back-foot straight-bat shots with the front side of the body pointing in the direction of the intended stroke and the toes of the feet pointing towards point. Force is then imparted to the stroke by the vertical forward rotation of the shoulders around the axis of the head and the sideways movement of the weight of the body into the stroke. Many players try to hit back-foot shots hard by using the arms and hitting strongly with the natural bottom hand on the bat handle. This causes a wide lateral movement of the shoulders, which in turn makes the batter swivel on the rear foot. The result of this action is that the bat descends from the top of the backlift in a wide arc from off to leg and across the line of the ball, thus minimising the chance of making contact with the ball.

CORRECTION STRATEGIES
Use verbal cues: 'Move back to see the ball, advance to hit it'; 'Side on'; 'Rock your shoulders, pointing your front side at the ball'. Place a piece of coloured sticky tape on the inside of the batter's leading shoulder, so that it remains visible to the player as the shot is played, thereby ensuring the side-on position. Place 'footprints' in the appropriate spot to ensure the correct positioning of the back foot and the maintenance of that position during the stroke.

- MOVEMENT OF THE SHOULDERS AND ARMS
See *Detection and correction of faults in front-foot strokes* (page 32).
- BATSWING
See *Detection and correction of faults in front-foot strokes* (page 33).
- FOLLOW-THROUGH
See *Detection and correction of faults in front-foot strokes* (page 34).
- RESULT OF THE STROKE
See *Detection and correction of faults in front-foot strokes* (page 34).

2 Back-foot cross-bat strokes — the cut

The correct model

Comments on the reasons behind the skill and possible faults

- GRIP
See *Detection and correction of faults in front-foot strokes* (page 29).
- STANCE
See *Detection and correction of faults in front-foot strokes* (page 29).

- THE BACKLIFT
1 The bat should be horizontal at the top of the backlift
2 The backlift should be high behind the batter's head.

The horizontal posture of the bat at the top of the backlift results from the batter's bottom hand on the handle taking charge of the movement after it has been initiated by the top hand. This position is essential to the execution of a cross-bat stroke. The backlift should be high to facilitate the batter hitting down on the ball and keeping it on the ground. One of the most common faults in this shot is the batter lofting it as a catch to the gully or slip fielders.

CORRECTION STRATEGIES
Use a 'tee-ball' tee, placing a ball on it at waist height. The batter takes up a position on the leg side of the tee and about a bat-and-arm's length from it. The striker then practises lifting the bat back, before striking down on the teed ball. This motor skill may also be practised without a ball with the batter standing in front of a full-length mirror to observe the correctness of the backlift.

- BACK-FOOT MOVEMENT
1 The back leg moves back towards the off side
2 The back foot stabilises with the toes of the rear foot pointing towards backward point
3 The rear knee is slightly bent.

The movement of the rear foot takes the batter's body back towards the off side of the stumps. It brings the batter into a position where contact can be made with the ball with the arms and bat fully extended. The batter adopts a posture in which the chest faces mid-off. The rear foot is firmly planted to permit a stable base for the summation of forces which will impart the greatest power to the stroke. The rear knee is slightly bent to facilitate the batter's balance. The batter must not let the head go beyond the bent rear knee in an off-side direction otherwise a loss of balance will result. The rear knee must not be too bent otherwise the striker will crouch in playing the stroke, thus increasing the chances of hitting the ball upwards as a catch to the slips cordon. The movement of the rear leg in the cut is of paramount importance since it brings the batter's body into the correct position – not too close to the line of the ball and not too far away from it. If the striker is too close to the ball's line, he or she will be too cramped to play the stroke; too far away, and the ball will be out of reach.

CORRECTION STRATEGIES

Use 'footprints' to indicate the correct placement of the rear and front feet in the execution of the stroke. From a distance of about 10 metres, throw short balls bouncing waist-high on a line about 1 metre outside the batter's off stump; the batter practises the cut, trying to steer the ball through a 10-metre-wide target area designated by stumps and situated about 20 metres from the batter in the point region. The batter must hit the ball through the target area along the ground. A fielder retrieves the ball. Use verbal cues to prevent the batter crouching: 'Stand up on the stroke'; 'Don't crouch.'

It is best to use simulated match and group-activity situations to correct faults in this stroke, since one of the most common errors in its execution is that of playing it to an inappropriate delivery, i.e. a ball which is too close to the batter's body, is too full-pitched, is too wide to reach or bounces too high to hit along the ground. Game situations present the batter with the opportunity to refine his or her judgement about when to play the stroke.

• POSITIONING OF THE HEAD AND EYES

1 The head and eyes move to a position which is exactly a bat-and-arm's length away from the line of the approaching ball
2 The eyes sight the approaching ball from alongside the leading shoulder.

As always in playing a stroke, the head and eyes remain steady, level and still throughout the execution of the stroke. They do not move behind the line of the ball in playing the cut. The stroke demands great perceptual judgement to determine the line and speed of the approaching ball very early in its flight. The positioning of the rear foot in the stroke hinges on this tracking of the ball by the eyes. Thus the batter sights the ball early in its flight along the line of the front shoulder, makes the decision to cut and moves the rear foot into a position which brings the head and eyes to a spot a bat-and-arm's length from the line of the ball. The batter keeps the head down and looks at the point of contact as the ball is struck.

CORRECTION STRATEGIES

Use verbal cues: 'Head down'; 'Sight the ball along your arms'. Use simulated match situations as suggested under Back-foot movement as above.

• BODY MOVEMENT

1 The batter's body is in an open position with the chest facing mid-off
2 The batter does not crouch.

There is no need for the batter to maintain a side-on position since this is a cross-bat stroke demanding a lateral rather than vertical swing of the shoulders and bat. The 'chest-on' position during the execution of the stroke suits this movement. The body should be erect so that the batter hits down on the ball from above its line of flight.

CORRECTION STRATEGIES

Use simulated game and group activity situations as under Back-foot movement as above. Employ verbal cues: 'Stand up when you play the stroke'; 'Don't crouch'.

• MOVEMENT OF THE SHOULDERS AND ARMS

1 The arms and shoulders swing from a high position at the top of the backlift, horizontally and down to the

The downward swing of the shoulders and arms ensures that the bat swings down on the ball. If this does not occur the ball may be lofted as a catch into the slips cordon. The straightening of the arms

height of the ball's bounce
2 The arms straighten during the batswing and are fully extended at the point of contact.

means that contact between bat and ball is made at the appropriate distance outside the off stump. If the arms are not fully extended, the batter's elbows are tucked into the side of the body, impeding the full swing of the bat and cramping the striker in the execution of the stroke. When this occurs, the ball is too close to the off stump to play the cut.

CORRECTION STRATEGIES
Make the batter model the shoulder and arm action without a ball. Feedback for the striker can be provided by executing the movement in front of a full-length mirror or videotaping and replaying it to the player. Use simulated game and group activities to practise the skill and provide verbal cues: 'Swing down on the ball'; 'Arms fully extended'.

- BATSWING
1 The bat swings horizontally and slightly down on the ball
2 The bat face is angled slightly downwards towards the ground at the moment of impact.

The downward horizontal swing of the bat and its closed face guarantees that the ball will be hit into the ground, thereby avoiding giving a catch to the fielders behind the wicket on the off side. The batswing should be controlled and not too forceful. The batter exploits the speed of the ball to guide it away on the off side. Contact with the ball is made when the ball is level with the batter's body for the square cut and when the ball has just passed the striker's rear hip for the late cut.

CORRECTION STRATEGIES
Use the drills outlined under Movement of the shoulders and arms as above.

- FOLLOW-THROUGH
1 Across the front of the batter's body with the bat swinging horizontally and slightly downwards
2 Not too forceful or full.

The downwards horizontal follow-through indicates that the ball has been struck downwards with a cross bat. Since the ball is guided and not struck violently, the follow-through reflects this lack of force whilst indicating that the face of the bat was moving at the point of contact. The fact that the cut is a cross-bat stroke means that the follow-through is lateral and not in the same direction as the stroke.

CORRECTION STRATEGIES
The follow-through reflects the correct execution of the previous phases of the stroke. Strategies to ensure a correct follow-through should therefore have been carried out at earlier stages of the stroke.

- RESULT OF THE STROKE
The stroke has been performed a) correctly, b) incorrectly.

The desired result from the stroke usually indicates its correctness; an incorrect result indicates the necessity for remedial procedures previously outlined.

3 Back-foot cross-bat strokes — the pull and hook

The correct model

Comments on the reasons behind the skill and possible faults

- GRIP
- STANCE

See *Detection and correction of faults in front-foot strokes* (page 29).

- BACKLIFT

1 The bat is horizontal at the top of the backlift
2 The backlift is high behind the batter's head.

The horizontal position of the bat at the top of the backlift results from the batter's bottom hand on the handle taking charge of the movement after it has been initiated by the top hand. This position is essential to the execution of a cross-bat stroke. The backlift is high to facilitate hitting down on the ball and keeping it on the ground. One of the most common faults in the pull and hook strokes is the batter lofting the ball as a catch to fielders on the leg side.

CORRECTION STRATEGIES
The batter models the backlift in front of a full-length mirror. Feedback as to the correctness or incorrectness of the backlift can be provided by the comments of a partner. A videotape facility can also provide the same information. Carry out these procedures without using a ball.

- BACK-FOOT MOVEMENT

1 The back foot moves backwards and across the wicket towards the off side to an appropriate position relative to the line of the ball
2 The back-foot movement is quick, decisive and of an appropriate length
3 The back foot stabilises
4 The weight of the body is on the ball or toes of the back foot
5 In the case of the pull stroke, the batter moves first on to the back foot, but as the stroke is executed moves forwards again on the front foot which is advanced in the direction of the intended stroke
6 In the case of the hook stroke, the back foot acts as a pivot around which the front foot swings in a wide arc.

The back foot moves back to afford the batter extra time in which to see the ball and execute the stroke by increasing the distance between the approaching ball and the striker.
  If the pull stroke is played to a short ball outside the off stump the back foot moves across the wicket to a position closer to the stumps than the line of the ball. This movement brings the body and arms into a position from which the ball can be struck with the arms fully extended from a spot in front of the batter's body and slightly to its off side.
  If the pull stroke is played to a delivery bouncing waist- or chest-high in line with the stumps, the foot movement is slightly to the off side of the line of the ball. This brings the body and arms into a chest-on position in front of the stumps from which the ball can be struck with the arms fully extended from a spot directly in front of the batter's body.
  If the pull stroke is played to a ball outside the line of the leg stump, the back foot moves to a position well to the off side of the line of the ball. This brings the batter's body into an open position in front of the stumps from which the ball can be struck with the arms fully extended from a spot in

61

front and slightly to the leg side of the batter's body.

For the hook stroke the back-foot movement takes the batter's body well to the off side and inside the line of the approaching high-bouncing delivery. This means that should the bat fail to make contact with the ball, the batter is so far inside its line that there is no danger of being struck on the body or head. Hesitancy in the execution of the back-foot movement entails superfluous movements, thus increasing the reaction and movement time needed to play the shot.

A back-foot movement which is too long and pronounced also augments movement time and causes mis-timing of the stroke.

The back foot must stabilise and bear the batter's weight since it provides the firm base from which the summation of forces begins, enabling the batter to put power into the stroke.

The batter's weight for the execution of the pull stroke is borne on the ball of the rear foot, since this provides a broader centre of gravity from which the force of the stroke may be launched forwards on to the front foot.

For the hook stroke the batter's weight is carried on the toes of the rear foot because in this instance less forward momentum is required. Since the stroke is played behind square leg, the back foot acts not as a launching pad for the shot, but rather as a pivot around which the body swivels.

In the hook stroke the batter's weight swivels on the rear foot as the ball is helped on its way to fine leg. This causes the front foot to swing in an extended arc around the back foot, sometimes finishing on the off side of the stumps with the batter facing the wicketkeeper.

Correct positioning is a key factor in the execution of the pull and hook strokes and hinges on the correct placement of the feet. Most errors which occur in this skill have their origins in the incorrect movement of the feet and transference of weight.

CORRECTION STRATEGIES

Using a tennis or bouncy ball on a hard true surface, throw deliveries onto a target area 5 metres in front of the batting crease, in line with or on either side of the wicket so that they bounce chest- or head-high as they come within the batter's striking range. The batter uses a paddle bat or the hands to hit the ball, or may catch the ball after positioning the feet. Against the bouncer, the batter must decide when to play the hook shot or avoid the ball by ducking. A wall behind the batter obviates the necessity of retrieving the ball. Use 'footprints' (shoe insoles) to reinforce the placement of the feet, and provide the batter with verbal cues: 'Feet astride facing mid-off'; 'Plant yourself firmly on the back foot'.

- **POSITIONING OF THE HEAD AND EYES**

1 The head and eyes are stable, level and do not lift on contact between bat and ball
2 The head and eyes are positioned appropriately for the stroke to be played: to the leg or off side of the line of the ball or behind it for the pull, inside the line of the ball for the hook.

Since there is often a risk of being struck and injured by the rising ball in the execution of a pull or hook stroke, the apprehensive batter sometimes averts the eyes in playing the shot. Taking one's eyes off the ball drastically reduces the chances of hitting it, and greatly increases the risk of injury. The position of the head and eyes will vary for the execution of the pull stroke. When pulling a ball from outside the off stump the head must be slightly to the leg side of the line of the ball; when playing the same stroke to a ball on the wicket the head and eyes must be diametrically behind its line; when pulling a ball which pitches outside the leg stump the batter's eyes must be to the off side of the ball's line. In each instance, the eyes line up the ball so that it may be hit with the arms fully extended either in front of or to the side of the batter's body.

For the hook stroke the head and eyes are well inside the line of the delivery and line up the ball so that the stroke may be carried out with the arms fairly straight. In playing the hook stroke the head must never be positioned in line with the ball: it is in these circumstances that batters are struck and injured. The position of the head and eyes in playing the pull and hook strokes is contingent on correct foot movement and body positioning.

CORRECTION STRATEGIES
Insist that batters wear helmets at practice and in matches. Such protection reduces the chance of serious injury, anxiety levels and improves skill performances. Carry out the correction strategies outlined under *Back-foot movement* (page 63) for the movement of the feet.

- **BODY MOVEMENT**

1 For the pull stroke the body assumes an open position facing mid-off, the bowler or mid-on
2 For the pull stroke the transference of weight occurs firstly onto the back foot and then forwards onto the front foot in the direction of the intended stroke
3 For the hook stroke the body retains a side-on position as the back foot moves back and across the stumps
4 For the hook stroke the weight is transferred onto the toes of the rear foot and swivels on that axis.

In the pull stroke the weight moves back on to the firm base of the back foot, as the body assumes the chest-on position necessary to play a cross-bat stroke in front of the batter. The chest usually faces the point of contact between bat and ball. After establishing a stable base on the back foot, the batter then moves his or her weight forwards onto the front foot in the direction of the intended stroke in order to impart power into it.

In playing the hook it is advisable to retain a side-on position until such time as the body swivels on the rear toes. If a batter is compelled to duck to avoid a bumper, a side-on position ensures that the evasive action will be towards the off side and inside the line of the approaching ball. A chest-on posture causes the batter to duck forwards towards the ball rather than out of its line.

The swivelling movement on the toes of the back foot imparts power to the hook whilst ensuring maximum control. It is important to note that not much power is required for the hook stroke since the batter is harnessing the speed of the fast bowler and merely helping the ball on its way to fine leg. Control of the stroke is far more important: one of the most common faults in playing the hook is to try to hit the ball too hard and in so doing loft the stroke to deep fine leg. Balance is of paramount importance in playing the pull and hook strokes. Often batters fail to establish a firm centre of gravity on the base of their rear foot, allowing their weight to pass beyond that fulcrum towards the off side. With their weight falling towards point, away from the line of the ball, they are therefore unable to control the stroke and loft the ball to the fielders on the leg side.

CORRECTION STRATEGIES
Carry out the correction procedures outlined under *Back-foot movement* (page 63) for the movement of the feet.

- MOVEMENT OF THE SHOULDERS AND ARMS

1 The shoulders and arms move through a horizontal arc and down on the ball when it is in front of or as it passes the batter
2 The arms are fully extended throughout the batswing.

The most common fault in the execution of the pull and hook strokes is failure to keep the ball on the ground. Difficulty is created for the batter by the abnormally high bounce of the ball and the attendant problem of hitting down on it. It is therefore imperative that the movement of the shoulders in the backlift should take the rear shoulder to a very high position, thus enabling the batter to lift the bat very high. From this position the lateral movement of the shoulders must involve a pronounced downward swing if the ball is to be hit into the ground.

As in the cut, the arms must be straight in the playing of the pull and hook strokes, since the power in the shot depends upon a full swing of the bat. Strokes played with a horizontal bat also require the batter's elbows to be a long way from the body in order to permit the uninhibited swing of the bat. The point of contact between bat and ball in the pull and hook strokes is always a bat-and-arm's length in front of or to the side of the body. A common fault amongst batters is that of trying to play the hook or pull to balls which are too close to the body.

CORRECTION STRATEGIES
Carry out the correction procedures outlined under *Back-foot movement* (page 63) for the movement of the feet.

- BATSWING

1 The bat swings horizontally with a pronounced downward movement on the ball
2 The face of the bat is angled downwards at the point of contact with the ball.

The failure of the bat to swing down on the ball is the natural consequence of an insufficient elevation of the rear shoulder and arm in the backlift and causes the common fault of lofting the hook and pull as a catch to leg-side fielders. Rolling the lower hand (i.e. the hand closest to the blade of the bat) over the top of the handle at the moment of impact with the ball accentuates the closed face of the bat. Such sensitivity of touch, however, occurs only in the skilled batter and it is safer to ensure the closed face of the bat by emphasising its downward horizontal swing on the ball.

CORRECTION STRATEGIES
Carry out the correction strategies outlined under *Backlift* (page 62) to ensure that the backlift is sufficiently high and that the bat will consequently swing down on the ball. Place the ball on a 'tee-ball' tee in an appropriate position for the stroke – i.e. high to the off, in front of or to the leg side and in front of the batter for the pull stroke, level with and to the leg side of the batter for the hook shot. Using two stumps 20 metres apart establish a target area on the leg side through which the ball must be struck along the ground. Such target areas will be in front of the wicket for the pull and level with or behind the wicket for the hook stroke. Measurement of the effectiveness of the stroke may be achieved by awarding the batter 4 runs each time the ball is struck through the target area. A similar strategy may be carried out against a moving ball. In this case the ball is projected by a bowling machine or a player throwing the ball onto a designated spot on the pitch 8–10 metres in front of the batting crease so that the ball rises to chest or shoulder height when it is level with the batter. The batter then strikes the ball through the target area on the leg side along the ground.

● FOLLOW-THROUGH

1 The follow-through should be full, indicating power in the pull stroke, but controlled in the case of the hook
2 The follow-through is horizontal in a downward arc slightly lower than the point of contact with the ball and around the axis of the batter's body
3 In the pull, the follow-through will be initially more in the direction of the intended stroke, before swinging in the downward arc in front of the batter's body.

More power is required for the pull because the stroke is played in front of the wicket. The hook shot uses the pace of the bowler and deflects the ball behind the wicket on the leg side; therefore it requires less power and this is reflected in the follow-through, which is full because the batter is pivoting on the rear foot, but controlled because the aim is to keep the ball on the ground. The follow-through is lower than the point of contact with the ball, indicating that the bat has swung down on the ball. In the pull stroke it is further forward and in the intended direction of the stroke because the batter's weight is moving forwards at the moment of contact with the ball. In the case of the hook the follow-through almost describes a circle around the axis of the batter's body because the stroke entails the body pivoting on the toes of the back foot.

CORRECTION STRATEGIES
The follow-through reflects the execution of the previous phases of the stroke. Strategies to ensure a correct follow-through should therefore have been carried out in the earlier stages of the stroke.

● RESULT OF THE STROKE

The stroke has been performed a) correctly, b) incorrectly.

The desired result from the stroke usually indicates its correctness; an incorrect result shows the necessity for the remedial procedures previously outlined.

The attacking strokes

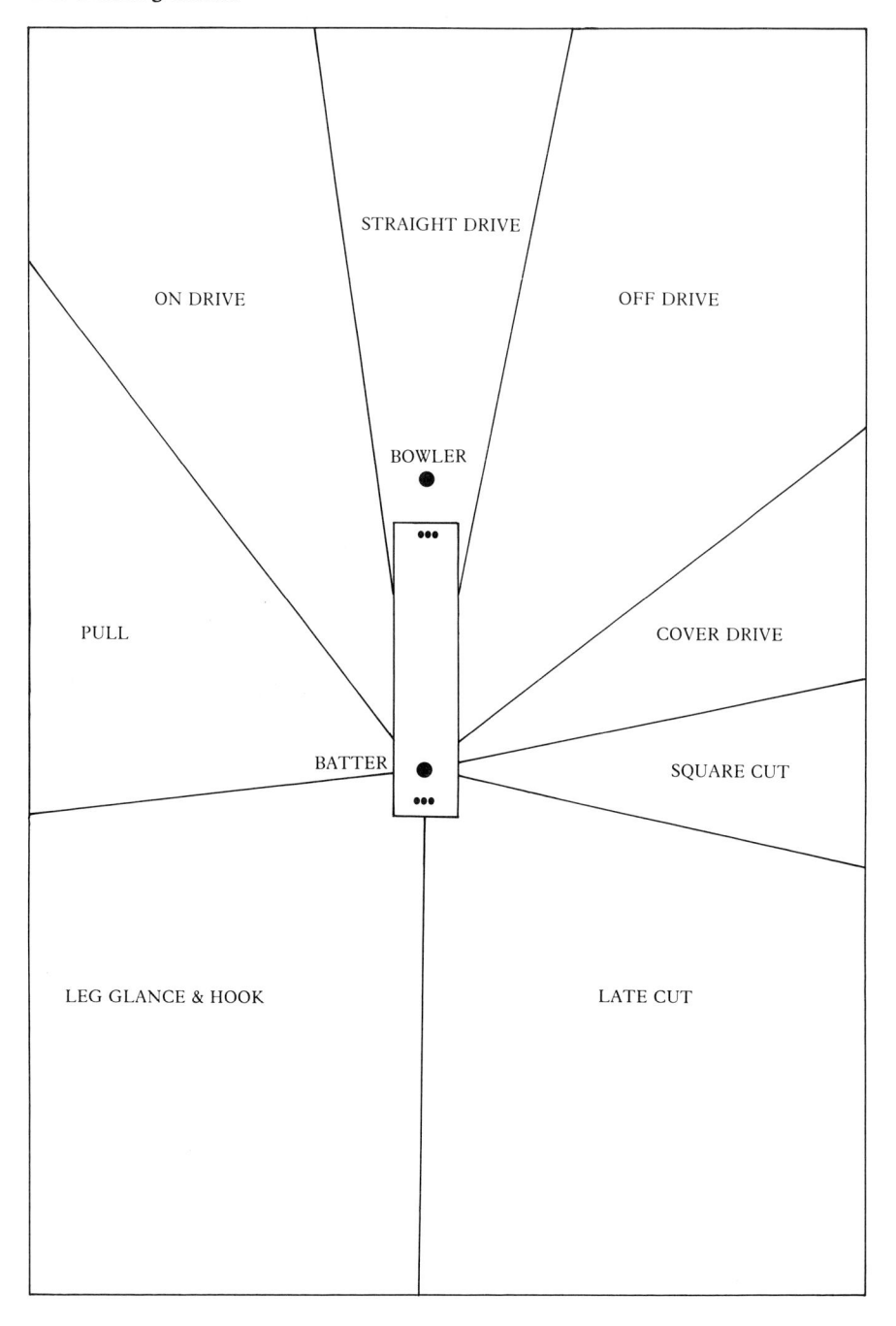

STRAIGHT DRIVE

ON DRIVE

OFF DRIVE

BOWLER

PULL

COVER DRIVE

BATTER

SQUARE CUT

LEG GLANCE & HOOK

LATE CUT

Running between the wickets

The batter should learn to run well between the wickets to score the maximum number of runs and avoid being run out unnecessarily. Correct placement of shots and good running between the wickets can dictate bowling tactics and field settings.

REMEMBER: BE BALANCED. WATCH THE BALL AND THE FIELDER.

How to run well between the wickets

1 KNOW THE BOWLER'S TACTICS, THE FIELD AND YOUR PARTNER The batter should acquire a knowledge of the bowler's intentions, e.g. whether he is concentrating on the off stump short of a length. This will enable you to know where your best chance of runs lies. Watch where the field is placed and note their positions before taking strike. Pinpoint the good, mobile, strong-throwing fielders and take no risks with them. Learn the right- and left-handed throwers. You would normally be able to run a single to cover's left hand but *not* if he or she is left-handed. You should also know your partner: whether he or she is a fast or slow runner, hesitant or reliable. Most good partnerships are based on trust and understanding.

2 THE CALL The call is short for an immediate response and loud and clear for understanding. There are three calls: 'yes', 'no' and 'wait'. Beware of calls which may be misinterpreted, e.g. 'go', which could be misheard as 'no'. 'Wait' is used only when there is some doubt that the ball will pass the fielders.

Call immediately after every ball and after each run call again to indicate the possibility of an additional run. As you and your partner cross in mid-wicket indicate your intentions about the next run.

If there is any doubt about a run the call should always be 'no'. An extra run is not worth a wicket. Always call 'no' for a misfield when it is impossible to judge how quickly the fielder will recover.

The batter who has the clearer sight of the ball should always call. For strokes in front of the wicket, the striker has the clearer view and calls. For those strokes travelling behind the wicket, the non-striker calls. This may vary in certain instances; for example, a striker deflecting the ball fine past leg slip may see the fielder miss the ball and block the view of the non-striker. In this instance the striker calls for the run.

The batter who is running to the 'danger-end' – that is, to the stumps to which the ball is being returned on the completion of two, three, four or five runs – always has the final say.

The caller must always guarantee his or her partner a safe passage, otherwise trust and understanding between them disappear. The non-caller must always trust the caller.

3 BACKING UP Never regard backing up as 'stealing a metre' at the beginning of a run. It is merely a 'moving barrier' start by the batter as the ball is in the air and before it is struck (approx. $1/2$–1 second). The non-striking batter walks up with the bowler in the last few strides of the run-up. The non-striker is on the opposite side of the wicket to the bowler, watching his hand, advancing sideways, chest-on to the bowler and trailing his bat in his rear hand. If you are backing up always keep some part of your bat or body behind the batting crease until *after* the bowler has released the ball. While the ball is in the air, take two or three steps down the pitch before the ball is struck and the call for runs made or until it passes through to the wicketkeeper. From this position you can go through for a run or quickly regain your crease.

If the batter tries to steal a start before the bowler releases the ball, it is within the Laws of Cricket for the bowler to run the batter out without prior warning.

4 THE RUN Run the first and subsequent runs as quickly as possible. Never slow down until there is no possibility of any more runs. In

completing the final run ground your bat 20 cm (8 in) in front of the popping crease and slide it in at arm's length.

Never run too far beyond the wicket in case of overthrows.

5 THE TURN When running between the wickets, always watch the ball and the fielder chasing it. Transfer the bat into the hand opposite to the side of the wicket to which the ball has been hit. Stop for a fraction of a second at the end of the run in a side-on position with your chest and head facing the ball. At full stretch reach out, grounding your bat lightly behind the batting crease, before calling for another run, receiving the agreement of your partner and embarking on the additional run.

A good shot does not automatically mean a run. Quick singles result largely from the placement of the stroke and touch: that is, if you place the ball short of the fielders and into vacant spaces in the field. Understanding between the partners is essential. This understanding will only come from batting and practising together.

The batters must think when running between the wickets. 'When in doubt, never run out' should be the golden rule.

Simplified hints and checklist

1 Know your partner and the oppositon
2 Yes, no and wait. No other loud and clear commands but these. Call for every ball. When in doubt stay at home. Those who see call. Danger – batter running to get home. Trust your partner and do not hesitate
3 Don't steal but borrow a few metres after the bowler has released the ball
4 Run every run as though it were the winning run. Stop when hope of further runs has gone. Slide your bat home. Don't run too far beyond the stumps
5 Face the ball when turning, call and run again.

REMEMBER: WATCH THE BALL. BE BALANCED.

Group activity

RUNNING BETWEEN THE WICKETS
- Feeder A bowls 6 deliveries to batter B on or outside off stump
- The batter hits the ball on the off side and runs are taken as in normal cricket
- Fielders rotate positions at the end of each 6-ball over
- Batters may be dismissed bowled, caught, stumped or run out. In addition, failure to call correctly, back up, turn, or complete a run in the appropriate manner will also constitute a dismissal
- A batter once dismissed may bat again after all other batters have had a turn
- Each team bats for a specific time or number of overs
- The team scoring the higher number of runs in the allotted time is the winner.

Number of players: 2 teams of 6-10 players
Equipment: 2 bats, 1 ball, 1 set of stumps.

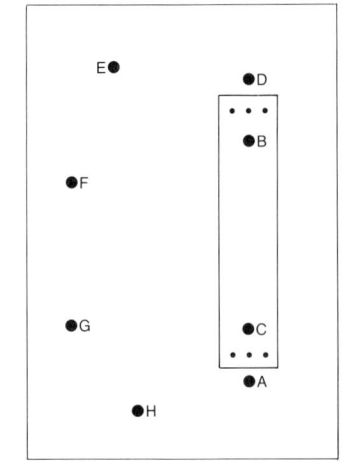

Bowling

Bowling: the run-up

The bowler runs up before delivery in order to add the impetus of forward movement to body weight and muscular strength. The bowler's approach contributes 20 per cent of the ball's speed and enables a slow bowler to move the bowling arm and hand around the ball more quickly and thereby spin the ball more. The run-up also adds to a bowler's pace by accentuating the 'rock-back' body movement in the delivery stride. If a fast bowler leans forward whilst running in, the body has to move through a greater angle in the 'rock-back' and the force imparted to the ball will be correspondingly greater. Most important of all, the run-up is the principal determinant of a bowler's accuracy. If a bowler moves consistently towards the target of the batter's wicket in the approach, this forward impetus propels the ball along the same straight line. It is virtually impossible to project a ball accurately in one direction whilst running in a different one. If the bowler permits the direction of the approach or a loss of balance to divert the body's forward movement from the line of the batter's wicket, a loss of accuracy will result.

Consistent body impetus at the moment of release also produces a steady length. The bowler has no need to determine the amount of force to put behind the ball in order to bounce it on the desired spot. The automatic movements of the body obviate the need for such judgements.

The length of the run-up depends on each individual's action and physique. It should not be too long and tiring but carried out with the correct degree of acceleration and deceleration within a minimum number of metres. The bowler should be moving at the maximum speed compatible with balance in the last-but-one stride of the approach. The bowler starts the run slowly before accelerating evenly to top pace and then slowing up slightly and executing a jump as the body turns sideways in the final stride of the approach. The last-but-one stride of the run-up is the longest and the fastest. The last pace is one of the shortest since it facilitates the gymnastic sideways action necessary to deliver the ball. Then follows the very long delivery stride.

The run-up provides the basic rhythm of a bowler's action. Some bowlers approach the crease in rhythmic units of three strides, others in units of four or five. The ideal approach incorporates the minimum number of these units compatible with correct acceleration, deceleration and balance in the delivery stride.

The run-up may be straight or at various angles from the mid-off position. The more oblique the approach, the easier it is to turn into the action in the delivery stride. Always remember however, that the angle of the approach should not divert the bowler from moving consistently and steadily towards the target of the batter's wicket.

1 LENGTH AND RHYTHM Establish the length, speed, angle and rhythm of the run-up by beginning at the batting crease at the bowler's end of the wicket. Turn your back on the batter's wicket and run away from the bowling crease. Begin with the foot opposite the bowling arm on the batting crease. Start slowly and accelerate to attain the fastest speed suited to you in the last-but-one stride of the approach. Decelerate as you jump high and sideways into the bowling action and rock back, keeping your arms tucked into your body. Once you have established the length, speed, angle and rhythm of your run-up by these natural methods, measure it in even walking strides so that you can establish a constant appreciation of how long it should be. The natural running method of measuring a run produces variations in its length according to the temperature of the day and the degree to which your body is warmed up. Place a marker at the end of your run.

2 ACCELERATION Begin your run-up from the marker which you have placed on the ground. Begin slowly, gain momentum with a few rhythmic strides, then accelerate, gradually at first but then faster towards the end of your run. It may help to place a second marker on the ground at the point at which you begin to accelerate.

3 DECELERATION The last-but-one stride in your run-up is the longest and fastest, and ends on the foot opposite your bowling arm. Take off from that foot, jumping high into the air and twisting sideways in the air until you are side-on, with the side of your body opposite your bowling arm facing down the wicket towards the batter. This jump slows the forward momentum of the body and produces a short step, but under no circumstances should it stop the body moving forward towards the batter's wicket. As you land on the foot on the same side of the body as your bowling arm, rock back away from the batter at an angle of about 15 degrees, keeping both arms close to the body to facilitate the fast movement of the trunk. Your back foot should point towards the stumps at the bowler's end and should be parallel to the bowling crease. This step is the beginning of the bowling action and the delivery stride.

4 FOLLOW-THROUGH The follow-through is the shock absorber of the action and the run-up. It provides the slow deceleration which places

as little strain on your body as possible. It must be long enough to fulfil this function and not so long as to be tiring. It also provides an indicator of whether your action is correct; if your forward momentum has been maintained it will be straight for two or three paces, before you move off the wicket to avoid running into the 'danger area' 1.2 metres (4 ft) in front of the batting crease and 30 cm (12 in) either side of the middle stump. A slow bowler will follow through less than a faster bowler: some two or three paces.

5 PRACTICE HINTS The run-up must be practised until it is automatic. The no-ball law dictates that some part of the bowler's front foot must be behind the rear edge of the batting crease at the moment of delivery. Since it is impossible for you to watch your front foot at the very moment of releasing the ball – a time when you should be concentrating on where you are going to pitch the ball – you must ensure that you do not bowl a no-ball by placing your back foot far enough behind the bowling crease as you begin the delivery stride. Place a marker on the spot where your back foot should land so that if you begin your delivery stride from that position, your front foot will remain behind the batting crease.

Simplified hints and checklist

1 Practise running up from the batting crease at your end with your back towards the direction in which you are going to bowl. When you feel like bowling, bowl. Now measure out the run-up in even strides.

2 You are a car. Move into first gear, then second, then third. Now brake

3 Jump high, twist and gather yourself as though you are going to do an astride jump facing the bowling wicket

4 Run after the ball. It is impossible to bowl the ball in one direction whilst running in another

5 Perfect practice makes perfect in a simple automatic skill.

REMEMBER: WATCH WHERE THE BALL WILL BOUNCE.
BE BALANCED.

Group activity

BOWLING – THE RUN-UP
- Bowler begins at a set of stumps with feet together, moves off and bowls when it feels comfortable
- Partner places a marker on the ground where the bowler's back foot lands in the delivery stride
- This procedure is repeated until the bowler consistently hits the same spot with the back foot
- The distance from the marker to the stumps is measured by the bowler using normal walking strides. The distance measured represents the length of the bowler's run-up
- Players change roles once the first bowler has established the length of his or her run-up.

Number of players: 2
Equipment: 1 ball, 1 set of stumps, 1 marker.

The basic action

The orthodox side-on action is essential if a bowler is to bowl consistently straight on a desired line, bounce the ball on a good length and obtain the greatest amount of speed, swing, spin or flight.

It should not be presumed that a slow bowler's action is not energetic. The spinner's body action should be strong and his or her bowling arm speed almost as fast as that of a quick bowler. In slow bowling, however, the weight of the body and arm moves quickly around the side of the ball rather than remaining behind it as in fast bowling. The slow bowler who has a strong body action is able to spin the ball more, since the speed and weight of the body and arm moving around the side of the ball complements the strength of the wrist and fingers.

NOTE: These directions are for a bowler delivering with the bowling arm over the top of the wicket at the bowler's end.

REMEMBER: BE BALANCED. WATCH WHERE THE BALL WILL BOUNCE.

The bowling stride

The last-but-one stride of your run-up is the longest and fastest and ends with the foot opposite your bowling arm landing on the ground. Move into the bowling stride by jumping off this foot high into the air, twisting your body until the side of the body opposite the bowling arm points down the pitch towards the batsman. Your body maintains its forward impetus towards the batsman, but the jump in the last stride of the run-up slows down your forward momentum. You move into your bowling stride as you descend on your back foot, which is the foot on the same side of your body as your bowling arm. The toes of your rear foot point towards the stumps at the bowler's end and your foot is parallel to the bowling crease. Your body is now in a side-on position with your chest facing the bowler's stumps. The bowling stride then becomes a sideways step towards the batter with your front hip and leading side of the front leg pointing down the pitch, initially slightly towards the batter's body or fine leg. Your head should be upright and steady and your eyes fixed on the spot where the ball will bounce.

Front-arm and trunk movement

As you spring onto the rear foot in the bowling stride, rock your trunk back, keeping both elbows close to your side. Since you were leaning forward in your approach, the rock-back of the trunk moves the body through an angle of approximately 30 degrees, lifting the front leg high off the ground. Your front arm is thrust upwards and forwards towards the batter as you look behind it and over your front shoulder. Your head is steady and your eyes still on the spot where you hope to bounce the ball. Your weight is on the back leg and your back slightly arched as you continue your forward movement towards the batter. As your front arm moves forwards and upwards along the intended line of the delivery, bring your front elbow down suddenly, tucking it into your front hip where it stops and stabilises before dragging your bowling arm over.

The bowling arm

As your front arm moves away from the body after the rock-back of the trunk, so does the bowling arm. Initially it is extended and close to the front arm high on the leading side of the body before moving downwards and backwards in a circular movement alongside your chest. It is fully extended and straight behind the body when the front elbow is tucked into your hip where it stabilises. This sudden lowering of the leading elbow drags the bowling arm over quickly, high and straight alongside your head. The ball is released in this position. For slower bowlers the point of release is generally just before the bowling arm reaches the vertical position. For faster bowlers the release occurs just after the bowling arm has passed the vertical point. It is important to ensure that the shoulders are in line throughout the delivery swing and rotate vertically towards the batter. If you are a faster bowler, keep your hand behind the ball at the moment of release. Lay your wrist back before flicking it through behind the ball towards the batter.

Front-foot position

As you step down the pitch towards the batter, transfer your weight from the back to the front foot. The toes of your front foot should point towards fine leg or straight down the wicket. The swing of your bowling arm from behind your body causes the hips to rotate over the pivot of the front leg, which should be braced as the ball is released at the top of the action. Make sure that some part of your front foot is behind the rear edge of the popping or batting crease at the moment of release. Maintain your forward momentum towards the batter.

Follow-through

In the follow-through the front arm resumes its movement downwards and back behind the body, absorbing the impetus of the bowling arm. The bowling arm comes over and across the front of the body, finishing alongside and outside the front knee. Bend your back to allow the bowling hand to come as close to the ground as possible in front of your body. Swing your rear leg as close as possible past the front with the knee bent and moving forward in a straight line – not in a semicircle. Follow through for two or three strides down the wicket before moving off to the side and avoiding the 'danger area' on the pitch 1.2 m (4 ft) in front of the batting crease and 30 cm (12 in) either side of the middle stump. If your follow-through is initially straight you have maintained your forward momentum towards the batter in your action.

The basic action is suited to bowling outswingers, off spinners, off cutters and leg spinners.

The **outswinger** is a ball which swings in the air from the leg side to the off before it bounces. It is generally bowled at medium or fast pace.

The **off spinner** is a ball which turns in from the off side after it bounces because of the spin imparted by the bowler. Generally it will curve away before spinning back and is bowled at slow speed.

The **off cutter** is a ball which turns in from the off side after it bounces because of the cut imparted to the ball by the bowler. The difference between cut and spin is that spin is imparted by both the wrist and finger movement of the bowler's hand, whereas cut is obtained by the wrist action which drags the fingers of the bowling hand down the side of the ball. The off cutter is bowled at medium pace.

The **leg spinner** is a ball which turns from the leg side after it bounces because of the spin imparted by the bowler rotating the wrist and fingers. It is bowled at slow speed.

Simplified hints and checklist

1 Jump onto the back foot as though you are going to do a feet astride jump facing the umpire
2 Rock back, elbows in. Throw your front arm and leg forwards towards the batter. Tuck your front elbow in
3 Drag your bowling arm over with your front elbow. Almost brush your ear
4 Step forward towards the batter. Brace your knee
5 Run after the ball. You can't bowl in one direction and run in another.

REMEMBER: BE BALANCED. WATCH WHERE THE BALL WILL BOUNCE.

Group activity

THE BASIC ACTION
- Bowler A bowls 10 deliveries using the basic action
- A hoop with a cone inside is placed on a good length, 2 metres in front of the stumps
- The bowler attempts to land the ball in the hoop
- Wicketkeeper B and the bowler swap positions after 10 deliveries
- Scoring: 3 points if the ball lands in the hoop; 2 points if the stumps are hit; 5 points if both events occur; and 20 points if the cone is hit.

Number of players: 2
Equipment: 1 set of stumps, 1 ball, 1 hoop and 1 cone.

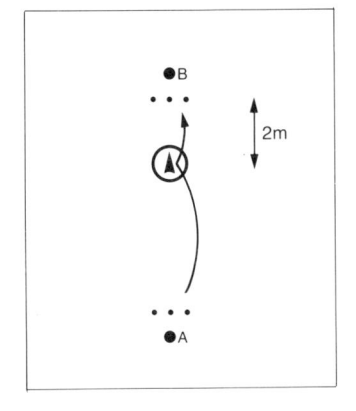

The outswinger

An outswinger is a delivery which moves in the air from leg to off before it bounces. A batter may be bowled by such a ball by trying to play it on the leg side, consequently hitting across the line of a ball which is curving in the opposite direction. The batter may also follow the ball outside the off stump and edge a catch to the wicketkeeper or slip fielders. The outswinger is more easily bowled with the assistance of a wind blowing from the leg to the offside of the wicket. The ideal winds for the outswinger are those which come from deep fine leg and mid-on. Humid, overcast conditions also assist the outswinger, as does a head wind, though the latter situation reduces the pace of the bowler. The new ball, because of its shine and pronounced seam, helps the bowler to swing the ball more.

REMEMBER: BE BALANCED. WATCH WHERE THE BALL WILL BOUNCE.

How to bowl an outswinger

1 ACTION The basic bowling action is ideal for the outswinger since it imparts a body action which 'drags' the ball from leg to off. (This applies to right-handed bowlers bowling to right-handed batters or left-handed bowlers bowling to left-handed batters.)

2 GRIP Hold the ball with the seam running vertically and pointing at the moment of release towards first slip. The index and second finger grip the ball at the top, one finger on each side of the seam. The side of your thumb should be on the seam at the bottom. Hold the ball well out of the palm and by the top joints of the fingers and thumb. Your third and little fingers are placed down the side of the ball. If there is a shiny side of the ball, place that side on the side opposite the direction of the desired swing.

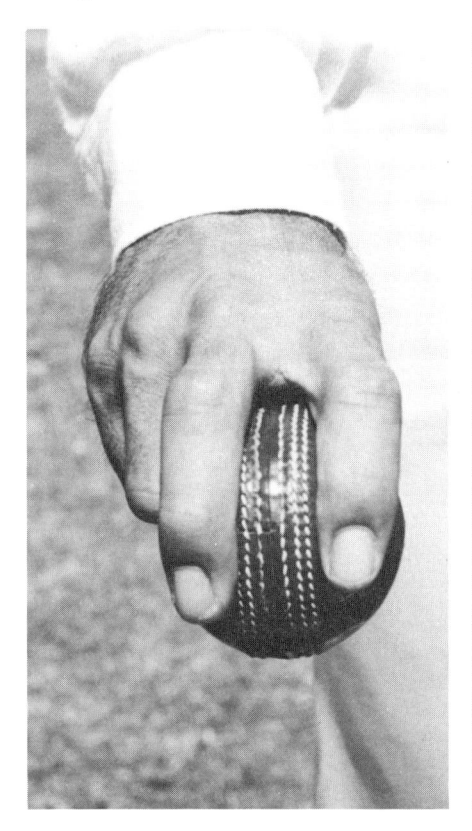

3 RELEASE At the moment of release point the index and second fingers in the direction in which you want the ball to swing. Your hand comes slightly around the outside of the ball, pushing it towards the slips.

Simplified hints and checklist

1 The basic closed action
2 Hold the ball in the three prongs of your first two fingers and the side of the thumb with the seam between the first two fingers and pointing vertically towards the slips
3 Steer the seam towards first slip as you release the ball.

**REMEMBER: WATCH WHERE THE BALL WILL BOUNCE.
BE BALANCED.**

Group activity

THE OUTSWINGER
- Players bowl a ball back and forth which has been painted one half white, the other half red
- Each player tries to deliver the ball with the seam vertical using the outswing action and grip
- Score 1 point if the ball moves through the air without wobbling and the seam vertical. If the ball swings in the direction of an outswinger, score 2 points.

Number of players: 2
Equipment: 1 red/white ball.

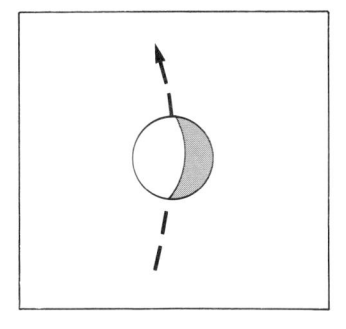

The off cutter

The off cutter is a medium or medium-fast delivery which turns after it bounces from off to leg. Sometimes the off cutter curves away from the bat before it cuts back in.

An off cutter is bowled against a batter who does not play close enough to his pads with the bat, leaving a gap through which the ball can pass and hit the stumps. If a batter does not push the ball into the ground, he will play an off cutter into the air as a catch to close fielders on the leg side.

The off cutter is used with great effect on a dry pitch which 'dusts' or crumbles and helps the ball turn, as does a wet wicket. Since the cutter is bowled at medium pace with the wrist 'cutting' the fingers down the side of the ball, the ball turns quickly even on the slowest wickets. It also tends to lift suddenly.

A breeze blowing from the leg side helps the off cutter since it blows the ball away to the off in the air, before it turns back in the opposite direction.

REMEMBER: BE BALANCED. WATCH WHERE THE BALL WILL BOUNCE.

How to bowl an off cutter

1 ACTION The basic action is ideal for the off cutter.

2 GRIP Hold the ball with the top joints of your fingers around the seam and well out of your palm. Grip the top of the ball with your index and second fingers in the 11 and at 12 o'clock positions, with your thumb at twenty to the hour and your third finger at twenty past. Your grip should be firm and tension exists between your first, second and third fingers.

3 RELEASE Release the ball when your bowling arm has just passed its highest point in the delivery swing. At the moment of release, angle the seam in a line between cover and backward square leg. With your wrist drag your index and second fingers sharply downwards and forwards in the direction of backward square leg.

Simplified hints and checklist

1 The basic closed action
2 Grip the ball around the seam, with the index and second fingers on top of it in the 11 and 12 o'clock positions and pointing down the wicket. Your thumb is at twenty to the hour and your third finger at twenty past
3 At the moment of release, turn the seam of the ball like a door knob, with your wrist and fingers towards backward square leg.

REMEMBER: BE BALANCED. WATCH WHERE THE BALL WILL BOUNCE.

Group activity

THE OFF CUTTER
• A line is drawn on the ground in front of the stumps just outside off stump
• Bowler A attempts to land the ball outside the line so that it cuts back to hit the stumps
• Keeper and bowler change positions every 10 deliveries
• Score 1 point if the ball crosses the line and 3 points if it also hits the stumps.

Number of players: 2
Equipment: 1 ball, 1 set of stumps.

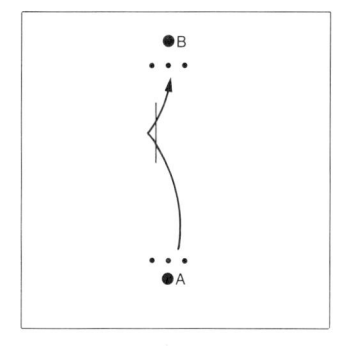

The off spinner and its variations

An off spinner is a delivery which turns at slow pace after it bounces from off to leg, and because of flight creates uncertainty in the batter's mind about whether to play forward or back. Because the closed action is used the ball curves away in the air before it spins back.

It is bowled to a batter who does not play close enough to the front pad with the bat and leaves a gap through which the ball can pass and hit the stumps. The batter may also hesitate in deciding whether to play forward or back to the flighted off spinner which drops on a shorter length than expected and, not reaching its bounce, hit a catch in the air. When the batter does not play the off spinner to ground a catch to the close fielders on the leg side may result.

The off spinner is used to advantage on a dry pitch which 'dusts' or crumbles, helping the ball turn, or on a wet wicket. The speed with which the ball turns is determined by the dustiness or wetness of the pitch. The greater the dustiness of the pitch, the quicker the turn of the ball. Quick turn also occurs on a sticky wicket – when a wet wicket is drying. A breeze blowing from the leg side helps the off spinner since it blows the ball away to the off in the air – curving it away before it turns back. A headwind makes the off spinner drop in the air and makes the batter uncertain about whether to play forward or back.

REMEMBER: BE BALANCED. WATCH WHERE THE BALL WILL BOUNCE.

How to bowl an off spinner

1 ACTION The basic action is suitable for the off spinner. In the delivery stride, accentuate the movement of your front foot to the leg side by pointing your front toe towards fine leg. Bowl against your braced front leg and swivel on your front toe. This will increase the amount of 'drift' towards the off side in the air and the degree of spin.

2 GRIP Hold the ball around the seam and in the top joints of your index

and either the second or third fingers. You should be able to see light between the ball and the palm of the hand. Your index finger should be bent and you should exert tension between the top joints of the two fingers gripping the ball. Rest your thumb and little finger lightly on the seam.

3 RELEASE Release the ball at the top of the bowling action, early for more flight and late for a quicker delivery. At the moment of release the seam should be angled in a line between cover and backward square leg. Impart spin by pushing the index finger and wrist sharply towards backward square leg, and over the ball.

Simplified hints and checklist

1 The basic closed action. Front foot in front of the stumps and swivel on its toes
2 Grip the ball tightly around the seam in the top joints of the fingers. Squeeze the ball between the first, second and third fingers until it hurts
3 As you release the ball, push your first finger hard with a turn of the wrist towards backward square leg.

**REMEMBER: WATCH WHERE THE BALL WILL BOUNCE.
BE BALANCED.**

Group activity

THE OFF SPINNER
- Two single stumps are placed 5 metres apart with bowlers A and B standing a pitch length away from the stumps on either side of them directly in line
- Using the off-spin grip and action, each bowler attempts to bowl the ball so that it passes between the stumps after bouncing
- Score 1 point each time the ball passes between the stumps.

Number of players: 2
Equipment: 2 stumps, 1 ball.

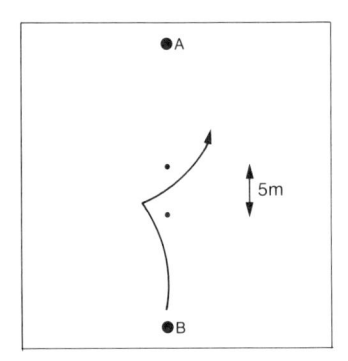

The left-handed finger spinner

The left-handed finger spinner is the left-handed version of the off spinner. The left-handed finger spinner turns the ball after it bounces from leg to off.

The delivery is suited to the same climatic and pitch conditions as the off spinner. The ideal breeze for the ball blows from off to leg and floats the ball in that direction before it turns in the opposite one. This ball is most effective against the batter who plays across the line of the ball towards the leg side and against the direction of the spin. It is also a threat to the batter who follows the ball which spins away towards the slips outside the off stump, and edges it to slip. All the details of the action, grip and release for the off spinner apply to the left-handed finger spinner.

ff spinner    Arm ball    Top spinner

How to vary off-spin bowling

The batter may become accustomed to dealing with the off spinner which consistently turns in from outside the off stump. The bowler must therefore seek to confuse the batter by varying the delivery. This variation is achieved by flighting the ball more or less, or by sending down a ball which does not turn.

1 THE DRIFTING DELIVERY The drifting delivery, or 'arm ball', is a disguised off spinner which does not turn but curves away in the air towards the slips. The batter, expecting turn, plays inside the line of the ball and as a result edges the delivery as a catch to the slips. You should bowl the 'arm ball' when the batter plays shots with the bottom hand in control and consequently hits across the line of the delivery towards the on side. The suitable breeze for the ball blows from the leg side, curving the ball in the air towards the off. It is not necessary for the wicket to be taking spin.

Point the seam of the ball vertically towards the slips and grip it with the first and second fingers, not around the seam, but on either side of it. Hold

the ball loosely and conceal your grip with your non-bowling hand. You should deliver the ball from close to the stumps at the bowler's end and as you deliver it, accentuate the swivel on your front foot. The bowling hand pretends to spin the ball but at the moment of release slides around it, steering the upright seam towards the slips.

2 THE OVERSPUN OFF SPINNER The overspun off spinner, or 'top spinner', is spun forwards towards the batter. This makes the ball drop or 'loop' in the air so that it drops on a length shorter than that expected by the batter. Because the delivery is released earlier in the swing of the bowling arm it has a higher trajectory and consequently bounces more after pitching. The batter who misjudges the flight of the ball and fails to reach its pitch before playing a stroke will loft the ball in front of the wicket.

The 'top spinner' should be bowled to the batter who is not a good judge of flight and who is hesitant or rash in moving down the wicket to reach the bounce of the ball.

Grip the ball as for the normal off spinner, but at the moment of release angle the seam vertically towards the batter by cocking your wrist inwards towards your body. Spin the ball forwards by pushing the first finger over the top of it. Let go of the ball just before the delivery arm reaches the top of its swing.

3 THE UNDERCUT OFF SPINNER The undercut off spinner is spun horizontally towards the batter, with the ball rotating from leg to off. It is also a slightly faster version of the off spinner and this factor, combined with the direction of its spin, makes the ball skid after pitching. If the delivery is deliberately pitched short, it may trap the batter into thinking it can be pulled, in which case, attempting the cross-bat shot, the batter is often dismissed l.b.w. because of the ball's lower bounce. You should grip the ball as for the normal off spinner, but lower your arm as you deliver it so that the palm of the bowling hand faces upwards. Push the first finger of the bowling hand horizontally from leg to off so that the ball rotates laterally. Bowl the delivery quicker and with a much flatter trajectory, releasing it late in the swing of the bowling arm.

The right-handed wrist-spun leg spinner and its variations

A right-handed wrist-spun leg spinner turns even on good wickets from leg to off. Its flight makes the batter uncertain about whether to play forward or back. It can bowl the batter who plays across the line of the ball towards the leg side and against the direction of the spin, hitting with the bottom hand in control and the chest facing the bowler. The batter may also follow the ball which spins away outside the off stump, edging a catch to the keeper or slips. The leg spinner which is not played quickly to ground may result in a catch to the close fielders on the off side.

The leg spinner is suited to a good hard wicket, which enables the ball to turn slightly and makes it bounce. A dry pitch which 'dusts' or crumbles slightly enables the leg-spin bowler to turn the ball a long way, quickly. A wet pitch helps the ball turn slowly but without much lift unless the pitch is drying.

A breeze blowing from the off side helps the leg spinner since it floats the ball in that direction before turning back from leg. A headwind makes the leg spinner drop in the air, increasing the batter's uncertainty about whether to play forward or back.

REMEMBER: BE BALANCED. WATCH WHERE THE BALL WILL BOUNCE.

How to bowl a right-handed leg spinner

1 ACTION In general the basic action is well suited to leg spin. The side-on position, the high delivery arm and bowling against the braced

front leg place weight behind the delivery, imparting more spin and making the ball turn quickly.

2 GRIP Hold the ball between the top joints of your index and third fingers, around the seam and well out of the palm. Your thumb and second and little fingers rest on the seam with the tension between the top joints of the index and third fingers.

3 RELEASE Release the ball at the top of the bowling action, earlier for more flight and later for a quicker delivery. At the moment of delivery angle the seam between mid-wicket and gully. In the swing of the bowling arm bend the hand inwards towards the inside of your wrist and then rotate it down and outwards until your wrist is straight and your palm faces the leg side. Spin is imparted when the wrist pushes the third finger towards gully and over the ball.

Simplified hints and checklist

1 The basic closed action
2 Grip the ball around the seam with the top joints of the fingers as though a tight elastic band has been placed around the tops of the fingers and thumbs. Squeeze the ball hard between the knuckles of the first and third fingers.
3 As you release the ball turn the wrist as though you are swimming the Australian crawl. Push your third finger with your wrist hard towards gully.

**REMEMBER: WATCH WHERE THE BALL WILL BOUNCE.
BE BALANCED.**

Group activity

THE LEG SPINNER
- A pair of parallel lines is drawn in front of the stumps
- Bowler A, using the leg-break grip and action, tries to land the ball between the lines or to the right of them
- Wicketkeeper and bowler change positions after 10 deliveries
- Scoring: 1 point if the ball lands between the parallel lines and hits the stumps; 2 points if it lands on the right-hand side of the lines and hits the stumps; 3 points if it lands between the lines but misses off stump.

Number of players: 2
Equipment: 1 ball, 1 set of stumps.

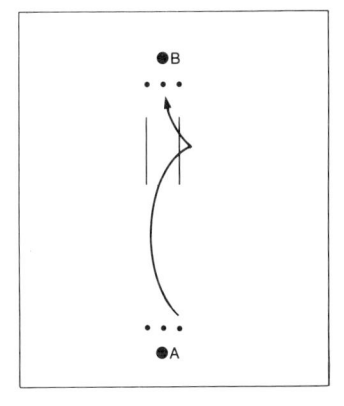

Leg spinner

'Wrong 'un'

Top spinner

Flipper

How to vary right-handed wrist-spun leg breaks

1 THE 'WRONG 'UN' The batter may become accustomed to playing the ball which spins consistently from the leg side after bouncing. The bowler must therefore deceive the striker by presenting all of the clues which indicate that the delivery will turn from leg, and then spinning it in another direction. The leg spinner is varied by the use of the 'googly', 'wrong 'un', or 'bosie', all of which terms describe a disguised ball which looks like a leg spinner but turns after it bounces like an off spinner.

The 'wrong 'un' is intended to puzzle the batter, who cannot detect which way the ball will turn from the action and wrist movement of the bowler. The batter who does not play the straight-bat strokes with the bat close to the pad is especially vulnerable to this delivery, which may pass between bat and pad to hit the stumps. The flight of the 'wrong 'un' causes problems for the batter who is uncertain about playing forward or back; failing to reach the bounce of the ball when moving forward, he or she may hit a catch to the fielders on the leg side. It is also an effective delivery against the batter who fails to push the ball into the ground when playing defensively and as a result provides a catch for the close fielders on the leg side.

The 'wrong 'un' should be bowled when a good hard pitch provides turn and bounce. A dry wicket which 'dusts', or 'crumbles', accentuates the delivery's turn and bounce. On wet surfaces, the ball turns a long way, but slowly, unless the pitch is drying out and 'sticky'.

A breeze blowing from the leg side drifts the ball away in the air before the 'wrong 'un' spins back from outside the off stump. A headwind makes the 'wrong 'un' loop in its flight and poses problems for the batter about whether to play forward or back. The ideal wind for the delivery comes from fine leg.

The 'wrong 'un' is bowled with the basic open action used in the inswinger and described later. Grip the ball as if you are bowling a leg spinner, but at the moment of release accentuate the 'Australian crawl' movement of the bowling hand and wrist and push your third finger towards backward square leg rather than gully. Your elbow points towards the sky and the back of your hand to the ground as the ball spins out of your hand over the top of your third finger.

2 THE WRIST-SPUN TOP SPINNER The wrist-spun top spinner rotates forward towards the batter, turning neither from off or leg, but 'looping' in the air to drop on a shorter length than that expected by the striker and bouncing higher than normal. The batter who does not reach the bounce of the top-spinner when attempting a drive will hit the ball into the air as a catch. If the batter does not play close to the pad and allow for turn, he or she may be bowled by the ball which passes between pad and bat. Bowl it when a batter picks up the direction of your spin easily and expects every ball to turn or is hesitant or rash in moving down the wicket.

Use the basic bowling action and the same grip as for a leg spinner. At the moment of release, however, push your third spinning finger forwards over the top of the ball so that the seam rotates vertically towards the batter. The back of your hand should face down the pitch as the wrist rotates outwards and forwards.

3 THE FLIPPER The 'flipper' is a wrist-spun back spinner, which turns neither from the off or leg, but skids quickly on to the batter after pitching because of its flipped spin and low trajectory. The ball rotates backwards away from the batter as it progresses down the pitch. You should bowl the 'flipper' against a batter who likes to cut or pull the ball which pitches in line with the stumps. Because it comes through quickly and does not bounce very high the delivery often dismisses such a player l.b.w.

Use the basic bowling action and the same grip as for a leg spinner. At the moment of release, however, as your bowling hand is rotating in the 'Australian crawl' motion, flip your first finger back over the ball and your thumb forwards in front of it in a snapping motion. This will impart backspin. The delivery is a difficult one to master since the body, arm and hand are moving forwards while your fingers are rotating in the opposite direction.

The inswinger

An inswinger is a medium-pace or fast delivery which moves in the air from off to leg before it bounces. Bowl an inswinger against a batter who does not play close to the pads with the bat, leaving a gap through which the ball may pass and hit the stumps. The batter who does not play the inswinger quickly to ground may present a catch to close fielders on the leg side.

A breeze blowing from the off side helps the movement of the inswinger from that direction. The ideal breeze for this delivery is from deep third man or mid-off. A headwind will increase the swing of the ball but decreases the speed of the ball.

REMEMBER: BE BALANCED. WATCH WHERE THE BALL WILL BOUNCE.

How to bowl an inswinger

1 GRIP Hold the ball well out of the palm of the bowling hand in the top joints of the index and second fingers. The flat of the thumb supports the ball underneath. The seam is vertical, pointing towards fine leg with the index and second fingers slightly across and on top of it. Your third and little fingers are positioned lightly alongside the ball.

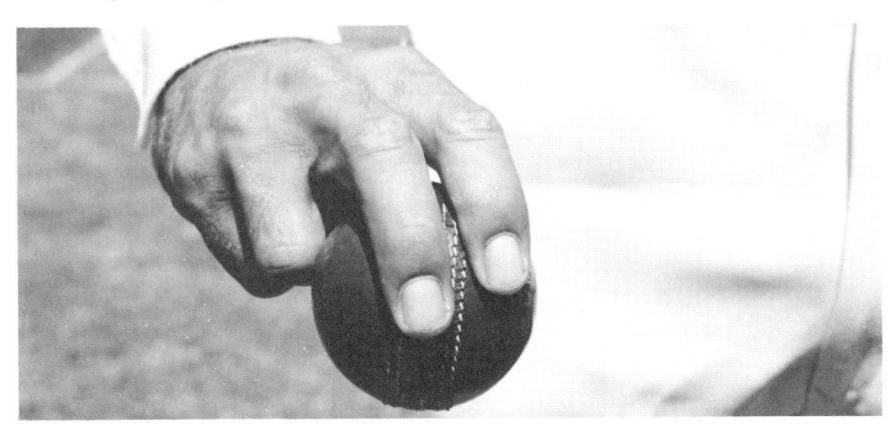

2 DELIVERY STRIDE As you approach the bowling crease, gather yourself by jumping high and placing your weight onto your back foot, which is on the same side of the body as your bowling arm. The rear foot should not be as parallel to the bowling crease as in the basic action. The toes point more towards mid-wicket. Move your front foot down the wicket towards the batter's off stump and not towards fine leg as in the basic action. The delivery stride and subsequent movements must maintain the bowler's momentum towards the batter's wicket.

3 FRONT ARM AND TRUNK Jump onto your rear foot, rock back and reach upwards with your front arm, turning your body so that your front shoulder and hip point down the wicket and at the batter's off stump. Your chest should be towards mid-on, your head upright and steady, and your eyes fixed on the spot on which you intend to bounce the ball. Look at this spot from a point in front of your front shoulder and not behind as in the basic action. Your front arm acts as a lever, pushing your trunk back from the forward angle adopted in the run-up, stretching the front side, and lifting your front foot clear of the ground. From this position throw your front arm and shoulder forward and upwards towards a point just outside the batter's off stump before suddenly lowering your front elbow and stopping it tucked into your leading side. Transfer your weight onto your front foot. Rotate your hips and open them early in the action, bringing your chest to face the batter.

4 THE FRONT FOOT Step down the wicket onto your front foot, transferring your weight onto it and landing so that some part of your foot is behind the rear edge of the batting or popping crease. Your toes should point towards the batter's off stump. Straighten your front knee and brace it as your body passes over it.

5 THE BOWLING ARM Raise your bowling arm at the beginning of the action with your front arm and in front of your body. Keeping your bowling arm straight, swing it downwards, backwards and then upwards, almost brushing the side of your head at the top of the delivery and the moment of releasing the ball. You should be upright at this stage, your front knee stiff, your bowling arm high, striving for maximum height.

6 RELEASE At the moment of release the seam of the ball should point to fine leg and your hand should pass down the side of the ball pushing it in to the right-handed batter. Your arm should be high. If there is a shiny side to the ball place it on the opposite side of the ball to the direction of the desired swing.

7 FOLLOW-THROUGH After releasing the ball, swing your bowling arm and shoulder slightly across your body and downwards, finishing on a line between your legs. As your bowling arm swings downwards as near the ground as possible, bend your back. Your front arm and elbow now resume their backward movement to absorb the energy of the action, brushing the outside of the front knee and finishing high behind your back. After taking one or two steps straight down the wicket after the bowling stride, swing off the pitch towards cover for a further three or four steps in your follow-through.

Simplified hints and checklist

1 Hold the ball in the three prongs of your first two fingers and the thumb. Seam vertical between the first two fingers and pointing towards fine leg

2 In the delivery stride do a feet-astride jump, landing first on your back foot, with your chest facing a spot just in front of the non-striker's wicket. Keep moving towards the batter

3 Reach for the sky with your front arm, looking on its leg side at the spot on the wicket where you hope to bounce the ball. Rock back before throwing your front arm forwards and upwards towards the batter's off stump and suddenly tucking your elbow into your side

4 Step forward on your stiff front leg towards the batter's off stump

5 Swing your bowling arm round like a windmill, brushing your ear and, in the follow-through, the inside of your back leg

6 Push the ball into the batter's body, steering it with the seam

7 Try to touch the inside of your front foot's big toe and veer off the wicket to the off side after you have let go of the ball.

**REMEMBER: WATCH WHERE THE BALL WILL BOUNCE.
BE BALANCED.**

Group activity

THE INSWINGER
• Players bowl a ball back and forth which has been painted with one half white and the other half red
• Using the inswing grip and action, each player tries to deliver the ball with the seam vertical and pointing towards fine leg
• Score 1 point if the ball moves through the air with the seam vertical and without wobbling. If the ball swings in the direction of an inswinger, score 2 points.

Number of players: 2
Equipment: 1 red/white ball.

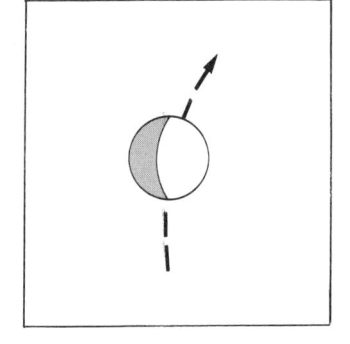

The leg cutter

The leg cutter is a medium or medium-fast ball which turns after it bounces from leg to off. Because the inswinger action is used, the ball usually swings in before cutting away. Bowl the leg cutter against the batter who anticipates inswing and will play inside the line of the ball, thus giving a catch to the keeper or slip fielders when the ball cuts away. The batter who follows the leg cutter outside the off stump will edge the ball in the same way, whilst the player who does not play the leg cutter downwards immediately after contact with the bat will give a catch to the close fielders on the off side.

The leg cutter is suited to a dry, 'crumbling' or 'dusting' pitch, which enables the ball to turn quickly, as does a sticky wicket. Since the cutter is bowled at medium or medium-fast pace with the wrist cutting the fingers down the side of the ball, it turns quickly on even the slowest of wickets. It also tends to lift suddenly.

A breeze from the off side helps the leg cutter since it blows the ball into the stumps before cutting it away in the opposite direction.

REMEMBER: BE BALANCED. WATCH WHERE THE BALL WILL BOUNCE.

How to bowl a leg cutter

1 ACTION The inswinger action is ideal for the leg cutter.

2 GRIP Hold the ball around the seam well out of the palm of the bowling hand with the top joints of your index, second and third fingers and the flat of the thumb. Your index and second fingers should be on top of the ball in the 11 o'clock and 1 o'clock positions with the thumb at

twenty to the hour and the third finger at twenty past. Your grip should be firm, with tension between the index, second and third fingers.

3 RELEASE Release the ball as the bowling arm begins to descend after reaching the top of its swing. At the moment of release, angle the seam between mid-wicket and backward point. Cut is imparted by the wrist drawing the index, second and third fingers sharply downwards in the direction of backward point. Your second finger is the main 'cutting' agent and your rear shoulder and body action in the delivery swing will add to the cutting movement by coming down on the off side of the ball.

Simplified hints and checklist

1 The basic inswinger action
2 Grip the ball around the seam with the first and second fingers on top of it in the 11 and 1 o'clock positions, pointing down the wicket and well spaced. The thumb is at twenty to the hour and the third finger at twenty past.
3 As you let go of the ball, push your fingers downwards and towards backward point with your wrist.

**REMEMBER: WATCH WHERE THE BALL WILL BOUNCE.
BE BALANCED.**

Group activity

THE LEG CUTTER
• A line 5 m long is drawn on the ground and bowlers A and B each stand 15 m beyond the ends of the line, facing each other
• Using the leg cutter grip and action, each bowler tries to bowl the ball so that it crosses the line after bouncing
• Score 1 point for each delivery which crosses the line after bouncing.

Number of players: 2
Equipment: 1 ball.

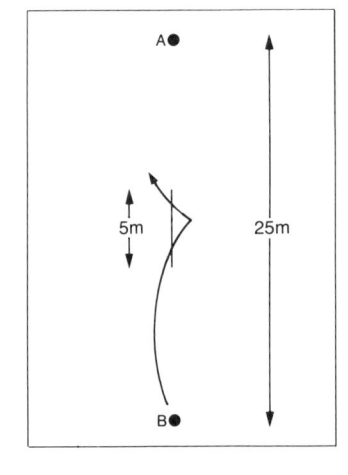

Outswinger

Off cutter

Inswinger

Leg cutter

Bowling tactics

Variety is one of a bowler's most important weapons. Varying deliveries has dangers, however, since few bowlers have complete mastery over every type of ball. Experimentation with a wide range of deliveries causes inaccuracy and brings the consequence of punishment. Bowlers should therefore cultivate a regular or 'stock' ball over which they have a high degree of control, before varying their attack around that delivery. Variety can be achieved by several simple methods.

The use of the bowling crease

The bowling crease is 2.64 m (8 ft 8 in) long between the return creases. The bowler can attack the batter by bowling over or around the wicket from any spot on the crease. This changes the angle of attack greatly and, combined with a variety of spin and swing, produces a wide range of different balls. An outswinger delivered from close to the bowling stumps and aimed at the batter's leg stump could yield an edged catch to the slips. A similar ball delivered from wide on the return crease and aimed at the batter's leg stump would probably hit the wicket. Bowling around the wicket accentuates the angle of the ball across the face of the stumps but diminishes the chance of an l.b.w. decision, because in order to fulfil the requirements of the l.b.w. law the ball must turn back towards the stumps to eventually hit them.

Change in pace

Bowlers vary their pace to make the batter play too early or too late and give a catch or be bowled. To achieve these results the difference in pace between deliveries need not be great, but it must not be discerned by the batter. The speed of your run-up must be the same, the position of your body unchanged and the speed of your bowling arm constant.

Vary your pace only occasionally to prevent the batter being constantly on guard. Variations in speed are usually produced by removing some part of the weight of the action or hand from behind the ball. The 'demon' Australian fast bowler, Fred Spofforth, used to bowl a 'half-ball', in which he held only half of the ball with half of his hand. Other fast and medium-pace bowlers send down off spinners or cutters, deliveries in which the hand draws down the side of the ball. Individual bowlers achieve spectacular success by their own unique methods and coaches should encourage this type of experimentation.

Variation in flight

The flight of the ball can be altered by varying the speed of the delivery or by increasing or decreasing the amount of top and side spin on it. The spin bowler can deliver a quicker ball by increasing the speed of the action, releasing the ball later and flattening the flight. It is possible to 'lob' a slower ball by means of a slower arm action and an earlier release point, but this is easy to discern. More difficult for the batter to see is the ball which is spun forward harder than normal. This makes the ball 'loop' in the air like an overspun table-tennis shot and drop suddenly before bouncing high off the pitch because of the delivery's higher trajectory. The wrist-spun top spinner and the overspun off spinner both achieve this end. The 'arm ball', or 'drifter', of the off spinner makes the ball float towards the slips in the air with the arm, whilst the back-spun leg spinner or 'flipper' (a specialist ball which is spun backwards with a flicking motion of the thumb and fingers) makes the ball skid through quickly off the pitch.

Varying the flight of the ball makes the batter uncertain about whether to play forward or back and often causes a shot to be lofted because the striker has not reached the bounce of the ball before playing the stroke. The bowler usually varies his or her flight when a batter is uncertain about moving forward or is rash in the execution of a front-foot stroke.

Length and line in bowling

Bowling on a good length and line is a great virtue in a bowler. A good length means that the batter is continually uncertain about whether to play forward or back and is forced to defend. A ball of good line is directed at the stumps. In the past these two qualities have always been extolled above the virtues of speed, swing, cut and spin, but this has produced players who have subordinated their natural abilities to bowl with exceptional speed, cut and spin to the necessity to bowl accurately. The coach's job is to improve natural ability, not to restrain it. Length and line evolve from the mastery of the basic action. Place these qualities second in coaching priorities to the ability to bowl fast, move the ball in the air and cut or spin it off the pitch.

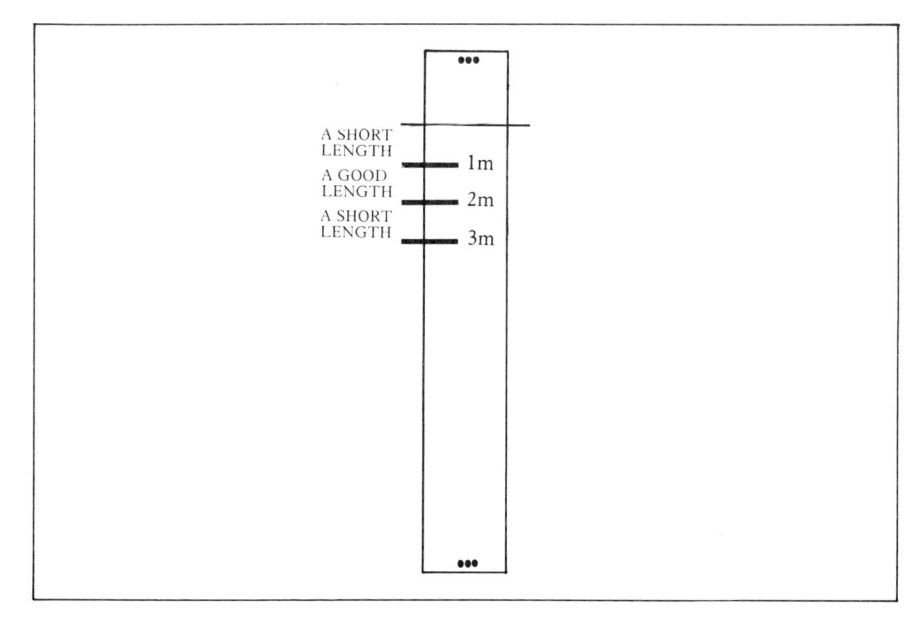

A SHORT LENGTH	1m
A GOOD LENGTH	2m
A SHORT LENGTH	3m

Detection and correction of faults in the run-up and basic bowling action

1 Run-up

The correct model

The length of the bowler's run-up should be appropriate to the speed of the delivery.
The bowler:
1 begins the run-up slowly
2 accelerates gradually to a top speed which is compatible with balance
3 achieves top speed in the last-but-one stride of the run-up, i.e. this stride is the longest and fastest of the approach
4 maintains a forward momentum during the run towards the target of the batter's wicket
5 approaches the delivery position on the bowling crease directly
6 leans forward in the run-up
7 decelerates in the last stride of the approach by jumping high off the foot opposite the bowling arm and turning sideways into the delivery position with the front side pointing down the wicket towards the batter.

Comments on the reasons behind the skill and possible faults

A run-up which is of a suitable length permits acceleration to a speed appropriate to the delivery over the shortest possible distance. A bowler's ideal running speed should be suited to the pace of the delivery and compatible with a balanced delivery stride. Some faster bowlers run long distances before bowling, without accelerating to top speed in their penultimate stride. They gain rhythm but waste energy. Other bowlers run very short distances quite slowly before bowling, relying on a violent body action for pace and spin. These bowlers operate off their strength, tire quickly and are susceptible to muscle injury because of the strain which they place upon their bodies. The bowler's run-up contributes 20 per cent of the speed of a delivery, if the maximum benefit is derived from it. It will also augment a slow bowler's spin since it causes the bowling arm to move more quickly around the side of the ball. It begins slowly with a gradual acceleration until the bowler attains the maximum speed compatible with balance in the last-but-one stride of the approach. At this stage the bowler must slow up slightly to jump into the air and turn sideways into the bowling action.

The bowler must always maintain linear momentum towards the target of the batter's wicket in the run-up to ensure accuracy. Any deviation from the direct linear movement towards the batter's wicket, e.g. by a curvature of the run-up towards the off side or a sideways step in the same direction at the end of the approach, causes the bowler's weight to fall away towards mid-off and will open the bowler's action, resulting in the ball being directed down the leg side.

Leaning towards the batter's wicket assists forward momentum and accentuates the bowler's rock-back in the delivery stride, enabling him or her to make greater use of the large body mass of the trunk. Bowlers who are upright throughout their run-up only rock back through an angle of approximately 15 degrees. Bowlers who lean forward as they run up, are able to move their trunks through an angle of about 30 degrees. It is permissible for a bowler to approach the bowling crease at an angle from the mid-off position provided, that in the last few strides of the run-up, forward momentum is maintained towards the batter's wicket and towards the point on the bowling crease from which the ball will be delivered.

Bowlers who run too fast in their approach do not slow up sufficiently in their last stride to enable them to turn their bodies into a suitable side-on position to deliver the ball. Thus they bowl with the toes of their back feet and their chests pointing down the wicket and are unable to fully utilise the rock-back and the large mass of the body to project the ball. The swing of their shoulder line is also towards the off side, deviating from the desired forward movement towards the batter's wicket.

Bowlers who approach the wicket too slowly are able to turn into the side-on position to deliver the ball, but never have any follow-through because the body lacks forward momentum. The absence of a follow-through means that the leading foot and front side of the body absorbs all the shock of the bowling action, placing a tremendous strain on these parts.

Some bowlers have irregular or hesitant run-ups and frequently change feet, shorten step or shuffle at some point in their approach. This is caused by the bowler arriving at a point in the run-up at which it is obvious that he or she will either overstep the bowling crease and bowl a no-ball or fall short of the stumps. Such a change of running speed in the run-up makes it impossible to attain maximum momentum in the penultimate stride. The fault is caused by a lack of graded acceleration and consistently regular strides in the approach.

CORRECTION STRATEGIES

The establishment of the run-up (as explained under *Bowling: the run-up*, page 00) should enable the bowler to decide upon a comfortable, balanced and gradually accelerating run to the wicket. Standing at deep mid-off, cue the bowler's acceleration verbally: 'Slow start ... accelerate ... gather yourself ...'

The directness of the run-up can be governed by planting stumps at strategic points in the approach and instructing the bowler to run alongside and just inside the line of the stumps. To regulate the bowler's length of stride place visible markers (e.g. small witch's hats) alongside each ideal foot placement of the bowler in the run-up. The bowler will then be able to see these markers from the corner of the eye and strive to place the feet alongside them. The ideal foot placements can be worked out by observing where the bowler places the feet during a satisfactory approach and marking them accordingly.

For bowlers who are extremely hesitant in their approach or who bowl off the wrong foot, 'backward-shape' the run-up. From a position just behind the bowling crease, the bowler takes one step onto the foot opposite the bowling arm before jumping onto the natural foot and bowling. Then the bowler adds two more paces to the run, stepping off onto the 'unnatural' foot, then the natural foot, and onto the unnatural foot again before jumping on to the natural foot to bowl. Build up the run in units of two steps in this way until a satisfactory length is established. Then quicken the approach to a jog, then to a run, lengthening it to accommodate the extra speed and to enable the bowler to place the front foot in the delivery stride behind the popping crease.

For bowlers who approach the wicket too quickly or too slowly, use the verbal acceleration technique outlined above. Bowlers with a slow approach will be assisted by insisting that they follow through past a stump placed by the side of the pitch at the bowler's end 3 m in front of the batting crease. In an effort to lengthen their follow-through they will increase the speed of their approach.

For bowlers who do not turn into a side-on position in their delivery stride, place a length of rope on the ground in the middle of the last stride of the run-up and parallel to the bowling crease. Ask the bowler to jump high above the rope to turn into the bowling stride. The height of the jump will then facilitate the twisting action of the body into the side-on position in the delivery stride.

2 Basic bowling action

The correct model

Comments on the reasons behind the skill and possible faults

- PLACEMENT OF THE FEET

1 The bowler jumps onto the rear foot, which is parallel to the bowling crease
2 The bowler steps down the wicket with the front leg towards the target of the batter's wicket. The toes of the front foot point towards the batter or fine leg
3 The front foot is raised high in the rock-back and remains braced once it is planted in the delivery stride.

The placement of the feet in the delivery stride is the result of the bowler jumping high in the final pace of the run-up and turning into a side-on position with the line of the shoulders pointing directly towards the batter's wicket. The bowler maintains forward momentum in this direction.

In the rock-back, the front leg is raised high in front of the body before being stamped into the ground as the bowler steps down the wicket towards the batter. If the front leg is not raised high in front of the body, the rock-back is inadequate. If the front foot does not point towards fine-leg or the batter, the hips have assumed an open position. This indicates that the bowler has probably stepped down the pitch, not towards the batter, but towards first slip and consequently has not maintained momentum towards the target of the wickets.

Once the front leg has been planted in the delivery stride, it remains braced to ensure that the bowler delivers from the greatest possible height. This produces maximum bounce, speed and spin since it increases the arc through which the bowling arm must pass as quickly as possible. A collapsed front knee is a common fault which dramatically reduces a bowler's effectiveness.

- BODY MOVEMENT

1 The body rocks back away from the batter through an angle of approximately 30 degrees.
2 The body is in a side-on position in the delivery stride, with the front shoulder, side and hip pointing and moving forwards towards the batter after the rock-back.

The side-on position of the body makes it easier to maintain forward momentum towards the batter's wicket along the line of the shoulders. If the bowler is chest-on to the batter in the delivery stride, the shoulders describe a sideways arc, not in the desired direction of the batter's wicket, but towards slips. Consequently, if the bowler releases the ball at the wrong moment, it will pass either to the leg or off side of the wicket.

The rock-back of the body increases the arc through which the trunk will move forward as the bowling arm swings over. If the bowler leans forward in the run-up, the trunk will rock back through an angle of 30 degrees before moving sideways towards the batter through an angle of 80 degrees. An absence of rock-back causes the bowler to lose the benefit of the trunk's weight and strength behind the delivery, with a consequent minimisation of speed and swing. If the body only rocks back from an upward posture through an angle of 15 degrees, this too reduces the extent of the trunk movement and consequently the bowler's speed and spin.

• FRONT-ARM MOVEMENT

1 As the body rocks back, the front arm is bent at the elbow and raised, but remains close to the body
2 When the body is in the 'cocked' position, at the end of the rock-back, the front arm is extended upwards and forwards in the direction of fine leg. The bowler looks over the front shoulder and behind the front arm at the batter
3 The front arm moves forwards and upwards towards fine leg before bending as the leading elbow is depressed quickly into the leading side
4 The front elbow stabilises and stops.

In keeping the arms close to the trunk during the rock-back, the bowler facilitates the quick movement of the large mass of the body, thus increasing speed and spin. The forward and upward movement of the front arm pulls the bowler up to full height and maintains the forward movement of the body towards the batter's wicket. Looking over the front shoulder and behind the front arm maintains the body in a side-on posture, thus preserving forward momentum towards the batter and increasing accuracy. The degree to which the front arm moves forwards and upwards before the leading elbow is lowered determines the length of the delivery. The earlier the lowering of the elbow, the shorter the length of the ball, since the downward movement of the front and rear shoulder – and consequently the bowling arm – will occur earlier in the delivery stride. Insufficient elevation of the front arm and a failure to look behind it is one of the most common faults in the bowling action.

• MOVEMENT OF THE BOWLING ARM

1 The bowling arm is raised alongside the front arm when that arm begins its forward and upward movement
2 The bowling arm moves downwards and backwards before beginning an upward and forward movement as the front elbow stabilises
3 The bowling arm moves forward towards the batter alongside the bowler's head. The ball is released just after the arm has reached the highest point of its swing for the faster bowlers, just before for the slower bowlers.

The sudden dropping of the front elbow accelerates the swing of the rear shoulder and bowling arm. It is easier to move the short upper arm down quickly than the whole front arm and this movement drags the bowling arm over faster. The stabilisation of the front elbow alongside the leading hip accentuates the drag on the bowling arm and the speed of its swing. Many bowlers lower the whole of the front arm rather than just the elbow and thereby lose speed and spin.

The longer the swing of the bowling arm from in front of the body, the faster it moves and the greater the speed of the ball. The bowling arm begins to move at its fastest after the front elbow has stabilised. This occurs when the bowling arm is behind the body.

The bowling arm must swing in the same linear direction as the shoulders – directly towards the batter's wicket. Keeping the arm close to the head maximises the height of the release and gains extra bounce. (Many bowlers fail to keep their bowling arms high and 'sling' the ball.) Releasing the ball just before the bowling arm has reached its highest point enables the slower bowler to flight the ball and gain overspin. Releasing the ball after the bowling arm has reached its highest point flattens the ball's flight and increases its speed.

- FOLLOW-THROUGH

1 After the release of the ball, the leading arm resumes its movement, swinging downwards and backwards alongside the body to absorb the force of the bowling arm
2 The bowling arm swings across the body and downwards and backwards alongside the leading leg
3 The rear leg bends and moves forwards alongside the leading leg
4 The bowler takes two or three steps down the wicket towards the batter before moving off the pitch towards the off-side.

Swinging the leading arm past the body in the follow-through absorbs the force of the bowling arm. Swinging the front arm directly backwards indicates that the bowler has maintained forward momentum.

The swing of the bowling arm across the body in the follow-through indicates that the bowler has maintained a side-on position in the delivery stride for as long as possible. If the bowling arm swings too wide of the leading side of the body, the bowler's momentum in the delivery stride has deviated towards the slips and away from the target of the batter's wicket.

The forward movement of the back leg and the body straight down the wicket after the ball indicates continued forward movement towards the batter. If the back leg swings in an arc around the front leg and the bowler runs off the wicket too quickly towards the off side, there is too much lateral shoulder movement in the delivery stride and forward momentum has not been maintained.

CORRECTION STRATEGIES

To correct an open hip and leg placement in the delivery stride make the bowler bowl through a 'gate' formed by one stump placed 60 cm wide of the bowler's wicket on the off side of the bowling crease and another placed on the batting crease 45 cm wide of the stumps on the off side.

To increase a bowler's rock-back, provide verbal cues to ensure that he or she leans forward in the run-up, using the arms to 'pump' the body forward towards the batter.

A closed shoulder action can be facilitated by placing a piece of coloured sticky tape on the outside of the bowler's leading shoulder and insisting that it should be visible to the bowler throughout the bowling action.

To increase the height of a bowler's action and avoid a collapsed front knee and low arm, suspend a piece of string or a bird bell just above the spot where the front and bowling hand pass in the delivery stride. Ask the bowler to brush the string or bell with both the front and rear hands.

Use verbal cues for the sudden dropping of the front elbow and to ensure that the bowler 'brushes the ear' with the bowling arm, keeping it high.

To guarantee that the bowler maintains forward momentum towards the batter's wicket, plot the run-up and follow-through with the aid of stumps or miniature witch's hats. The bowler then runs up, bowls and follows through, keeping just within the line of the plotted course. Use the 'bowling through the gate' procedure for the delivery stride.

- RESULT OF THE DELIVERY

The ball has been delivered:
a) on the appropriate, straight line
b) with the optimum amount of speed and swing, cut or spin.

The desired result from a ball usually demonstrates its correctness; an incorrect result indicates the necessity for the remedial procedures previously outlined.

Wicketkeeping

Wicketkeeping

The wicketkeeper is the most important fielder in cricket. Theoretically he or she may have to stop every ball. The 'keeper' takes more catches, stumps more batters, and runs out more players than any other fielder. There is no substitute for a good keeper, who has to be consistently proficient and can inspire the side.

REMEMBER: BE BALANCED. WATCH THE BOWLER, THE BATTER AND THE BALL.

How to keep wicket

1 EQUIPMENT Always wear and use comfortable clothes and equipment – small light pads and gloves are preferable to big and heavy ones. The gloves protect the hands but must allow you to 'feel' the ball as you take it. A pair of inner chamois gloves should always be worn in addition to the wicketkeeping gloves themselves. Push fingers of both your hands hard into the tops of the inners and gloves. It is an idea to shorten the length of the protective hard stall at the end of fingers. The stall protection is standard in most gloves but it can reduce the flexibility of the fingers. Your gloves should have a good hollow or 'cup' in the palm. Never allow the glove surface to become worn and smooth. Comfortable boots are essential. To avoid sore feet on hard grounds wear insoles or two pairs of socks. Clothes should be loose fitting for comfort and quick movement. A cap helps concentration and reduces glare from the wicket.

2 STANCE It is difficult to set a standard stance for wicketkeepers. Some prefer to squat on their toes, others balance on the balls of their feet. Whichever stance you adopt, it should be comfortable with your weight distributed evenly between your legs and feet. The comfortable balanced squatting stance ensures essential speedy footwork.

For fast bowlers, stand back far enough to receive the average ball as it stops rising. Judge how far outside the off stump you should stand. Naturally this will vary with different bowlers and conditions. A left-handed bowler over the wicket on a 'green' pitch will demand a different wicketkeeping position than a right-handed bowler on a good wicket. The critical point is that the bowler's hand must be clearly visible throughout the run-up and delivery.

For slow bowlers you must judge how far outside the off stump you need to stand. It will generally be just outside the off stump but will vary according to the type of bowler. It is essential that you are near enough to the stumps to reach them with one movement and effect a stumping when the opportunity arises. For medium-paced bowlers you must decide whether you will stand up to the stumps or back. This will depend on the state of the game and the wicket. If in doubt it is better to stand back, since

The stance, standing back

Standing up

in that position you will take a higher percentage of the straightforward edged catches.

3 MOVEMENT OF THE FEET Quick movement is essential to good wicketkeeping. You will need at all times to drive your legs to achieve this. Try to move sideways into a position behind the ball or where you can take the ball on the side of the body closer to the stumps. Use the drop and cross-over steps to facilitate this sideways movement. When standing up to slow bowlers, work in a semicircle around the stumps so that they always remain within striking distance.

Thrust sideways, cross-over step

Thrust sideways

Taking the ball on the leg side

High take

Taking returns

When standing back to any bowler, be prepared to spring up to the stumps, every ball if necessary, to deter the batter from taking quick singles and to be prepared for run-out attempts. Unless there is a chance of a run-out, you should always move to the thrown balls and try to take returns from the fielders on the full toss, thus preserving the shine of the ball for the faster bowlers and showing the batters that you are alert. If you

The hands

cannot take the ball on the full toss, move back to take it after it has bounced, gaining time to see its height and direction and minimising the risk of an awkward bounce and possible injury.

4 THE HANDS To avoid damage to the fingers in taking the ball it is essential that you should always point your fingers up or down when taking the ball, sometimes slightly to the side. Never point them towards the ball.

Give with your hands, arms and body as you take the ball to prevent it bouncing out and to avoid sore hands. Rise with the ball to absorb its shock and never snatch at it.

5 HEAD AND EYES Never take your eyes off the ball while it is in play. Ignore the swing of the bat and assume that every ball will come to you. Hold your head steady.

Stumping on the off side

6 STUMPING Always be in a position to stump the batter who has left the crease. Keep the stumps within reach in a single movement. Never retreat to take the ball. Watch the batter's feet and the ball all the time. Rise with the ball according to its bounce and let the hands give as you gather it. Concentrate on taking the ball before moving your hands towards the stumps. When you see the batter leave the crease, never be hurried into snatching at the ball.

Stumping on the leg side

Simplified hints and checklist
1 Make sure that your equipment is comfortable and efficient
2 A comfortable, balanced stance for speedy footwork. Always have the ball in sight. Stand back to the fast bowlers, taking the ball as it stops rising. When standing up, always have the stumps within reach
3 Drive your legs sideways when standing back and take the ball on the side of your body closer to the stumps. When standing up, work in a semicircle around the stumps. Drive your legs up to the stumps to take fielders' returns
4 Fingers sideways or downwards, never towards the ball. Soft hands. Rise with the ball
5 The batter does not exist. Take every ball
6 When stumping, first things first. Take the ball before striking at the wicket.

REMEMBER: WATCH THE BOWLER, THE BATTER AND THE BALL. BE BALANCED.

Group activity

WICKETKEEPING
- Wicketkeeper A tries to take each delivery with batter B 'shadow' batting, i.e. attempting to obscure the keeper's view of the delivery
- On taking each delivery the keeper goes through the stumping motion
- Players swap positions after 10 deliveries
- The keeper scores 1 point for each delivery taken cleanly and correctly.

Number of players: 3
Equipment: 1 bat, 1 ball, 1 set of stumps.

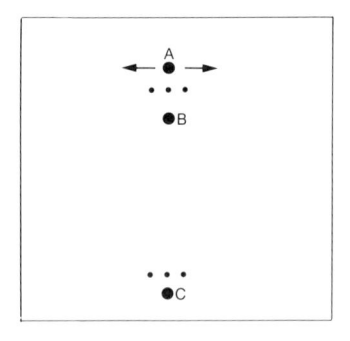

The following are the most frequent wicketkeeping faults:
- Incorrect gloves and equipment
- Faulty balance
- Poor footwork
- Wrong positioning at the stumps
- Uncomfortable stance
- Lack of drive in the movement to the ball
- Inability to reach the stumps standing up
- Wrong positioning of the hands when taking the ball
- Snatching at the ball and not allowing the hands to give
- Taking the eyes off the ball
- Trying to stump the batsman before taking the ball
- Retreating when taking the ball.
- Rising too early.

Fielding

Basic principles of fielding

When the ball is struck, the fielder must move quickly either to take a catch or stop the ball. The first movement depends on the direction of the ball and whether it is travelling along the ground or in the air. A batter can run approximately 60 cm (2 ft) in a tenth of a second; consequently, fielders should strive to save tenths of a second during the pick-up and throwing phases.

To minimise the time taken returning a fielded ball, the fielder will need to use different footwork and throws in different situations.

Moving to field the ball

1 FORWARD Begin from a balanced position, with your feet shoulder-width apart, weight evenly distributed on the balls of the feet, knees bent, slightly crouched with hands hanging between your legs.

Run quickly with your body square on to the ball, keeping the ball directly in front of your body.

As you approach the ball ensure that your hands are in front of your body and shorten your steps, keeping low to the ground by bending at the knees and hips.

If the ball is bouncing, adjust your running speed to take the ball at waist height or in a comfortable position, i.e. at the top of the bounce or just after the ball bounces.

2 SIDEWAYS: THE CROSS-OVER STEP Make a short quick sideways step with the foot closer to the line of the ball transferring your weight onto this foot.

Take a cross-over step with the other foot.

Run in a direction to get the ball, throwing target and your body in a straight line whenever possible.

Cross-over step

Drop step

3 BACKWARDS: THE DROP STEP Move the foot closer to the line of the ball backwards approximately 20 cm (8 in), at the same time turning the foot and your hips in the direction of the ball.

Throw your other leg around to begin running towards the ball.

Preparing to throw the ball

1 THE CROW HOP The crow hop is used to turn the body into the correct side-on throwing position and to add distance to a throw.

Pick up the ball with your body almost square on to the ball, toe of the foot closer to the target and heel of the other foot approximately in line.

Transfer your weight quickly on to the foot closer to the target, then move the other foot forward to a position at right angles to the direction of the throw by using the cross-over step.

Step forward with the foot closer to the target, then push off the right foot and complete the throw.

2 THE REVERSE TURN The reverse turn is used when the fielder is forced to field the ball out to the side with the non-throwing arm and is running at right angles to the eventual throwing direction.

When the ball is collected, stop your movement by planting the foot on the same side of your body as the throwing arm firmly on the ground.

Swivel on the planted foot turning your back to the target whilst transferring the ball to your throwing hand.

Throw the leg opposite to your throwing arm around until it is in line with the target and complete the throw.

If a long throw is required, use the crow hop after the turn has been completed.

3 THE PIVOT TURN The pivot turn is used by a short cover or short mid-wicket fielder to throw the ball for a run-out at the bowler's end.

In fielding the ball, lead with the leg opposite to the direction you wish to throw.

Point the other leg at the throwing target.

In making the throw, turn your body only.

4 THE JUMP TURN The jump turn is used to turn the body into the throwing position when a longer throw is required than can be executed using the pivot turn.

When you have collected the ball, rotate into a position side-on to the target by jumping vertically and twisting with both feet off the ground.

Throwing

1 THE GRIP Grip the ball with the first and second fingers across the seam and the thumb and third finger directly underneath.

When fielding the ball, ensure that your fingers are in the correct position on the ball before the throw is commenced, i.e. find the seam.

2 THE OVERHAND THROW This throw is used when distance, speed and accuracy are required.

Turn your body into the correct side-on throwing position by using the crow hop.

From the side-on position, step forward with your front leg towards the target.

At the same time, move the throwing arm in a large arc, beginning in front of the body, then moving down, back and up to a point where the elbow is shoulder high.

During this preparatory throwing phase, keep your hand on top of the ball.

As the throw is made, lead with the elbow of the throwing arm and, at the point of release, snap the wrist.

Release the ball with backspin to obtain maximum distance.

Follow through towards the target.

3 THE SHORT ARM THROW When speed rather than distance is the crucial factor, the short arm throw is needed.

Shorten the arc of the throwing arm by taking the elbow straight back to the throwing position.

Keep the ball in front of the elbow.

Follow through after the throw.

4 THE SIDE-ARM THROW To save time in fielding a ground ball, the side-arm throw is used when only a short throw is required.

Collect the ball with the leading leg pointing towards the target.

After the ball is fielded, stay down with your back in a horizontal position.

Draw the throwing arm back quickly to a throwing position.

Make the throw from a bent position, throwing arm almost horizontal so that the ball travels on an upwards path towards the target.

Additional power may be generated by turning the hips quickly just before you release the ball.

If you are required to field and throw whilst still in motion, field the ball with the opposite leg to your throwing arm forward and follow through on to the right foot as the throw is made.

5 THE UNDERHAND THROW When you are very close to and in front of the throwing target, use the underhand throw.

Move quickly behind the line of the ball, picking it up on the throwing-arm side of your body.

Use a one-handed pick-up in front of your body and beside the same leg as your throwing arm.

Lock the wrist and elbow as the throw is made.

Follow through with your arm and body directly towards the target.

6 THE BACKHAND FLIP This throw is used when the throwing target is to the left or right of the direction you are facing as you field the ball.

Collect the ball in the same hand as the direction it is to be thrown in.

Take the throwing arm across in front of the body away from the target.

The ball must always face the target.

As the throw is made, stiffen the wrist and allow your arm to follow through towards the target.

Simplified hints and checklist

1 Find the seam before throwing
2 Overhand throw for distance, speed and accuracy
3 Short arm throw for speed
4 Side-arm throw for a short distance
5 Underhand throw when close to the target
6 Backhand flip when the target is to the left or right.

Examples of specific fielding techniques

A Underhand throw
B Backhand flip
C Reverse turn with short-arm throw
D Reverse turn with crow hop
E Pivot turn with leading right leg and short-arm throw
F Pivot turn with leading left leg and short-arm throw
G Jump turn and short-arm throw.

NB Assume fielder is right handed and all throws are to the bowler's end.

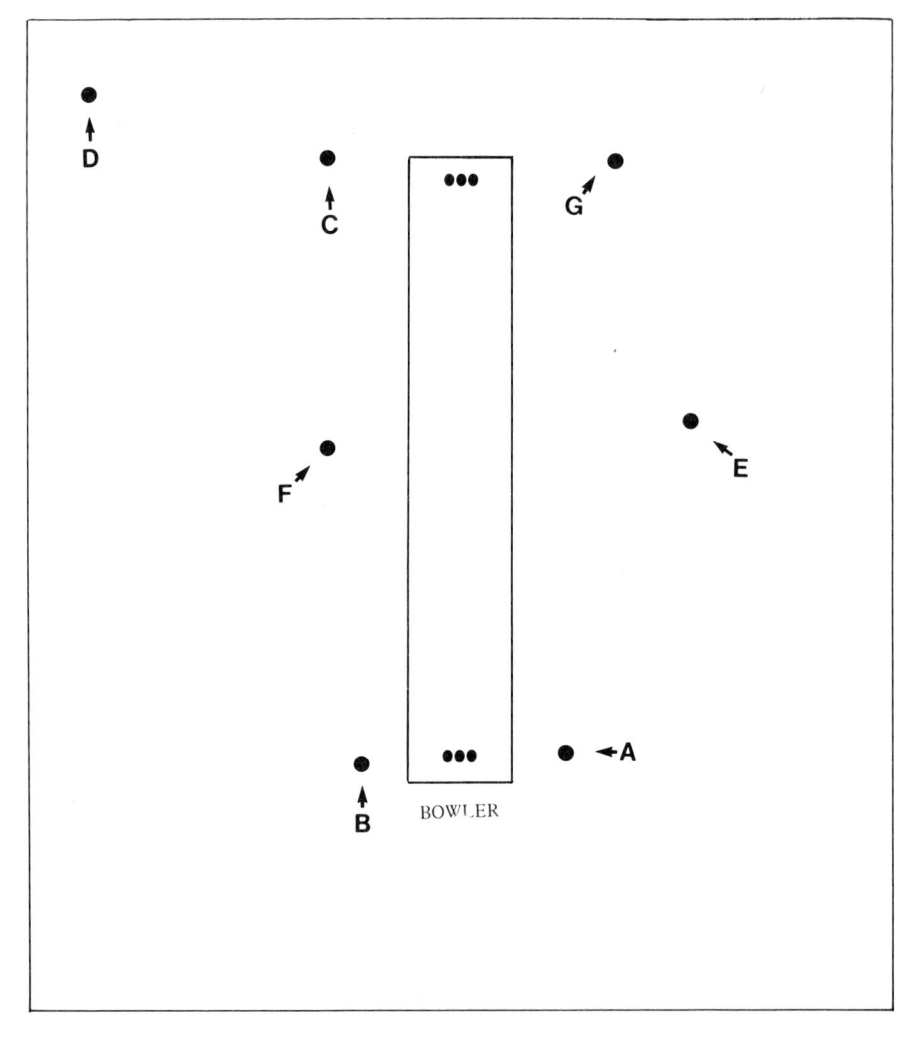

Field placements (to a right-handed batter)

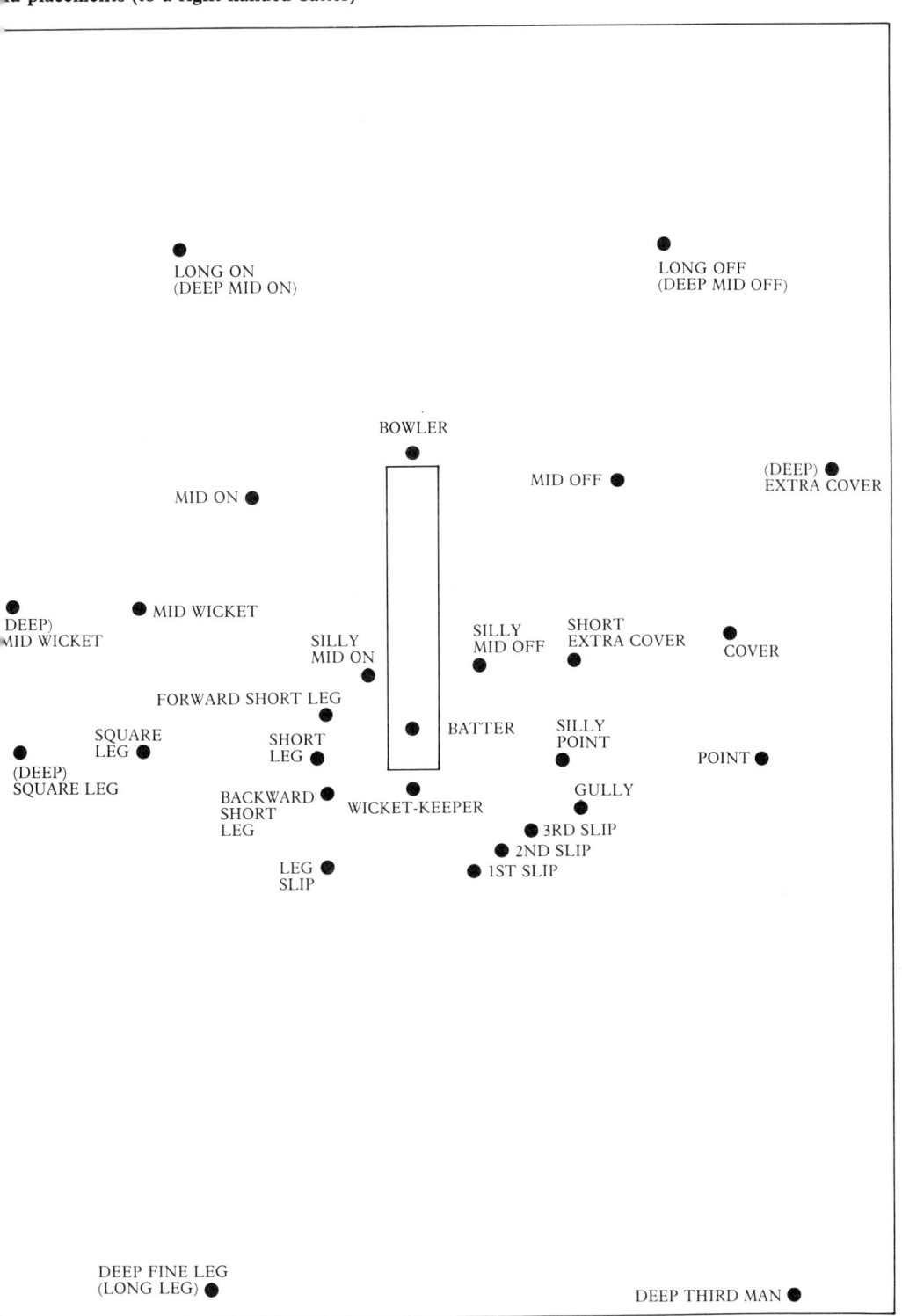

- LONG ON (DEEP MID ON)
- LONG OFF (DEEP MID OFF)
- BOWLER
- MID OFF
- (DEEP) EXTRA COVER
- MID ON
- MID WICKET
- SILLY MID ON
- SILLY MID OFF
- SHORT EXTRA COVER
- COVER
- (DEEP) MID WICKET
- FORWARD SHORT LEG
- SQUARE LEG
- SHORT LEG
- BATTER
- SILLY POINT
- POINT
- (DEEP) SQUARE LEG
- BACKWARD SHORT LEG
- WICKET-KEEPER
- GULLY
- 3RD SLIP
- 2ND SLIP
- LEG SLIP
- 1ST SLIP
- DEEP FINE LEG (LONG LEG)
- DEEP THIRD MAN

The attacking outfielder

A player fields in an attacking way in the outfield in order to assist the bowler and wicketkeeper to dismiss the batter by catching or running them out. The attacking outfielder not only helps dismiss batters, but saves runs and makes the batting side unsure in the judgement of runs and pressurises them into mistakes.

The close-to-the-wicket fielders attack by catching the batters. The attacking outfielder is to be found in all positions away from the wicket: the third man area, deep point, cover, extra cover, mid-off on the off side, mid-on, mid-wicket, square leg, fine leg on the on side. The outfielder should defend only when the ball is struck past him or her or hard enough to make stopping the ball the first consideration.

REMEMBER: BE BALANCED. WATCH THE BALL AND THE BATTER.

How to field in an attacking way

1 STANCE As the ball is bowled you should be upright, on your toes, leaning forward slightly and moving in at a walk towards the pitch or batter, ready to accelerate in any direction towards the ball.

2 HEAD AND EYES Hold your head steady. Your eyes should be fixed first on the ball and bowler, and then on the batter, whose actions will lead you to anticipate the direction of the stroke. After the ball is struck the eyes should be firmly on the ball until it is out of play, or it comes right into your hands and you return it to the keeper or the bowler.

The stance   The stop

3 MOVEMENT TO THE BALL As the ball is struck, move quickly to a position where your body is in line with the ball. Your initial foot movement is determined by the direction of the ball. When moving sideways use a cross-over step (p.116). A backwards movement commences with a drop step (see p.117).

4 THE STOP As you stoop to pick up the ball, bend at the knees and the hips. Place your rear foot in line with the ball, front leg points slightly to the side of the throwing target and shoulders almost square on to the ball. Pick the ball up in front of your rear foot, the fingers of your hands pointing downwards and both hands cupped together. Watch the ball right into your hands.

5 THE THROW The attacking outfielder may use a variety of throws: the overhand (see p.119) for long distances; the short arm (see p.120) for shorter distances; and the side-arm (see p.120) when there is not enough time to throw from a standing position. With all throws, keep your eyes on the target as you throw and aim your return to arrive just over the top of the stumps on the full.

6 BACKING UP Outfielders should always back up the wicketkeeper or bowler when returns come to the stumps from the opposite side of the pitch, moving quickly into line behind the throw in case the wicketkeeper or bowler misses it. When a ball is struck and the batters think of a run, fielders such as mid-off and mid-on close to the bowler's stumps move to the wicket to take any return that may come to that end.

A fielder must never presume that the player closer to the wicket will stop the ball. Back up your team member in case the batter's stroke penetrates the first line of defence.

7 CATCHING IN THE OUTFIELD When a catch comes your way, don't move forward too early. Watch the ball closely and judge the flight of

Catching in the outfield

the catch and the spot where it should bounce before moving into position. If a catch goes over your head, turn in the direction of the ball using a drop step (p.117), and run sideways using a cross-over step by crossing the trailing leg in front of the leading leg.

The most effective catching is achieved just above or just below eye level. Cup your hands together with your fingers upwards or downwards at those levels. Above eye level sight the ball between the back of the fingers of the hands cupped together level with the forehead. Watch the ball right into the hands and give with your hands as the ball enters them to stop it bouncing out, and avoid injury. Never snatch at the ball.

Simplified hints and checklist

1 Be ready to move quickly towards the ball
2 Keep your eyes glued on the bowler, the ball, the batters and the keeper until the ball is dead
3 Move quickly into line with the ball
4 Bend at the knees and the hips
5 Watch the target and return the ball over the top of the stumps
6 Back up
7 Look and judge before you catch and run.

Group activity

THE ATTACKING OUTFIELDER

- Wicketkeepers A and B roll the ball to fielders C, D, E and F in turn
- As the ball is rolled, the keeper nominates the end to which the throw is to be made
- Batters G and H try to complete a single
- In fielding the ball, the fielder uses the most appropriate footwork and throw
- Players rotate positions in pairs every 6 throws with the batting pair becoming the keepers
- One point is scored each time a batter is run out. The player with the highest score is the winner.

Number of players: 8
Equipment: 1 set of stumps, 1 ball, 2 bats.

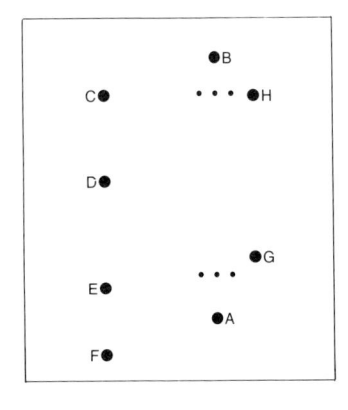

The defending outfielder

The object of fielding in the outfield in a defensive way is to prevent the batters scoring runs. All positions on the field are defensive when the ball penetrates that position or is struck hard towards it. Stopping the ball and saving runs is then the fielder's first consideration.

REMEMBER: BE BALANCED. WATCH THE BALL.

How to field in a defensive way

1 STANCE As the ball is bowled you should be upright, on your toes, leaning forward slightly and moving in at a walk towards the pitch or batter, ready to accelerate towards the ball in any direction.

2 HEAD AND EYES Keep your head steady and your eyes fixed first on the ball and the bowler, then on the batter whose actions will lead you to anticipate the direction of the stroke. After the ball is struck, watch the ball until it is dead or it comes into a fielder's hands and is returned to the keeper.

3 MOVEMENT TO THE BALL As the ball is struck, move quickly to a position where your body is in line with the ball. Your initial foot movement is determined by the direction of the ball. When moving sideways use a cross-over step (p.116). A backward movement begins with a drop step (p.117).

4 THE STOP In stopping the ball use your body as a barricade or second line of defence so that, if you miss the ball with your hands, your body will prevent it going for runs. Do this either by kneeling in a side-on position with the front side of the body behind the line of the ball and gathering the ball beside your front leg, or by standing with your feet and legs together and behind the ball as you stoop to gather it. Fingers point to 6 or 12 o'clock and the hands give as they gather the ball.

If the ball penetrates the field, chase it. As you arrive at the ball, step over it or alongside it with the foot on your throwing side so that your feet are in the correct throwing position. As you stoop to retrieve the ball your back will be towards the target wicket and your weight on your heels as you stop inside the boundary. Your back should be pointing directly at the target wicket so that when you pick up the ball, you can spin on your rear foot and throw accurately in the direction of the keeper or bowler's wicket. If a long throw is required, use the crow hop. In some instances close to the boundary if you are supported by another player, flick the ball backhand to the fielder backing you up to return it to the target wicket.

5 THE THROW To throw over a long distance, begin with a crow hop (see p.117) and use an overhand throw (see p.119). Don't run two or three steps to gain power as this wastes valuable time. Aim your return to arrive just over the top of the stumps on the full or after one bounce. The speed of a long return can be increased if the ball is relayed via a fielder who backs up halfway to the boundary. Your throw can then be flat, but it must be accurate.

6 BACKING UP Backing up is one of the most important aspects of defensive fielding. Outfielders should always back up the wicketkeeper or bowler when returns come from the opposite side of the pitch, moving quickly into line behind the throw in case the wicketkeeper or bowler misses it. When the ball is struck and the batters think of a run, fielders such as mid-off and mid-on close to the bowler's stumps move in to them to take any return that may come to that end. A fielder must never presume that the player closer to the wicket will stop the ball. Back that player up in case the batter's stroke penetrates the first line of defence.

Simplified hints and checklist

1 Be ready to move quickly towards the ball
2 Keep your eyes glued on the bowler, the ball, the batters and the keeper until the ball is dead
3 Move your body quickly in line with the ball
4 Put up the 'barricades' of your legs and body
5 Return the ball quickly using the crow hop and overhand throw
6 Back up your team mates.

Group activity

THE DEFENDING OUTFIELDER
• Batter A stands 20 m from the 'goal keeper' B and hits 10 catches or ground balls
• The goal keeper attempts to prevent the ball passing through the goals or takes the catches
• Fielders C and D retrieve misfielded balls
• Players rotate positions every 10 balls
• Score 1 point for each goal saved or catch taken.

Number of players: 4
Equipment: 1 bat, 1 ball, 1 pair of goals.

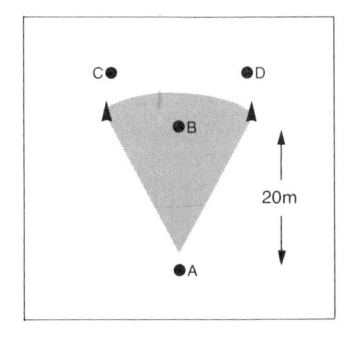

The close-to-the-wicket fielder

The close-to-the-wicket fielder's job is to assist the bowler to dismiss the batting side by catching or running them out. Most dismissals in cricket result from catches in the field when a bowler forces a batter into producing a false shot which travels in the air. Many of these catches are taken in close-to-the-wicket positions. The close-to-the-wicket fielder also has to stop the ball to prevent the scoring of runs.

How to field close to the wicket

1 POSITIONS The close-to-the-wicket fielders are positioned in front of the wicket and behind. Behind the wicket on the off side are the slips whose number can vary. Generally there are three slips standing in an arc from the wicketkeeper to the off side. Their distance back from the stumps is governed by the pace of the bowler and wicket so that an edged stroke from the batter which carries as a catch will reach the slips at a comfortable height between the knees and waist. The greater the contact a ball makes with the bat, the wider it will deflect from the bat, and the shorter the distance it will carry. Thus second and third slips and gully should be correspondingly closer to the bat and stumps in 'staggered' lines. The gully fielder is on a 45-degree angle behind the wicket, whilst point is at right angles to the stumps and close on the off side. First slip stands to the off side of the wicketkeeper and as wide as the keeper – who knows how much territory he or she can cover – wants. The slips and gully should be able to touch hands when their arms are outstretched leaving no gap through which a catch can escape.

Leg slips occupy the same position on the leg side as the orthodox slips on the off. Short leg corresponds to gully on the off side, whilst short square leg is the on side equivalent of point. In front of the wicket on the off side just off the pitch and at a distance which varies between half the length of the pitch and a few yards is silly mid-off. Wider on the off side of silly mid-off is short extra cover. Their equivalents on the leg side are silly mid-on and forward short leg. All the fielders in front of the wicket are stationed for the shot played in their direction and in the air.

2 STANCE Squat on the balls of your feet, with your feet comfortably apart and your weight evenly distributed. You must be able to move very quickly from this position. Move into your stance as the bowler turns to bowl.

3 HEAD AND EYES Your head should be still with your eyes fixed first on the bowler. As the bowler bowls, first slip should watch the ball, since its path and behaviour is clearly and constantly visible. The other slips, gully and point should watch the ball and the edge of the bat. The leg side fielder does not have as clear a view of the ball as the slips and gully and may need to anticipate a catch by the batter's movement. Your eyes must

follow the ball whenever possible but in the positions squarer of the wicket, you may have to anticipate a catch from the batter's movement.

4 THE CATCH Cup both hands together and point your fingers down or up, sometimes to the side but never at the ball. Give with your hands as the ball enters them to stop the ball bouncing out of them and to avoid injury. Never snatch at the ball. The most effective catching is done just above or just below eye level. Watch the ball right into your hands.

5 THE STOP When you stop the ball, use your body as a second line of defence, so that if you miss the ball, your body will prevent it going for runs. Kneel in a side-on position with the front side of your body behind the line of the ball or assume a crouched position leaning and shuffling forwards with your body behind the line of the ball as you stoop to gather it.

6 THE THROWS In close-to-the-wicket fielding positions the throw required is short and quick. The underhand throw (see p.121) and the backhand flip (see p.121) are most appropriate if the batter moves outside the crease. A throw to the bowler's end should be a short arm throw (see p.120) or a side-arm throw (see p.120).

7 BACKING UP Close-to-the-wicket fielders quite often need to back up the wicketkeeper who may not have time to come from a standing back position up to gather a quick return. On these occasions short leg, point, silly mid-off or -on fill the keeper's role. Close-to-the-wicket fielders also act as a second line of defence to the keeper for returns from the outfield or for short throws from fellow close-to-the-wicket fielders.

Simplified hints and checklist

1 Take up your stance an appropriate distance and angle from the batter
2 Be balanced and ready to move
3 Keep your eyes on the ball or the batter's movements, whichever is easier to see
4 When taking the ball, cup your hands like a bird's nest
5 Put up the 'barricades' of your body behind the line of the ball
6 Use short, quick throws
7 Back up throws at the stumps.

Group activity

THE CLOSE-TO-THE-WICKET FIELDER
- Feeder A throws balls on the full to batter B who hits catches to the slips cordon D, E and F
- Fielder C retrieves balls not hit by the batter
- If a catch is dropped, the fielder responsible moves to the third slip position and the other players move along one place towards first slip
- When first slip holds 3 catches he or she replaces the batter.

Number of players: 6-8
Equipment: 1 bat, 1 ball.

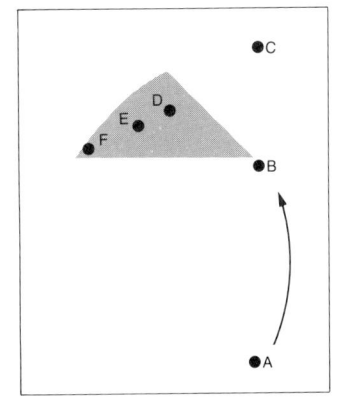

Detection and correction of faults in fielding

Whilst 75 per cent of a cricketer's playing time is spent on fielding, training sessions rarely reflect the importance of fielding. The most common errors and the easiest to eliminate are those which do not involve specific skills. The following fielding faults require constant drill in a simulated match situation at training:
- Inattention or failure to keep the eyes on the ball or the captain whilst the ball is in play and the game in progress
- Failure to be on the toes and on the move in the outfield when the ball is bowled
- Failure to move behind the line of the ball
- Failure to return the ball on the full to the keeper or bowler's wicket
- Failure to back up on both returns and on possible misfields
- Failure to support a fellow fielder in a chase to the boundary
- Failure to attack the ball whenever possible in the outfield
- Failure to adopt the correct position when fielding close to the wicket
- Failure to keep the eyes on the ball, bat or batter when fielding close to the wicket
- Moving from your position in the field without instructions from the captain or bowler.

There are also specific fielding faults:

1 Faults in throwing

Correction strategy **Comments on possible faults**

- INACCURACY IN LONG THROWS

To improve accuracy the coach should emphasise the importance of the correct throwing action, i.e. high throwing arm, stepping towards the target with the leading leg and following through.

The faults may be caused by imparting side spin to the ball at release resulting in the ball deviating from a straight path. Failure to follow through in the direction of the throw may also be a factor.

- RUNNING BEFORE THROWING

In order to return the ball in minimum time, preface a long throw with a crow hop and a lean back in the throwing position.

The tendency to run four or five steps before throwing over a long distance wastes valuable time and does not significantly improve throwing power as many fielders mistakenly believe. To stress this point, players could be timed for the time taken to return a ball using both correct and incorrect methods.

- **TAKING TOO LONG TO THROW THE BALL**

The coach should drill players in using footwork such as the reverse turn, pivot turn and jump turn. Whenever possible, the fielders' feet should be in the throwing position before the ball is picked up.

This fault is caused by the fielder taking unnecessary steps to get into the throwing position.

2 Faults in stopping

Correction strategy   **Comments on possible faults**

- **STUMBLING WHEN PICKING UP THE BALL ON THE MOVE**

To remain balanced when fielding a ball in front of the body, it is essential that the fielder is stationary just before pick up, feet apart with the knees and back bent.

This is a common fault caused by lack of stability and balance.

- **KNEELING ON THE INCORRECT KNEE WHEN USING THE 'LONG BARRIER'**

To develop confidence in using the non-preferred leg, the coach should simplify the skill by letting fielders stop a gently rolled ball from 5 metres.

All fielders have a preferred leg which they will use to block the ball unless a conscious effort has been made to develop the non-preferred leg.

3 Faults in catching

Correction strategy   **Comments on possible faults**

- **SNATCHING AT THE BALL**

To eliminate the forward hand movement, fielders should have their hands slightly out in front of the body to facilitate the movement back towards the body. Catching practice using a tennis ball will improve the ability to let the hands 'give'.

Fielders who snatch at the ball, particularly in slips, experience difficulty in taking the ball cleanly.

- **NOT WATCHING THE BALL INTO THE HANDS**

To encourage players to focus their attention on the ball, the coach could paint different coloured dots on the balls being used for catching practice. Players should identify the colour of the ball before taking the catch.

Successful catching demands that the fielder watches the ball until it is safely within his or her grasp.

Since you will be fielding for 75 per cent of the time you spend playing cricket, you must practise the skills you will need constantly. Fielding practice can be boring and can lack the glamour of the other skill practices so the coach should try to make fielding practice as varied and as interesting in match terms as possible.

The keeper should not practise only in the nets where the ball does not beat the bat enough to present the keeper with the varied situations which occur in a match. It is not possible to stand back nor to take returns from fielders in the nets so keeping should be practised constantly as a specific skill along the lines suggested in the group activities and situations practice sections of the book.

In fielding there are many useful skills which are only needed infrequently: the flick throw from close to the wicket, the flick back to a supporting fielder and the relay throw from the outfield. Remember to practise these skills.

A fielder is a pawn on the captain's chessboard and is moved around accordingly. When you are fielding watch your captain between balls and overs to find out what you are needed to do.

Fielding requires a lot of thought. Concentrate while the ball is in play. Think about throwing at the stumps when there is no-one to take the ball and no-one backing-up. Ask yourself 'is there a possible run-out here?' Think about the type of throw that you should make from the outfield: if there is no possibility of a run-out, it would be wiser to throw slowly and accurately rather than quickly and erratically (which increases the possibility of overthrows). Remember to ask yourself: 'Is this chance worth the risk of overthrows?'

Physical fitness

Physical fitness for cricket

The necessity to obtain and maintain a high level of physical fitness has become an increasingly important part of cricket at first class and club level. A high level of general endurance fitness allows a player to perform at a high level without becoming unduly fatigued. For example a fast bowler who cannot bowl more than three or four overs at top pace or a batter who cannot score past the 20s and 30s because of fatigue are simply not realising their potential for the team. Another important aspect of fitness is muscular fitness which allows the muscles to contract with force and power, and yet be flexible enough to offer a wide range of motion without incurring injury.

It is well known that as fatigue develops, skill deteriorates. 'When fitness fades, so too does skill' is often said. The bowler loses accuracy and length; the batter loses timing and placement; and the fielder loses reaction and concentration. Being physically fit delays the onset of fatigue. Fatigue is particularly noticeable in a bowler at the completion of several overs of fast deliveries, in a batter after a series of consecutive twos or threes, or in a fielder after several long chases to retrieve the ball. This type of fatigue is rather acute, is associated with shortness of breath, and results, in part, from the accumulation of lactic acid in the blood. Long periods of play on hot days can also produce a different kind of fatigue – a heavy legged feeling which disrupts concentration and therefore performance.

THE FITNESS COMPONENTS FOR CRICKET
There are six fitness components important for cricket:
- general endurance
- speed endurance
- speed and agility
- muscle strength and power
- muscular endurance
- flexibility

General endurance
Also called 'aerobic capacity', 'stamina', 'cardiovascular' or 'cardio-respiratory' endurance, this is the capacity of the heart, lungs and blood vessels to pump oxygen and nutrients to muscles which are working over a prolonged period generally at a steady, sub-maximum rate. This type of endurance is particularly needed by fast bowlers and batters.

Speed endurance
Closely related to general endurance, speed endurance is the capacity repeatedly to sustain speed over a short distance over a period of time. Thus it incorporates heart and lung fitness with speed of movement. In

cricket, players have to sprint when running between the wickets, and chasing after the ball in the field, and fast bowlers have to accelerate in their run-up for each delivery throughout the day's play.

Speed and agility

Speed is the ability to perform fast movements. In cricket fast bowlers need fast arm movements, and need to accelerate quickly during their run-up. Running speed is largely an inherited ability and can only be improved to a small extent through training.

Agility is related to speed and signifies the ability to change body position and direction quickly. Fielders in particular need to be agile to stop the ball and return it quickly to the wicketkeeper.

Muscle strength and power

Strength is the ability of a muscle group to exert force against a resistance in a single maximum contraction or effort. In cricket strength is important both to batters and bowlers particularly in the muscles of the legs, arms, shoulders, hands and trunk.

Power allows a player to perform fast, explosive movements. It is a combination of strength and speed and is exhibited by top line fast bowlers who bowl at 160 kph (100 mph).

Muscular endurance

Muscular endurance is the capacity of a muscle to exert force repeatedly against some resistance over a period of time. Bowlers who can bowl for long spells and batters who can bat for over four hours to score a century are displaying sound muscular endurance fitness in the muscle groups responsible for those movements.

Flexibility

Flexibility is defined as the ability to use a muscle throughout its range of movement. It also refers to an ability to move joints, such as the shoulder, hip and wrist joints, easily. Being flexible means having a long, resting muscle length in the various muscle groups important for cricket, for example, the hamstrings (back of upper leg), shoulder, adductors (inner upper leg), quadriceps (front upper leg), calves (back lower leg) and trunk. Flexibility is an important asset in running and the development of flexibility helps prevent certain muscle injuries common in cricket. The persistent hamstring and groin injuries experienced by many fast bowlers can effectively ruin a season.

FITNESS COMPONENTS AND SPECIALISED NEEDS
Of the six components just outlined some are more crucial than others in a cricketer's fitness preparation. Some components need greater development than others, depending on which facet of the game the player specialises in. For example, a fast bowler needs greater levels of general endurance than a slow bowler. Spin bowlers will need strong, flexible wrists and fingers, whereas batters and all fielders will require speed and

agility in their movements. Fitness training programmes should be designed specifically for the different aspects and activities of cricket. However, a general all-round level of fitness is essential for all players.

TESTING FOR FITNESS

Regular fitness testing is now an important part of the preparation of Test, State and club teams. Results from testing can provide the coach with some indication of where individual weaknesses lie in the various components of fitness and what progress has been made in response to prescribed training programmes. The following are some of the most commonly used tests to measure physical fitness important in cricket; they are easily administered in a field situation and require very little specialised equipment.

1 **Physical characteristics**
  - height
  - weight
  - body fat

Measurement of skinfold thicknesses can be used to estimate the amount of fat in the body. This can be done with skinfold callipers in the preferred side of the body. The sites for measurement are as follows. Female players need to measure only (a) triceps and (c) supra-iliac.

(a) Triceps – the landmark is midway along the back of the upper arm, between the acromion and olecranon processes on the back of the upper arm. The skinfold is lifted parallel with the long axis of the arm with the arm hanging freely.

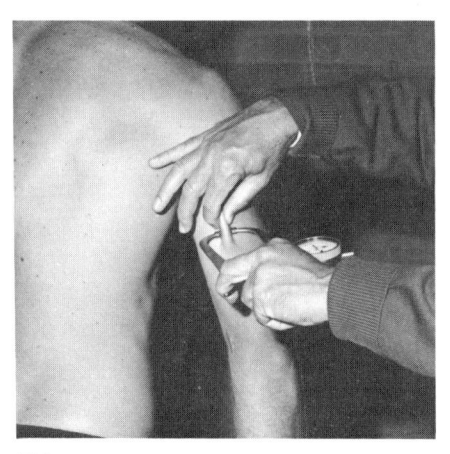

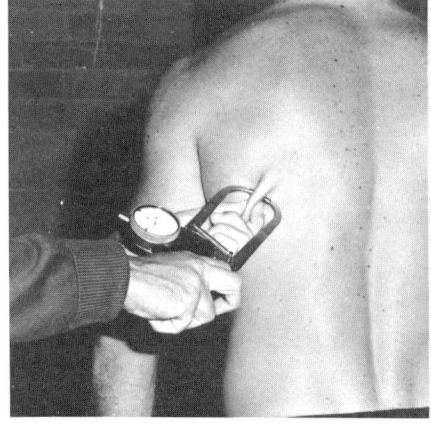

Triceps   Subscapula

(b) Subscapula – the landmark is one cm (½ in) underneath the scapula while the player stands in a relaxed manner. The fold is lifted downward and laterally in line with the ribs.

(c) Supra-iliac – the landmark is 5.0 cm (2 ins) vertically above the anterior superior iliac spine of the hip bone. The fold is lifted in line with the fibres of the external oblique muscle.

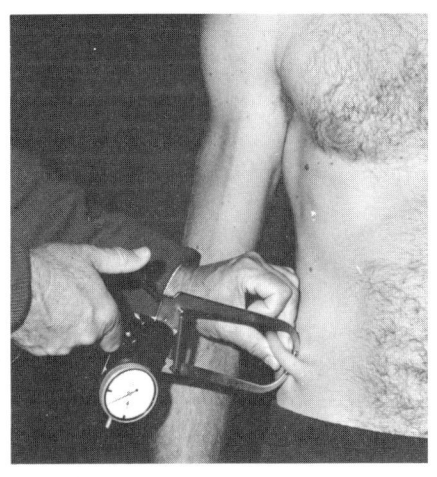

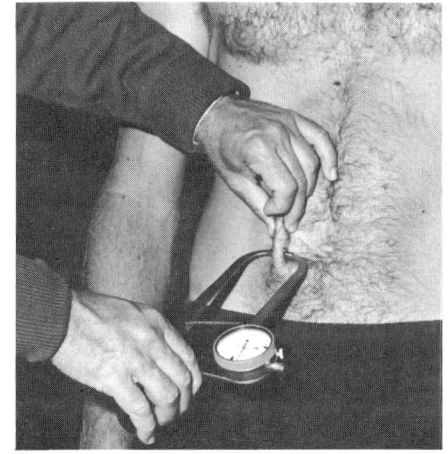

Supra-iliac   **Mid-abdominal**

(d) Mid-abdominal – the landmark is 5.0 cm (2 ins) adjacent to the umbilicus. The fold is lifted in the vertical plane.

Each skinfold should be measured in millimetres.

2 Running speed/agility

The time taken to complete three runs without a break is measured. Markers are placed on a firm grass surface 17.7 m (19.3 yds) apart, that is, the distance between the popping creases. Wearing non-slip shoes and holding a cricket bat, the player completes three runs as quickly as possible. The player should run between the markers as in a game, with the bat rather than the player crossing the lines. The best time in seconds in two trials is then recorded.

3 Muscular endurance

Sit-ups – the number of sit-ups completed in 60 seconds is measured. The player starts by lying on his or her back with knees flexed, feet on the floor, with the heels between 30 and 40 centimetres from the buttocks. The hands should be clasped behind the head and remain there throughout the test. The feet should be held by a partner to keep them in touch with the testing surface. The sit-up is completed when the elbows pass the line of the knee joints. To resume the starting position for each sit-up the back must make contact with the floor.

Press-ups – the number of press-ups completed in 30 seconds is measured. Starting with the player lying face-down with the hands directly under the shoulders, the arms are straightened whilst the rest of body is kept straight. A full press-up is counted when the chest is lowered to touch the ground. If a player is having real difficulty with full press-ups, from the toes, press-ups can be done from the knees.

4 Running endurance

The players run as far as possible on a flat, grassed surface in 15 minutes. This can be done on an oval or circular track with each lap being 400 metres with cones 40 metres apart to measure the exact distance covered by each player. The players should warm-up before the run and be highly motivated for a maximum effort. It is recommended that the elapsed time be called after each completed lap by the players. The number of laps and the segments of a lap covered is then noted and converted into metres.

5 Flexibility

The flexibility of the lower back and hamstring regions can be measured with the sit and reach test. The player sits on the floor, legs extended and feet flat against a flexibility bench (box with a ruler attached). The trunk is then flexed and the fingers extended along the scale where they are held for a period of 3 seconds. The legs must remain extended at the knees throughout the test. The score is recorded in centimetres as either a plus if distances beyond the feet are recorded or a minus if the player cannot reach his feet. Three trials are given after the player has been thoroughly warmed up.

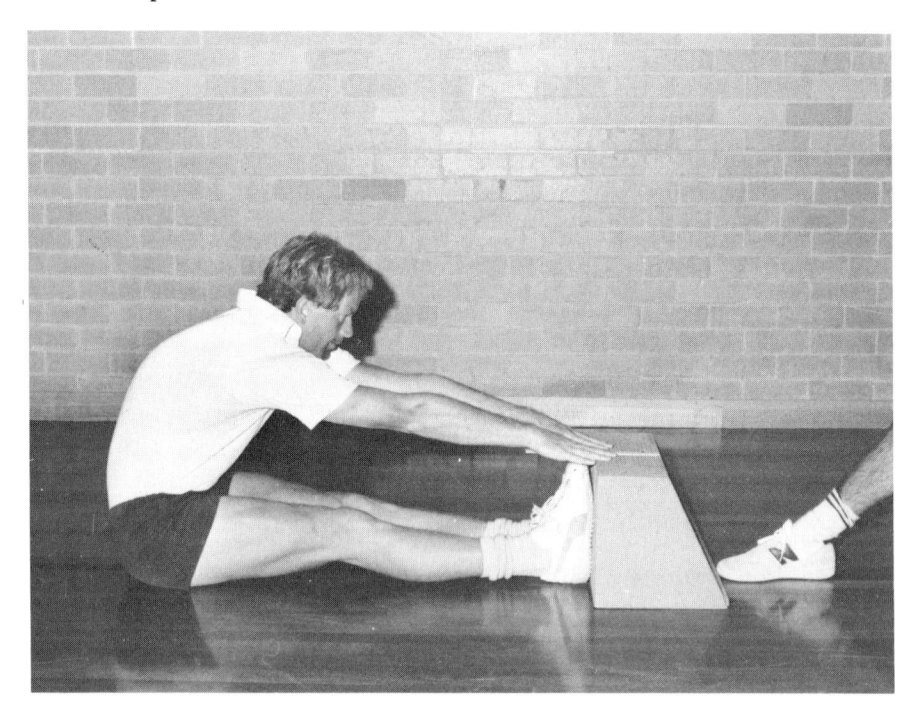

Order of testing

The recommended order of administering the test is:
   1 Height, weight, skinfolds.
10 minute period of warm-up comprising jogging and stretching.
   2 Run-a-three.
   3 Speed sit-ups and press-ups.
   4 15-minute run.
5-minute period of cool-down comprising jogging and stretching.
   5 Sit-and-reach.

Test standards
The minimum and desired standards for senior men and women at club level are presented in the following table:

		MEN		WOMEN*	
TEST		Minimum standards	Desired standards	Minimum standards	Desired standards
Body fat					
Triceps*	mm	14	10	13	10
Subscapula	mm	14	10	—	—
Supra-iliac*	mm	16	12.5	16	12
Mid-abdominal	mm	16	12.5	—	—
Total		60	45		
Per cent body fat		15	13	20	18
Running speed/agility	sec.	11.0	10.5	12	11.5
Muscular endurance					
Sit-ups (60 secs)	#	35	45	30	35
Press-ups (30 secs)	#	25	30	20	25
Running endurance					
15 min. run	m	3,300	3,600	2,800	3,200
Flexibility					
Sit-and-reach	cm	+3	+8	+8	+12

Once weaknesses have been identified in individual player profiles, training programmes can be followed to improve the situation.

Training programmes
PRE-SEASON FITNESS

The pre-season fitness stage should ideally begin three months before the season begins. The major aim of the pre-season fitness is to develop in each player a solid foundation of general fitness. From this base the more specific aspects of play-related fitness, for example, fielding drills, can be added.

As with most sports, cricketers need to build up their level of fitness as the season approaches. Training must be done regularly and must progressively overload the player. This means that the player must be subjected to training loads which are greater than those to which his or her body has been accustomed. Progressive overloading in training is influenced by the following variables.

(a) Frequency of training – this refers to the number of training sessions each week. Ideally players should work out three or four times per week.

(b) Duration of a training session – this refers to the amount of time given to each workload or session.

(c) Intensity of training – this indicates how much effort is put into the training session. For example, when running is part of the session, the intensity of effort is best measured by taking the player's heart (pulse) rate.

The higher the heart rate, the greater is the intensity of effort. A heart rate of over 160 beats per minute indicates a high intensity of work output.

(d) Training must be varied. Different methods to develop various aspects of fitness, and different venues for training will both help keep players motivated and interested in training.

General endurance

General endurance can be developed by daily running over relatively long distances (three to four kilometres (2–2½ miles) and upwards) at a steady pace. The player should start by running at a pace which can be handled comfortably. The intensity of the run can be gauged by measuring the pulse rate at the wrist. Approximately 160–70 beats per minute is sufficient intensity to have a training effect. At this intensity it should be possible to talk to a partner whilst running. Alternate days with shorter and long runs to allow some recovery between harder efforts.

Speed endurance

Speed endurance can be developed by the players engaging in short, fast interval training. Interval training is a series of repeated running efforts at a specific speed over a specified distance, alternated with prescribed periods of recovery. The recovery should take the form of a slow jog or walk rather than a complete rest. An example of this type of interval training which is suitable for cricketers is:

2 × 30 metres (yards)
2 × 50 metres
4 × 80 metres
2 × 50 metres
2 × 30 metres

at 80–90 per cent of maximum speed with a 1:4 to 1:6 work-rest ratio. If, for example, the 30-metre sprint took 4 seconds to complete, the player would then rest for 16 seconds before doing the next sprint using the 1:4 work-ratio regime. Similarly batters in full batting gear can repeat a series of ones, twos, threes and fours with appropriate recovery periods, and fielders can field four or five balls hit to different positions, recovering whilst another player is required to field the same number of balls. This type of activity done in small groups of four players is ideal for both speed endurance and fielding skills.

Speed

It is difficult to improve speed by more than approximately 10 per cent, but any improvement is obviously advantageous for fielding and running between wickets. Acceleration sprints over distances suggested in the speed endurance section using a good running technique are appropriate for speed development.

Muscular strength, power and endurance

Strength and power can be developed by doing a circuit without the need of sophisticated equipment. A bench or chair approximately 40 centimetres (16 ins) high and a stopwatch is all that is needed. The prescribed sets for each exercise should be completed before moving on to the next activity. The number of suggested repetitions can be raised or lowered according to the player's fitness level and the recovery period can also be altered.

A general circuit which is suitable for bowlers, batters and wicketkeepers is as follows:

1 **Bench steps**
- Step up and down 60 times on the bench in one minute.
- Recover for 30 seconds and repeat.
- Complete a minimum of three sets.

2 **Arm steps**
- Step up and down 15 times on the bench in 20 seconds.
- Recover for 40 seconds and repeat.
- Complete a minimum of three sets.

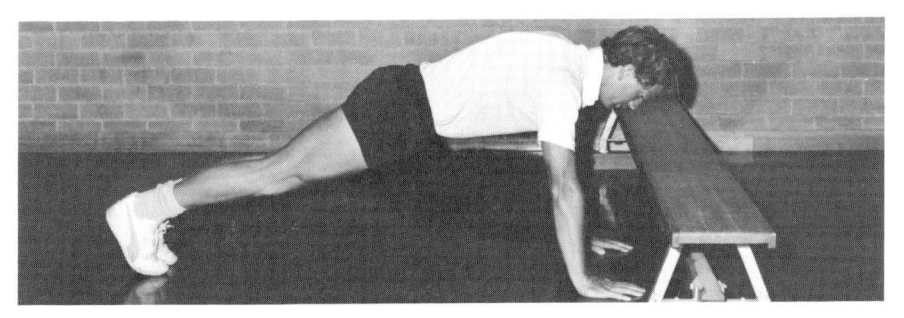

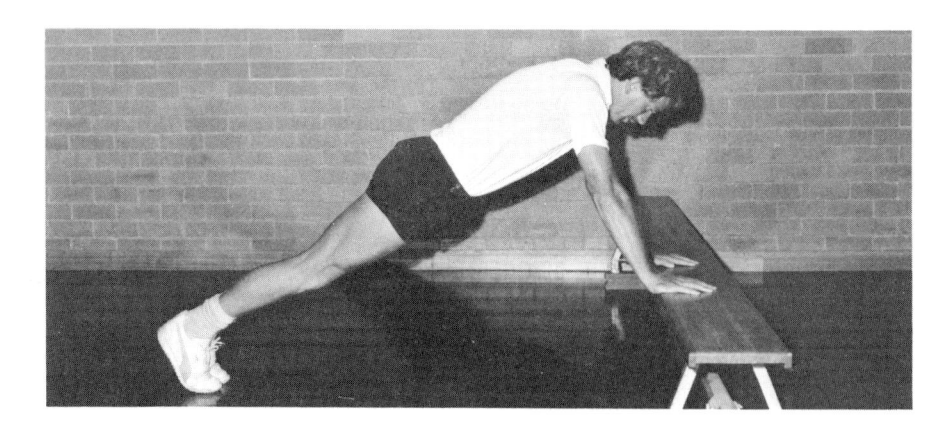

3 **Sit-ups** (bent legs)
  - Sit up and down 30 times in one minute.
  - Recover for 30 seconds and repeat.
  - Complete a minimum of three sets.

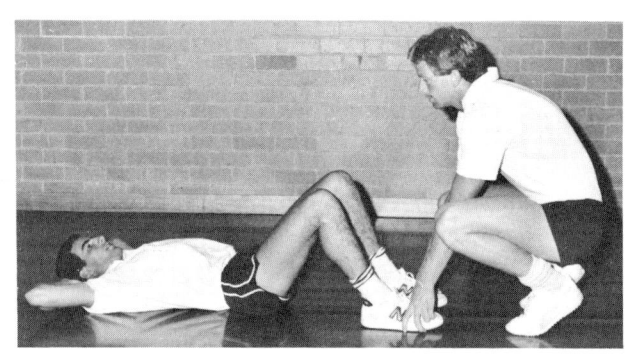

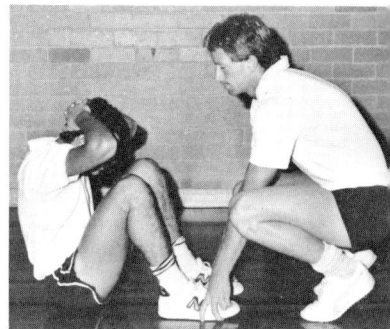

4 **Dips**
  - Dip up and down 15 times in 20 seconds.
  - Recover for 40 seconds and repeat.
  - Complete a minimum of three sets.

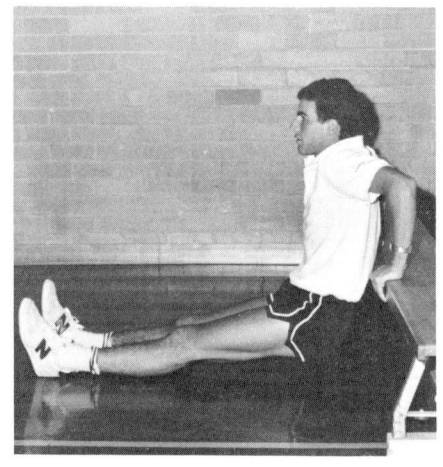

5 **Leg overs**
  - Touch both legs to each side of the body 15 times.

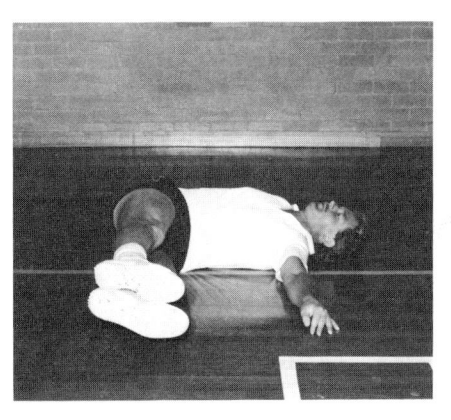

- Recover for 40 seconds and repeat.
- Complete a minimum of three sets.

6 **Bench blasts**
- Blast upwards, alternating legs on the bench top, 15 times in 20 seconds.
- Recover for 40 seconds and repeat.
- Complete a minimum of three sets.

7 **Press-ups**
- Press up and down 15 times in 20 seconds.
- Recover for 40 seconds and repeat.
- Complete a minimum of three sets.

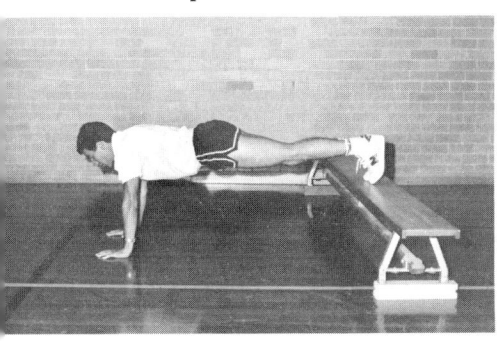

8 **Bench jumps**
   - Jump up and down on to the bench top 15 times in 20 seconds.
   - Recover for 40 seconds and repeat.
   - Complete a minimum of three sets.

As the player's fitness improves, the training load can be increased either by completing more sets or more repetitions in each set.

A player's strength and power can also be increased by the use of weight training equipment. Examples of this equipment include barbells and dumbbells where 'isotonic' work can be performed. In isotonic work two forms of muscle contraction occur. A concentric contraction where the muscle shortens as a weight is lifted, and an eccentric contraction where the muscle lengthens as the weight is lowered.

It is important that players learn correct lifting techniques. The lower back must be protected when performing any type of lifting exercises. Otherwise damage can occur to the discs or ligaments or muscles of the spine if weights are lifted incorrectly or carelessly. Good form and high quality execution of exercises is more important than lifting heavy weights. When lifting weights the following points should be stressed.
   - Always lift through a complete range of movement.
   - Always use the muscle groups involved in the exercise. For example, in bicep curls keep the back straight up against a wall. Any backward bending takes the load off the biceps.
   - The lowering phase of a movement must be controlled. The weight should not be allowed to drop quickly. Eliminate all bouncing, jerky or throwing-type movements.

SAMPLE WEIGHT TRAINING SCHEDULE

Exercise	Load	Muscle Group
Warm-up	(Skipping, jogging, riding a stationary bike 2-3 minutes)	
1 Seated military press	3 sets × 8-10 repetitions	upper arms, shoulders
2 Bicep curls	3 sets × 8-10 repetitions	upper arm
3 Half-squats	3 sets × 8-10 repetitions	upper legs
4 Inclined sit-ups	3 sets × 10-25 repetitions	abdominals
5 Overhead pull-downs	3 sets × 8-10 repetitions	shoulders, upper back
6 Leg extensions	3 sets × 10-15 repetitions	front upper leg
7 Leg curls	3 sets × 10-15 repetitions	back upper leg
8 Wrist curl	3 sets × 10-15 repetitions	forearm
9 Bench press	3 sets × 8-10 repetitions	chest, shoulders, upper arms

Seated military press

Bicep curl

Half-squat

Inclined sit-up

Overhead pull-down

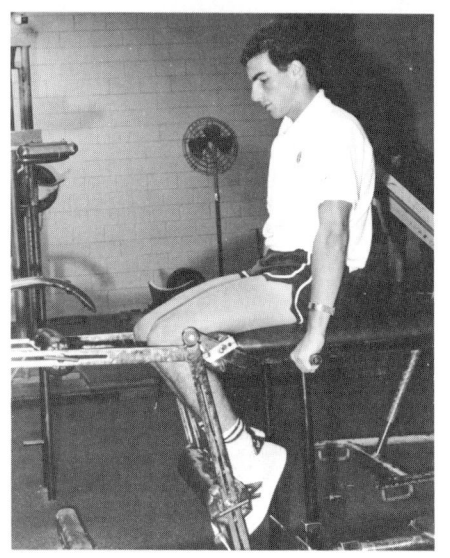

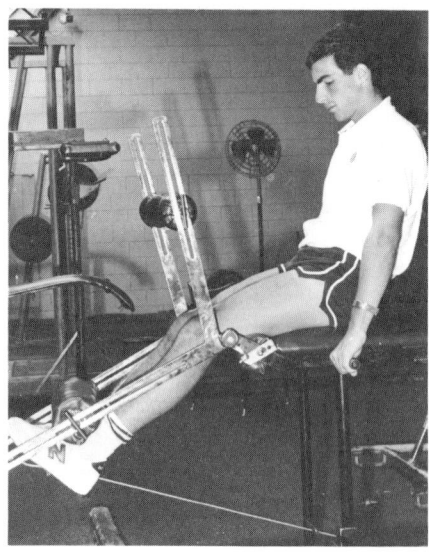

Leg extension

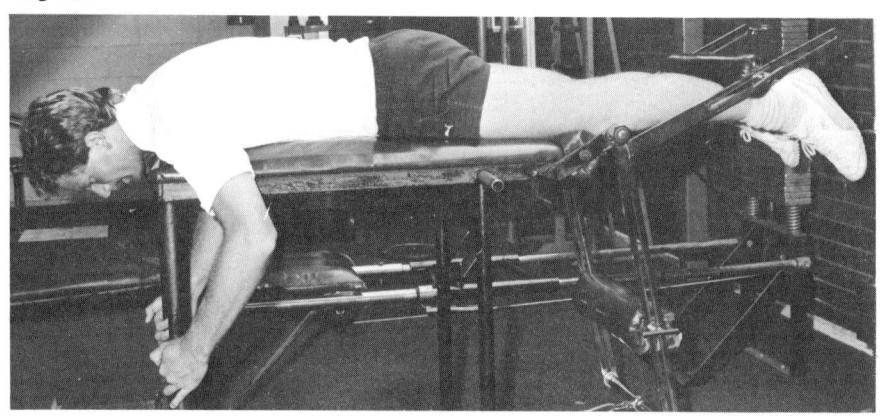

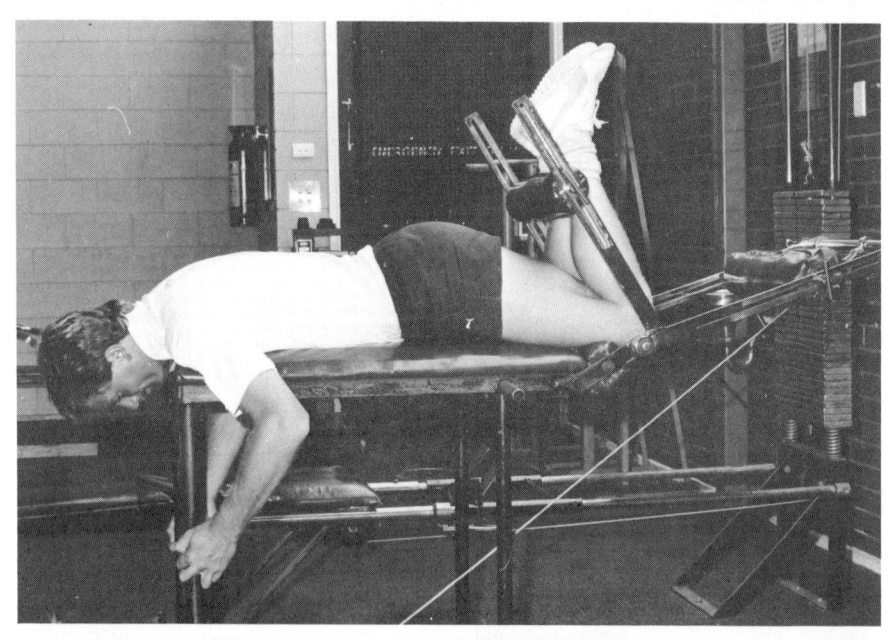

Leg curl

Wrist curl

Bench press

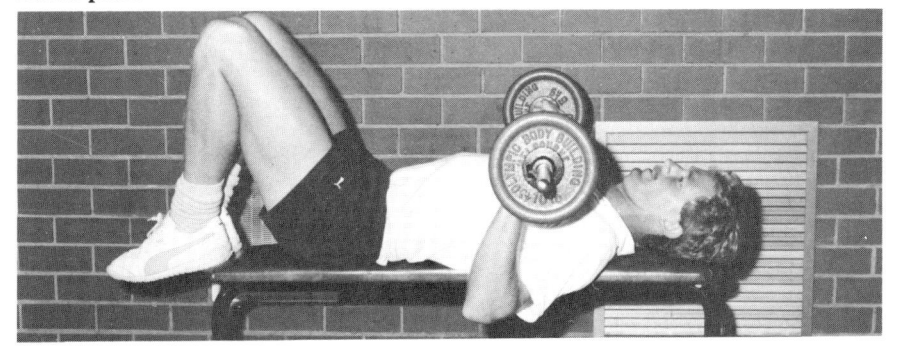

It is not possible to give details of resistance loads for each exercise without the knowledge of a player's strength capacities. If the player is a novice in weight lifting, then the load should be altered from the above sample. The inexperienced weight lifter should start with light weights which can be lifted 20–30 times and gradually work towards heavier weights which can be lifted 5–10 times.

The ultimate extension of any generalised weight training programme is progressively specialised to make it more specific to the game. Pulley systems and medicine balls can serve this end by permitting simulation of the bowling action. The rapid movement of lighter weights serve a similar function but should always be integrated with actual bowling practice.

The exercises in the sample weight training schedule can also be used with more sophisticated weight training equipment. An example of this is the Cybex equipment which uses the principle of isokinetic muscle contractions whereby speed remains constant throughout the range of movement. Here the player provides resistance against a mechanical device which moves at a pre-set speed. The device will alter the resistance during the exercise movement, according to how much force is being applied. This 'accommodating resistance' device, therefore, ensures that the muscle can be loaded as much as possible throughout the full range in every repetition.

Flexibility

Traditionally, there have been the two methods of stretching: ballistic and static. Ballistic stretching involves active movements of the body during the stretching movement, usually described as bobbing and bouncing. They should usually be avoided because the bouncing movement elicits a stretch reflex which actually inhibits and works against a full range of movement.

Static stretching is the preferred method. This is where the joint and muscle group is moved slowly into the stretched position until slight discomfort is felt. The position is held for a period of five to ten seconds. It is important to maintain a relaxed body without holding the breath and concentrate on stretching the specific muscle group.

Static stretching can be done by the player alone or with a partner. The following exercises are suitable for the 'hold stretch' technique:

1 *Arm and shoulder* – pull arms back horizontally.

2 *Trunk* – stand erect, then slide hands down the sides as far as possible.

3 *Front thigh* – pull up the leg and touch the heel on the buttock.

4 *Wrist* – pull hand back as far as possible.

Arm and shoulder

Trunk

Front thigh

Wrist

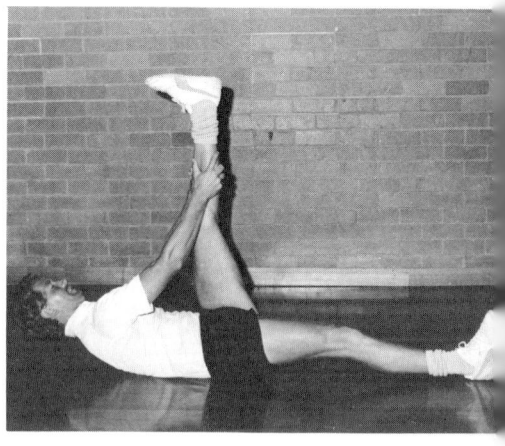

Groin **Hamstring**

5 *Groin* – one foot forward, one foot back in lunge position.
6 *Hamstring* – lie on the back, pull the leg up to a right angle.
7 *Groin* – sitting with legs bent and soles of the feet touching, push the knees outwards.
8 *Calf* – stand against fence, stretch out one leg and try to put the heel on the ground.

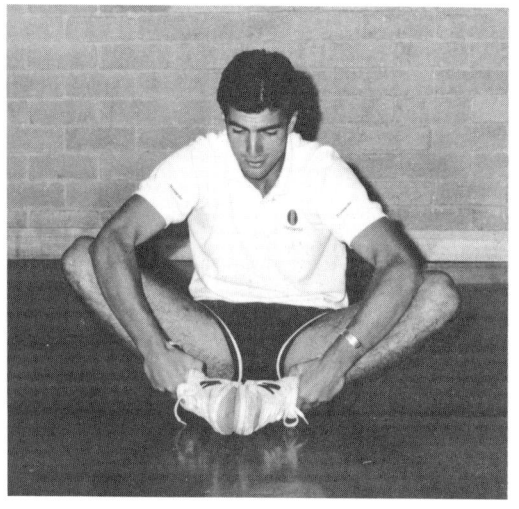

Groin **Calf**

9 *Trunk* – sit on the ground, trunk upright, and then twist to each side.

A recently introduced method of stretching which promotes both flexibility and strength in the muscle group being stretched is a technique known as 'PNF' or 'partner stretch' exercises. This technique involves players working in pairs, one assisting, whilst the other performs the exercise. The muscle group to be stretched is first contracted isometrically (held contraction) for 5 seconds against a resistance provided by

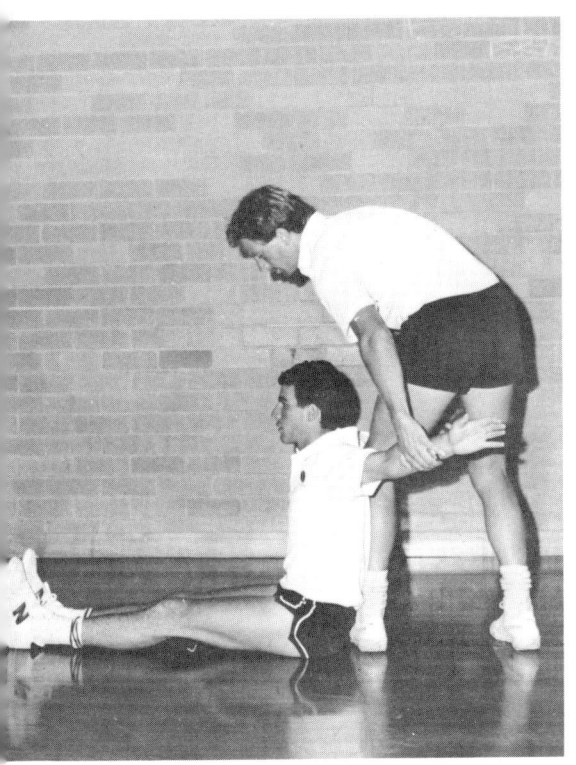

PNF: arms and shoulder
PNF: lower back

PNF: trunk

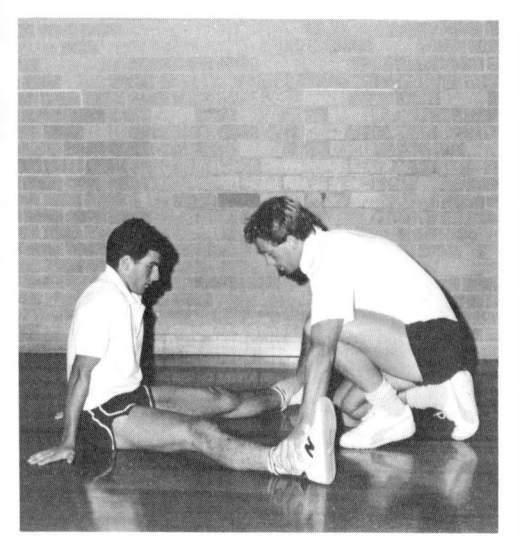

PNF: groin    **PNF: hamstring**

the partner. In a way that is not yet completely understood, the isometric effort decreases the sensitivity of the muscle to stretch and so allows it to move through a greater range immediately following the contraction effort. This procedure is repeated three to four times. The following muscle groups are suggested for stretching prior to training and matches:

1 Arms and shoulder
2 Trunk
3 Lower back
4 Groin
5 Hamstring.

The fitness aspect of cricket has received a great deal of attention in the past few years. Whilst fitness is certainly no substitute for the skills of the game, it nevertheless makes an important contribution to both individual and team performance. It gives a fit player a decided edge over less fit opponents. With the growing importance of fitness in modern cricket, it is important that players give it their fullest attention in order to realise their potential for their team.

Captaincy

A good captain provides a cricket team with a qualified leader, capable of executing a flexible, well-planned policy aimed at winning a match in an ethical manner. A captain guides the side tactically, ensuring maximum enjoyment for every player in it. A leader needs skills in personal communication to liaise with players, officials and outside agencies. In junior clubs, the skipper has to be an organiser who can co-ordinate selection, ascertain the availability of players, arrange transport and net duties, and supervise a practice routine which sets the players on the right path towards cricket proficiency.

There is no easy way to become a good captain. Experience is the best teacher. The coach may guide a captain's conduct and tactics or delegate the task, with the consent of the team, to the most experienced player.

The captain takes responsibility for the direction of the side on the field. The cricket leader is in authority but not necessarily authoritarian. He or she leads because the team supports an individual with a knowledge of tactics, a capacity to make incisive on-field decisions, playing skill, personality and an ability to command respect and obtain obedience.

The captain must communicate with and unify the team. In this respect the captain's role is like the coach's. It is one of encouraging players by praising success, criticising minimally and being objective and unemotional in any comments. Meetings before a game must outline and discuss the tactics to be adopted by the team, define the policy for the day and for the match, pinpoint the weaknesses and strengths of the opposition and in every way improve the side's appreciation of the approaching contest. A sound knowledge of the personalities of the team members is essential to good communication and the capacity to get the best out of players.

A skipper commands respect by being a good example of on-field alertness, sportsmanship, self-discipline, playing ability and by bringing out the best talents of the side. He or she must be a competitive, thoughtful and impartial leader.

As a tactician, the captain's first decision is whether to bat or bowl upon winning the toss. A side should bat if:

- The wicket is hard and firm, with little or no green grass in evidence on the surface
- The weather or wicket look as if they might worsen (onset of rain, or dampening or crumbling of the pitch)
- The wicket and weather are moderately good and look as if they might improve quickly.

A side should bowl if:

- The wicket is green, i.e. covered with green grass – a condition which normally helps the fast or medium-fast bowler 'to move the ball off the

seam' after it bounces. (The captain must have faster, 'seam' bowlers in the side if any advantage is to be derived from these conditions)
- The wicket is soft because of rain and will help the fast and slow bowlers to make the ball kick, turn, 'seam' or cut off the wicket
- The wicket is green or soft and it looks as if batting will be easier at a later stage of the day. Under these circumstances the captain takes advantage of temporarily good bowling conditions
- The day is overcast and humid and produces conditions suitable for fast or medium bowlers to swing the ball. The lack of oppressive heat means that bowlers will be more effective for longer periods of time
- The batting strength of the opposition appears suspect against the bowling team's attack. The opposition might have a poor record against fast bowling over the season, and the bowling strength of the captain's side might rest in two or three good fast bowlers.

In most instances the captain should decide to bat, to put 'runs on the board' and thus create a psychological hurdle for the side batting second.

The captain's responsibility does not end with the decision to bat or bowl. The players' performances in the match must be watched. Thus a bowler who pitches consistently short on a wicket helpful to seam bowling must be instructed to bowl a fuller length. The batter who fails to take advantage of a good wicket and a misdirected attack must be advised about how to attack the bowling. The leg spinner pitching too short on a slow wicket must be guided to bowl a fuller length. The counselling role of the captain never ends.

The captain must identify the strengths and weaknesses of the opposition. If an opposition batter reveals fallibility against inswing, leg spin or outswing, or proves rash in executing a favourite stroke, the captain must pick the faults and direct the attack accordingly, setting an appropriate field. If an opposing bowler has an effective and dangerous delivery, the team's batters must be warned about it. Should an opposing fielder excel in a certain position, that individual should be pinpointed.

It may become obvious that the opposition is attacking in a certain way, and that this tactic has to be countered. Thus a deep off side field with the bowlers attacking the off stump, short of a length, will call for instructions to the batter to concentrate on singles. A restrictive opposition bowling and fielding policy, with a declaration approaching, may call for adventurousness on the part of the batters. Aggression from the opposition batters or an inclination to go for quick singles demands a knowledge of sensible field changes to increase the batting risks and prevent the flow of runs.

The captain must know the strengths of the team's batters, bowlers and fielders. The batter who combats the new ball well should be sent in high in the order and the stroke makers shielded from the new ball. The fast bowler who swings the ball most should be given the new ball. The captain should be able to decide which of the bowlers will be most effective against certain batters and which of the batters will counter a certain attack most proficiently. Specialist fielders should be positioned in their correct places. The captain must be aware of the psychological make-up of the team: who will best stand up to crises and pressures. Bowlers who are tired must be relieved. The captain of the side must know when certain types of bowlers are ineffective – under certain conditions and against certain types of batters – and change them accordingly. A good skipper appreciates when to take the new ball, when to attack for quick runs, when to pressurise a batter newly arrived at the crease, and when to slow down the opposition's scoring rate. Judgement is needed to know when to enforce the follow-on and when to instruct batters to consolidate the team's position.

The captain's task is not easy. Specific instructions must be given to individuals. There must be a general plan of campaign drawn up whenever the side goes onto the field – but it must be adaptable, since original plans usually need modification. It is the captain's duty to keep the game moving and see that no time is wasted. A great part of the captain's responsibility on the field lies in consultation with the bowler and at times with other players, such as the wicketkeeper, before placing the field.

A few basic precepts need to be observed in the setting of a field.

In the close-to-the-wicket positions, such as the slips, there should be no gaps in the field. The slips should be able to touch each other's fingers at arm's length. They should be staggered, with the squarer fielders closer to the bat than the fine positions. The ball travels a shorter distance in the air when the hit is squarer. The distance back from the bat is governed by the state of the wicket and the distance travelled by the ball in the air when it is edged. The behind-the-wicket fielders should be placed so that they take the ball at a comfortable height according to its carry, between the waist and the knees.

No short fielder should be in the same line as a deeper fielder. This would mean that two individuals are covering the same angle of a possible hit, and the fielder at the rear does not have a clear sight of the ball because it is obscured by the closer player.

Boundary fielders should remain fairly close to the boundary. It is easier to run forwards than backwards. Moreover there is more time to prevent a shot reaching the boundary by running around the perimeter of the field. If a fielder comes in from the boundary, he or she must know the exact location of the fence and be able to move back comfortably to reach it.

The captain should insist that the fielders watch for instructions whenever the ball is not in play. There may be a need for a slight tactical change in the field.

The captain should place as many fielders as possible in catching positions. The fielders are there to catch and attack, to save a single, and to stop a boundary. There are no in-between positions. The field settings in the diagrams on pages 00 and 00 show the orthodox field placements for the different types of bowlers. Possible attacking variations are indicated.

A captain should field mostly at mid-off or mid-on where it is possible to observe the game from close to the centre of activity yet not be in a critical position which demands complete concentration on the fielding skill. The skipper needs time to think about captaincy and tactics. This is not an absolute rule, however, and varies when captains are specialist slip fielders or wicketkeepers. Watching senior games helps the captain to learn about field placements.

A captain should always observe a commonsense approach to field placements and set the field according to the standard of cricket in which the team plays. It is no use placing a fast bowler's field of five slips and no third man or fine leg if there is no genuinely fast bowler in the side. As a general rule, a junior captain should always place a deep third man and fine leg. Fielders in junior cricket should never be placed in positions of danger.

If there is any hesitancy on the part of two or more fielders going for a catch, the captain should nominate the fielder to take the catch. This will usually be the player running forward to take the ball.

Orthodox field placements for fast-medium, outswing, or leg-cutting bowler (to a right-handed batter)

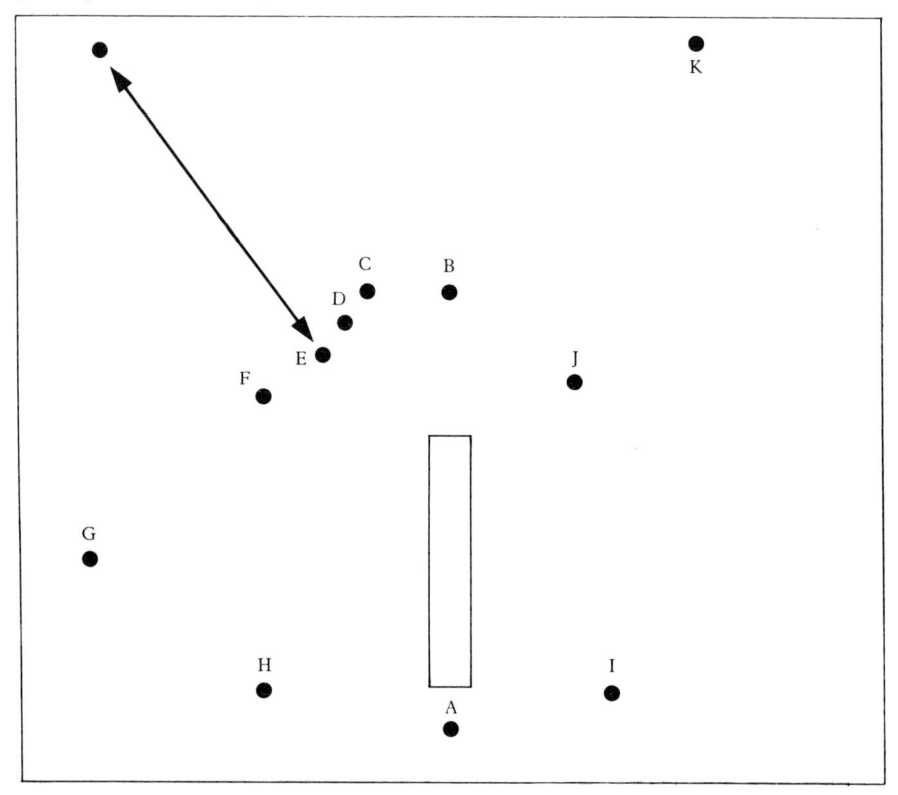

A BOWLER	E 3RD SLIP	H MID OFF
B KEEPER	OR DEEP THIRD MAN	I MID ON
C 1ST SLIP	F GULLY	J BACKWARD SHORT LEG
D 2ND SLIP	G COVER	K DEEP FINE LEG

Orthodox field placements for fast-medium, inswing, or off-cutting bowler (to a right-handed batter)

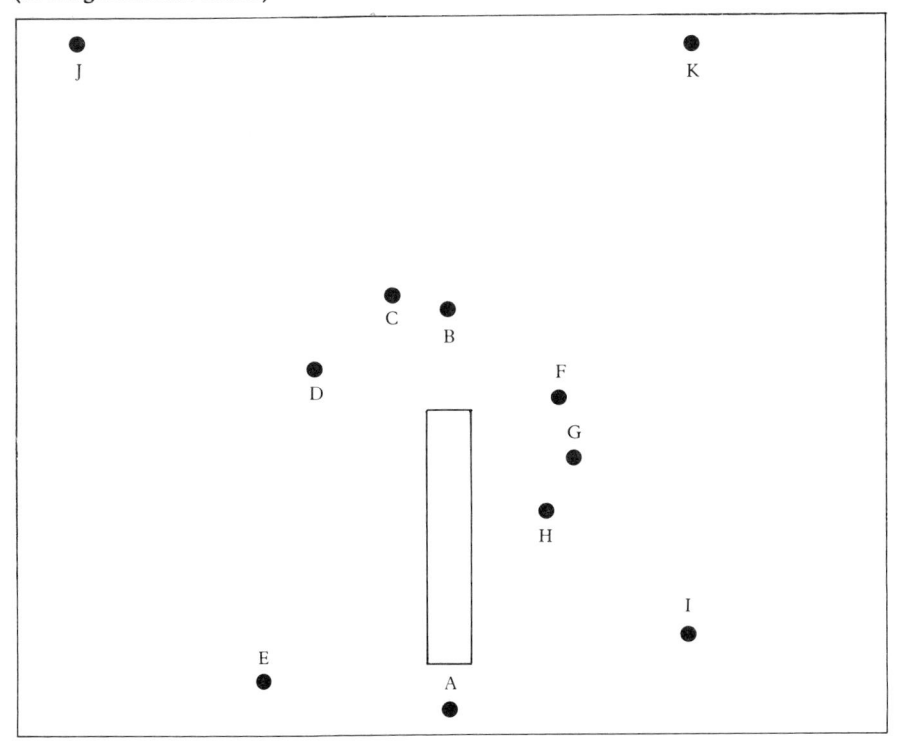

A BOWLER	E MID OFF	I WIDE MID ON
B KEEPER	F BACKWARD SHORT LEG	J DEEP THIRD MAN
C SLIP	G SHORT SQUARE LEG	K DEEP FINE LEG
D GULLY	H FORWARD SHORT LEG	

Orthodox field placements for a slow off-spin bowler (to a right-handed batter)

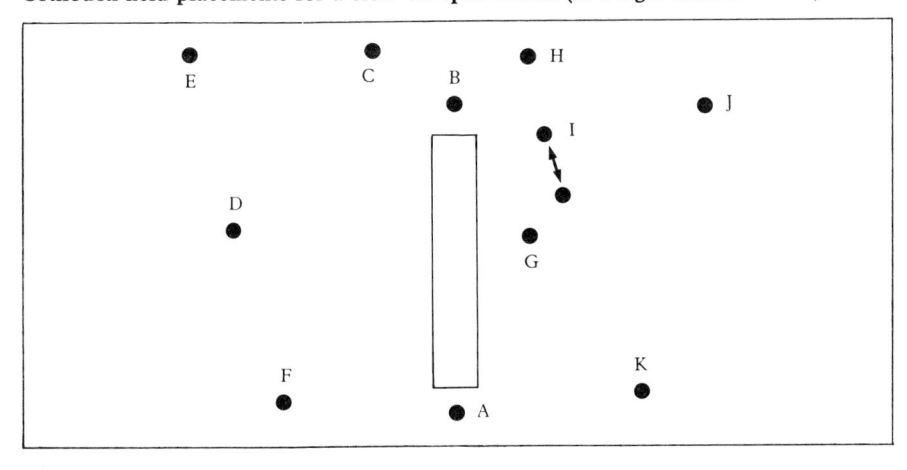

A BOWLER	E BACKWARD POINT	I SHORT SQUARE LEG OR
B KEEPER	F MID OFF	SHORT MID WICKET
C SLIP	G SILLY MID ON	J SQUARE LEG
D COVER	H BACKWARD SHORT LEG	K MID ON

161

Orthodox field placements for slow leg-spin bowler (to a right-handed batter)

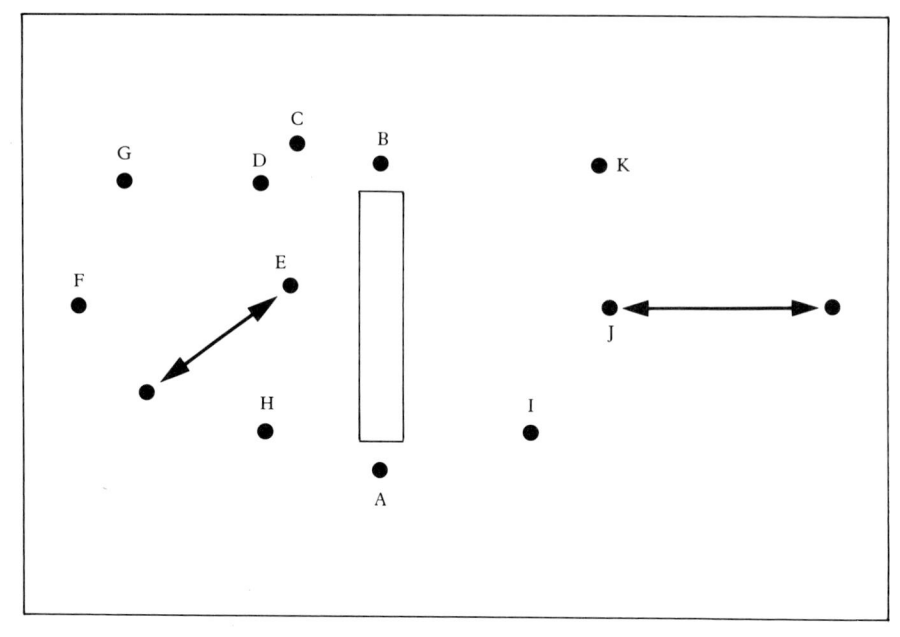

A BOWLER
B KEEPER
C SLIP
D GULLY
E SILLY MID OFF (ATTACKING/VARIATION) OR EXTRA COVER
F COVER
G BACKWARD POINT
H MID OFF
I MID ON
J MID WICKET OR DEEP MID WICKET
K SQUARE LEG

Modified cricket

The number of participants in organised cricket has increased dramatically in recent times. Ironically, the boom has not been evident in the traditional game, but in two alternative forms of cricket – modified rules for youngsters and indoor cricket. The common elements which make both new games so popular are maximum participation and an equalisation of opportunities for participants to both bat and bowl. Clearly, the time has arrived for all junior coaches, administrators and parents to evaluate critically the playing environment they create for young cricketers.

For too long it has been blindly assumed that all cricketers, irrespective of age or ability, are motivated by the desire to win and achieve personal success. The growing popularity of the alternative forms of cricket certainly negate this assumption. Participation, enjoyment and the opportunity to experience all facets of the game are factors which influence the continuing involvement of many players. Winning is a bonus, not the justification for playing.

An overemphasis on winning makes any mistake take on monumental proportions; for the player involved it becomes a personal tragedy. The mental anguish experienced by the young player who drops a catch, or the utter despair of a batter dismissed for a duck, are totally unnecessary, negative experiences.

The entrepreneurs responsible for marketing indoor cricket have cleverly modified the least desirable aspects of the traditional game. A soft ball was introduced, the playing area was made smaller, and all players must bat and bowl. Adults who accept the responsibility for organising under-age cricket have an obligation to ensure that youngsters are exposed to a similar ideal playing environment. Modifications to the adult game are essential if children are to experience the positive aspects of participation in cricket.

Modified rules are not a means to introduce children at an earlier age to a fiercely competitive environment. The ultimate objective of under-age cricket is to prepare young cricketers adequately to participate, eventually, in the adult game. The following general guidelines will assist in achieving this objective:
- Increase participation
- Make the game more enjoyable
- Ensure success is experienced
- Develop skill levels in participants
- Provide experiences which will ensure continued participation in cricket from childhood to adulthood
- Utilise equipment and rules appropriate to the participants
- Minimise the risk of pain, both physical and mental
- Provide a gradual progression towards the adult game.

Modifications to the adult game should take into account the age and skill level of the participants. As the children grow older and their skill levels improve, modifications should be gradually phased out. The following modifications are recommended:
- Reduce the team size
- Reduce the ground size to a maximum radius of 45 m from the pitch
- Reduce the pitch length to cater for the physical height of participants
- Use a small ball
- Batters bat in pairs for a specified number of overs
- Record wickets lost by each batting pair and calculate the team 'score' by dividing total runs made by the total wickets lost
- Batters change ends on the fall of a wicket or after three consecutive non-scoring shots
- No l.b.w.
- A player bowls a specified number of overs
- Bowlers operate from one end only to minimise time usage

Continuous Cricket (Ages 4-8)

1 Two teams of equal size (6-10).
2 The ball may be delivered by the bowler underarm or overarm to the first batter.
3 When the ball is hit, the batter must run to touch a marker approximately 5 m away and return to the batting positon.
4 One run is scored each time the batter touches the marker and returns safely.
5 The ball is always returned immediately to the bowler who bowls whether the batter has returned or not.
6 The batter may be dismissed bowled, caught or hit-wicket.
7 When a batter is dismissed, the next batter quickly comes in and the bowler may continue to bowl during the changeover.
8 Teams change over when all the batting side is dismissed.
9 The side scoring the greater number of runs wins.

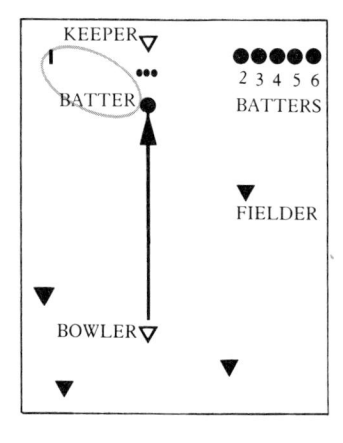

- Fielders rotate positions at the end of each over
- Fielders not to field in a designated area which is less than half the pitch length from the batters
- Helmets to be worn.

The purpose of modified games is to provide a smooth transition into the adult game. In the lower primary school grades, activities which develop hand-eye co-ordination and ball handling skills will provide an excellent grounding for the modified games described below.

The decision as to when children should be introduced to a more complex modified game will be influenced largely by the youngsters' skill development. Undue haste in moving towards the adult game could severely detract from the attraction of playing 'real' cricket.

Keeping in mind it is the 'game' which appeals to youngsters, Continuous Cricket followed by Diamond Cricket and then Pairs Cricket provides a suitable continuum to prepare children for the adult version of cricket. Additional games may be found in the Australian Kanga Cricket programme. Initial experiences of the adult game should incorporate the batting, bowling and fielding restrictions suggested earlier.

Diamond Cricket (Ages 8-10)

1 Two teams of equal size (10-16).
2 The batting team begins with one batter (B) at each set of stumps.
3 The fielding team has four wicket-keepers (W), one at each set of stumps.
4 To begin play, the first bowler bowls to the batter at the 'home base'.
5 Batters run around the bases in an anti-clockwise direction.
6 One run is scored each time the 4 batters safely arrive at the next base.
7 Batters may be dismissed at any base by any of the usual means except l.b.w.
8 If a batter is dismissed at 1st, 2nd or 3rd base, the other batters move anti-clockwise to the next vacant base.
9 At the completion of one or more runs from a scoring shot, the batter at the 'home base' is replaced by the next batter.
10 Batters who are dismissed or safely reach 'home base' continue to bat in order until the batting time has elapsed.
11 If a batter fails to score off 3 consecutive deliveries, the bowler bowls to the next base on the immediate right (turning clockwise).
12 Each member of the fielding team bowls one over in order.
13 Each team bats for a specified time, e.g. 10 minutes.

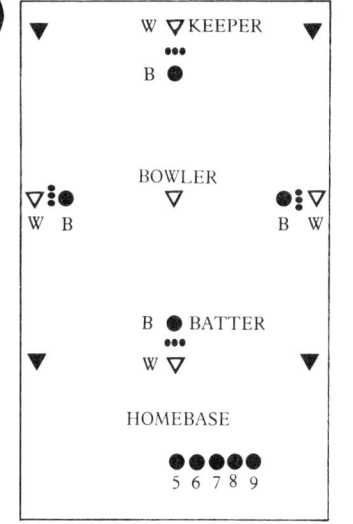

Pairs Cricket (Ages 9-12)

1 Two teams of 8 players.
2 The batting team is divided into 4 pairs.
3 Each batting pair bats for 4 overs irrespective of wickets lost.
4 Batters change ends at the fall of a wicket or after 3 consecutive non-scoring deliveries.
5 Batters may be dismissed by all of the usual means except l.b.w.
6 Each member of the fielding team bowls 2 overs.
7 The batting team's innings ends after 16 overs.
8 The total number of runs made by the batting team is divided by the total number of wickets lost to obtain an average.
9 The team with the higher average wins.

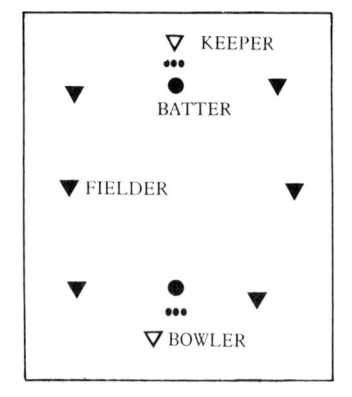

The Laws of Cricket

The Laws of Cricket and their interpretation

Some of the Laws of Cricket are clear and easily understood, others may need interpretation for the coach and player. The Laws are set out here in full, but where some explanation may be helpful, a brief comment is included in the right-hand column. The comments are subject to amendment under the provisions of local cricket associations.

LAW 1 THE PLAYERS
1 Number of players and captain
A match is played between two sides each of eleven players, one of whom shall be captain. In the event of the captain not being available at any time a deputy shall act for him.
2 Nomination of players
Before the toss for innings, the captain shall nominate his players who may not thereafter be changed without the consent of the opposing captain.

Notes
(a) More or less than eleven players a side
A match may be played by agreement between sides of more or less than eleven players but not more than eleven players may field.

LAW 2 SUBSTITUTES AND RUNNERS; BATSMAN OR FIELDSMAN LEAVING THE FIELD; BATSMAN RETIRING; BATSMAN COMMENCING INNINGS
1 Substitutes
Substitutes shall be allowed by right to field for any player who during the match is incapacitated by illness or injury. The consent of the opposing captain must be obtained for the use of a substitute if any player is prevented from fielding for any other reason.
2 Objection to substitutes
The opposing captain shall have no right of objection to any player acting as substitute in the field, nor as to where he shall field, although he may object to the substitute acting as wicketkeeper.
3 Substitute not to bat or bowl
A substitute shall not be allowed to bat or bowl.
4 A player for whom a substitute has acted
A player may bat, bowl or field even though a substitute has acted for him.
5 Runner
A runner shall be allowed for a batsman who during the match is incapacitated by illness or

LAW 1
The captain, or acting captain, must be one of the named eleven players.

LAW 2
A player, disabled at any time after he or she has been named in a side, must be allowed a substitute in the field or a runner whilst batting. In other circumstances the consent of the opposing captain is necessary.
  A fielding substitute may be any available person, but an emergency fielder is sometimes named. He or she may field anywhere, but if there is an objection from the opposing captain, may not keep wicket. A runner must be one of the disabled batter's side.
  A batter with a runner may not score by running between the wickets himself or herself. If, as the striker, the batter

injury. The player acting as runner shall be a member of the batting side and shall, if possible, have already batted in that innings.

6 Runner's equipment

The player acting as runner for an injured batsman shall wear batting gloves and pads if the injured batsman is so equipped.

7 Transgression of the Laws by an injured batsman or runner

An injured batsman may be out should his runner break any one of Laws 33 (Handled the ball), 37 (Obstructing the field) or 38 (Run out). As striker he remains himself subject to the Laws. Furthermore, should he be out of his ground for any purpose and the wicket at the wicketkeeper's end be put down he shall be out under Law 38 (Run out) or Law 39 (Stumped) irrespective of the position of the other batsman or the runner and no runs shall be scored.

When not the striker, the injured batsman is out of the game and shall stand where he does not interfere with the play. Should he bring himself into the game in any way then he shall suffer the penalties that any transgression of the Laws demands.

8 Fieldsman leaving the field

No fieldsman shall leave the field or return during a session of play without the consent of the umpire at the bowler's end. The umpire's consent is also necessary if a substitute is required for a fieldsman, when his side returns to the field after an interval. If a member of the fielding side leaves the field or fails to return after an interval and is absent from the field for longer than 15 minutes, he shall not be permitted to bowl after his return until he has been on the field for at least that length of playing time for which he was absent. This restriction shall not apply at the start of a new day's play.

9 Batsman leaving the field or retiring

A batsman may leave the field or retire at any time owing to illness, injury or other unavoidable cause, having previously notified the umpire at the bowler's end. He may resume his innings at the fall of a wicket, which for the purposes of this Law shall include the retirement of another batsman.

If he leaves the field or retires for any other reason he may only resume his innings with the consent of the opposing captain.

When a batsman has left the field or retired and is unable to return owing to illness, injury or other unavoidable cause, his innings is to be recorded as 'retired, not out'. Otherwise it is to be recorded as 'retired, out'.

10 Commencement of a batsman's innings

A batsman shall be considered to have commenced his innings once he has stepped on to the field of play.

leaves his or her ground to run or leaves it whilst the runner is running, he or she may be run out – but only at the wicketkeeper's end – and any runs made from the delivery shall be disallowed. Should the disabled batter be run out through the fault of the runner, runs shall be scored as in the case of a normal run-out dismissal.

A fielder absent for more than 15 minutes of playing time – having left the field during play or having failed to return after an interval – is not permitted to bowl on his or her return for a period of time equal to the period of absence. A stoppage for weather is treated as playing time; the luncheon and tea intervals are not. This restriction does not apply to absence at the start of the day's play – nor does it extend into the following day or a later innings.

Once play has started, an incoming batter's innings begins as soon as he or she crosses the boundary line. Any batter may leave or retire at any time, but the umpire must be informed of the cause. An unavoidable cause entitles a retired batter to return when another batter is out or retires. Otherwise, the consent of the opposing captain is required.

Notes
(a) Substitutes and runners
For the purpose of these Laws allowable illnesses or injuries are those which occur at any time after the nomination by the captains of their teams.

LAW 3 THE UMPIRES
1 Appointment
Before the toss for innings two umpires shall be appointed, one for each end, to control the game with absolute impartiality as required by the Laws.
2 Change of umpire
No umpire shall be changed during a match without the consent of both captains.
3 Special conditions
Before the toss for innings, the umpires shall agree with both captains on any special conditions affecting the conduct of the match.
4 The wickets
The umpires shall satisfy themselves before the start of the match that the wickets are properly pitched.
5 Clock or watch
The umpires shall agree between themselves and inform both captains before the start of the match on the watch or clock to be followed during the match.
6 Conduct and implements
Before and during a match the umpires shall ensure that the conduct of the game and the implements used are strictly in accordance with the Laws.
7 Fair and unfair play
The umpires shall be the sole judges of fair and unfair play.
8 Fitness of ground, weather and light
(a) The umpires shall be the sole judges of the fitness of the ground, weather and light for play.
   (i) However, before deciding to suspend play or not to start play or not to resume play after an interval or stoppage, the umpires shall establish whether both captains (the batsmen at the wicket may deputise for their captain) wish to commence or to continue in the prevailing conditions; if so, their wishes shall be met.
   (ii) In addition, if during play, the umpires decide that the light is unfit, only the batting side shall have the option of continuing play. After agreeing to continue to play in unfit light conditions, the captain of the batting side (or a batsman at the wicket) may appeal against the light to the umpires, who shall uphold the appeal only if, in their opinion, the light has deteriorated since the agreement to continue was made.
(b) After any suspension of play, the umpires, unaccompanied by any of the players or officials shall, on their own initiative, carry out an inspection immediately the conditions improve and shall continue to inspect at intervals. Immediately the umpires decide that play is possible they shall call upon the players to resume the game.

LAW 3
Umpires are required to show no bias in carrying out their functions. They alone resolve disputes and determine fair and unfair play. It is a tradition of cricket that their opinions are respected.

If the umpires decide that conditions are fit for play, play must go on. If at any stage, they decide that conditions are unfit, the captains must be given the opportunity to agree to proceed with play – despite the conditions. In the case of the light failing during play, only the wishes of the batters at the wicket are considered. Special regulations in some competitions may vary this law.

In keeping with the requirement that umpires shall stand where they can see best, there is provision in the accepted code of behaviour for the square-leg umpire to stand on the off rather than the customary leg side of the pitch – provided he or she announces his or her intentions. In exercising this right, the umpire should be careful not to be an obstruction.

Umpires are responsible for the accuracy of the scores. It is therefore of paramount importance that the scorers are properly informed. Where there is no appropriate signal with which the umpires may communicate with the scorers, direct verbal consultation may be necessary.

9 Exceptional circumstances
In exceptional circumstances, other than those of weather, ground or light, the umpires may decide to suspend or abandon play. Before making such a decision the umpires shall establish, if the circumstances allow, whether both captains (the batsmen at the wicket may deputise for their captain) wish to continue in the prevailing conditions: if so their wishes shall be met.

10 Position of umpires
The umpires shall stand where they can best see any act upon which their decision may be required.

Subject to this overriding consideration the umpire at the bowler's end shall stand where he does not interfere with either the bowler's run-up or the striker's view.

The umpire at the striker's end may elect to stand on the off instead of the leg side of the pitch, provided he informs the captain of the fielding side and the striker of his intention to do so.

11 Umpires changing ends
The umpires shall change ends after each side has had one innings.

12 Disputes
All disputes shall be determined by the umpires and if they disagree the actual state of things shall continue.

13 Signals
The following code of signals shall be used by umpires who will wait until a signal has been answered by a scorer before allowing the game to proceed.

Boundary 4
Bye

Dead ball

Boundary 6
Leg-bye

No ball    **Out**    **Short run**

Boundary – by waving the arm from side to side.
Boundary 6 – by raising both arms above the head.
Bye – by raising an open hand above the head.
Dead ball – by crossing and re-crossing the wrists below the waist.
Leg bye – by touching a raised knee with the hand.
No ball – by extending one arm horizontally.
Out – by raising the index finger above the head. If not out the umpire shall call 'not out'.
Short run – by bending the arm upwards and by touching the nearer shoulder with the tips of the fingers.
Wide – by extending both arms horizontally.

Wide

Cancel last signal

14 Correctness of scores
The umpires shall be responsible for satisfying themselves on the correctness of the scores throughout and at the conclusion of the match. See Law 21.6 (Correctness of result).

Notes
(a) Attendance of umpires
The umpires should be present on the ground and report to the ground executive or the equivalent at least 30 minutes before the start of a day's play.
(b) Consultation between umpires and scorers
Consultation between umpires and scorers over doubtful points is essential.
(c) Fitness of ground
The umpires shall consider the ground as unfit for play when it is so wet or slippery as to deprive the bowlers of a reasonable foothold, the fieldsmen, other than the deep-fielders, of the power of free movement, or the batsmen the ability to play their strokes or to run between the wickets. Play should not be suspended merely because the grass and the ball are wet and slippery.
(d) Fitness of weather and light
The umpires should only suspend play when they consider that the conditions are so bad that it is unreasonable or dangerous to continue.

LAW 4 THE SCORERS
1 Recording runs
All runs scored shall be recorded by scorers appointed for the purpose. Where there are two

LAW 4
Scorers should record runs – other than boundaries – and the bowling of legal deliveries

scorers they shall frequently check to ensure that the score sheets agree.

2 Acknowledging signals
The scorers shall accept and immediately acknowledge all instructions and signals given to them by the umpires.

LAW 5 THE BALL
1 Weight and size
The ball, when new, shall weigh not less than $5^{1}/_{2}$ ounces (155.9 g), nor more than $5^{3}/_{4}$ ounces (163 g), and shall measure not less than $8^{13}/_{16}$ inches (22.4 cm), nor more than 9 inches (22.9 cm) in circumference.

2 Approval of balls
All balls used in matches shall be approved by the umpires and captains before the start of the match.

3 New ball
Subject to agreement to the contrary having been made before the toss, either captain may demand a new ball at the start of each innings.

4 New ball in match of three or more days' duration
In a match of three or more days' duration, the captain of the fielding side may demand a new ball after the prescribed number of overs has been bowled with the old one. The governing body for cricket in the country concerned shall decide the number of overs applicable in that country which shall be not less than 75 six-ball overs (55 eight-ball overs).

5 Ball lost or becoming unfit for play
In the event of a ball during play being lost or, in the opinion of the umpires, becoming unfit for play, the umpires shall allow it to be replaced by one that in their opinion has had a similar amount of wear. If a ball is to be replaced, the umpires shall inform the batsmen.

Notes
(a) Specifications
The specifications, as described in 1 above, shall apply to top-grade balls only. The following degrees of tolerance will be acceptable for other grades of ball.
    (i) Men's grades 2-4
        Weight: $5^{5}/_{16}$ ounces (150 g) to $5^{13}/_{16}$ ounces (165 g)
        Size: $8^{11}/_{16}$ inches (22.0 cm) to $9^{1}/_{16}$ inches (23.0 cm)
    (ii) Women's
        Weight: $4^{15}/_{16}$ ounces (140 g) to $5^{5}/_{16}$ ounces (150 g)
        Size: $8^{1}/_{4}$ inches (21.0 cm) to $8^{7}/_{8}$ inches (22.5 cm)
    (iii) Junior
        Weight: $4^{5}/_{16}$ ounces (133 g) to $5^{1}/_{16}$ ounces (143 g)
        Size: $8^{1}/_{16}$ inches (20.5 cm) to $8^{11}/_{16}$ inches (22.0 cm)

on their own initiative. In other circumstances they should not record items until the umpires' signals are received and acknowledged.

LAW 5
There are special regulations for the use of balls in most grades of cricket. When the ball in use becomes unfit, the umpires shall select a suitable replacement from whatever balls are available.

LAW 6 THE BAT
1 Width and length
The bat overall shall not be more than 38 inches (96.5 cm) in length; the blade of the bat shall be made of wood and shall not exceed $4^{1}/_{4}$ inches (10.8 cm) at the widest part.

Notes
(a) *The blade of the bat may be covered with material for protection, strengthening or repair. Such material shall not exceed $^{1}/_{16}$ inch (1.56 mm) in thickness.*

LAW 6
Bats are not manufactured with any great deviation from the law's specifications.

LAW 7 THE PITCH
1 Area of pitch
The pitch is the area between the bowling creases – see Law 9 (The bowling, popping and return creases). It shall measure 5 ft (1.52 m) in width on either side of a line joining the centre of the middle stumps of the wickets. See Law 8 (The wickets).

2 Selection and preparation
Before the toss for innings, the executive of the ground shall be responsible for the selection and preparation of the pitch; thereafter the umpires shall control its use and maintenance.

3 Changing pitch
The pitch shall not be changed during a match unless it becomes unfit for play, and then only with the consent of both captains.

4 Non-turf pitches
In the event of a non-turf pitch being used, the following shall apply:
(a) Length: That of the playing surface to a minimum of 58 ft (17.68 m).
(b) Width: That of the playing surface to a minimum of 6 ft (1.83 m).
See Law 10 (Rolling, sweeping, mowing, watering the pitch and re-marking of creases), Note (a).

LAW 7
It is important to note that this law defines the legal pitch as having a fixed length and width. The clause governing non-turf pitches does not alter the legal pitch specifications, but defines the minimum length and width of non-turf playing surfaces, within the larger dimensions of turf pitch areas. This is significant in applying Law 41.3.

LAW 8 THE WICKETS
1 Width and pitching
Two sets of wickets, each 9 inches (22.86 cm) wide, and consisting of three wooden stumps with two wooden bails upon the top, shall be pitched opposite and parallel to each other at a distance of 22 yards (20.12 m) between the centres of the two middle stumps.

2 Size of stumps
The stumps shall be of equal and sufficient size to prevent the ball from passing between them. Their tops shall be 28 inches (71.1 cm) above the ground, and shall be dome-shaped except for the bail grooves.

3 Size of bails
The bails shall be each $4^{3}/_{8}$ inches (11.1 cm) in length and when in position on the top of the stumps shall not project more than $^{1}/_{2}$ inch (1.3 cm) above them.

LAW 8
The stumps should be set with the back edge of the bowling crease running through the centre of the stumps at their base. When bails are not in use, the provisions of Law 28.4 apply.

Notes
(a) **Dispensing with bails**
In a high wind the umpires may decide to dispense with the use of bails.
(b) **Junior cricket**
For junior cricket, as defined by the local governing body, the following measurements for the wickets shall apply:
  Width: 8 inches (20.32 cm)
  Pitched: 21 yards (19.20 m)
  Height: 27 inches (68.58 cm)
    Bails: each 3⁷/₈ inches (9.84 cm) in length and should not project more than ¹/₂ inch/1.3 cm above them.

LAW 9 THE BOWLING, POPPING AND RETURN CREASES
1 The bowling crease
The bowling crease shall be marked in line with the stumps at each end and shall be 8 ft 8 inches (2.64 m) in length, with the stumps in the centre.
2 The popping crease
The popping crease, which is the back edge of the crease marking, shall be in front of and parallel with the bowling crease. It shall have the back edge of the crease marking 4 ft (1.22 m) from the centre of the stumps and shall extend to a minimum of 6 ft (1.83 m) on either side of the line of the wicket. The popping crease shall be considered to be unlimited in length.
3 The return crease
The return crease marking, of which the inside edge is the crease, shall be at each end of the bowling crease and at right angles to it. The return crease shall be marked to a minimum of 4 ft (1.22 m) behind the wicket and shall be considered to be unlimited in length. A forward extension shall be marked to the popping crease.

LAW 9
Though the markings of creases have width, the creases themselves are the edges of those markings and have no width.

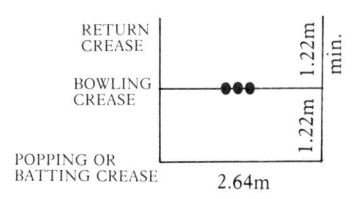

```
RETURN  |                      | 1.22m
CREASE  |                      | min.
BOWLING |----●●●---------------|
CREASE  |                      | 1.22m
POPPING OR |                   |
BATTING CREASE       2.64m
```

LAW 10 ROLLING, SWEEPING, MOWING, WATERING THE PITCH AND RE-MARKING OF CREASES
1 Rolling
During the match the pitch may be rolled at the request of the captain of the batting side, for a period of not more than 7 minutes before the start of each innings, other than the first innings of the match, and before the start of each day's play. In addition, if, after the toss and before the first innings of the match, the start is delayed, the captain of the batting side shall have the right to have the pitch rolled for not more than 7 minutes. The pitch shall not otherwise be rolled during the match.
  The 7 minutes' rolling permitted before the start of a day's play shall take place not earlier than half

LAW 10
Most provisions of this law are impracticable at levels below first-class cricket. The principles of the law, however, should still apply and be observed.

an hour before the start of play and the captain of the batting side may delay such rolling until 10 minutes before the start of play should he so desire.

If a captain declares an innings closed less than 15 minutes before the resumption of play, and the other captain is thereby prevented from exercising his option of 7 minutes' rolling or if he is so prevented for any other reason the time for rolling shall be taken out of the normal playing time.

2 Sweeping

Such sweeping of the pitch as is necessary during the match shall be done so that the 7 minutes allowed for rolling the pitch provided for in 1 above is not affected.

3 Mowing

(a) **Responsibilities of ground authority and of umpires**

All mowings which are carried out before the toss for innings shall be the responsibility of the ground authority. Thereafter they shall be carried out under the supervision of the umpires (see Law 7.2, Selection and preparation).

(b) **Initial mowing**

The pitch shall be mown before play begins on the day the match is scheduled to start or in the case of a delayed start on the day the match is expected to start. See (a) above (Responsibilities of ground authority and of umpires).

(c) **Subsequent mowings in a match of two or more days' duration**

In a match of two or more days' duration, the pitch shall be mown daily before play begins. Should this mowing not take place because of weather conditions, rest days or other reasons the pitch shall be mown on the first day on which the match is resumed.

(d) **Mowing of the outfield in a match of two or more days' duration**

In order to ensure that conditions are as similar as possible for both sides, the outfield shall normally be mown before the commencement of play on each day of the match, if ground and weather conditions allow (see (b) above).

4 Watering

The pitch shall not be watered during a match.

5 Re-marking of creases

Whenever possible the creases shall be re-marked.

6 Maintenance of foot holes

In wet weather, the umpires shall ensure that the holes made by the bowlers and batsmen are cleaned out and dried whenever necessary to facilitate play. In matches of two or more days' duration, the umpires shall allow, if necessary, the re-turfing of foot holes made by the bowler in his delivery stride, or the use of quick-setting fillings for the same purpose, before the start of each day's play.

7 Securing of footholds and maintenance of pitch

During play, the umpires shall allow either batsman

to beat the pitch with his bat and players to secure their footholds by the use of sawdust, provided that no damage to the pitch is so caused, and Law 42 (Unfair play) is not contravened.

Notes
(a) Non-turf pitches
The above Law 10 applies to turf pitches.

The game is played on non-turf pitches in many countries at various levels. Whilst the conduct of the game on these surfaces should always be in accordance with the Laws of Cricket, it is recognised that it may sometimes be necessary for governing bodies to lay down special playing conditions to suit the type of non-turf pitch used in their country.

In matches played against touring teams, any special playing conditions should be agreed in advance by both parties.

(b) Mowing of the outfield in a match of two or more days' duration
If, for reasons other than ground and weather conditions, daily and complete mowing is not possible, the ground authority shall notify the captains and umpires, before the toss for innings, of the procedure to be adopted for such mowing during the match.

(c) Choice of roller
If there is more than one roller available the captain of the batting side shall have a choice.

LAW 11 COVERING THE PITCH
1 Before the start of a match
Before the start of a match complete covering of the pitch shall be allowed.

2 During a match
The pitch shall not be completely covered during a match unless prior arrangement or regulations so provide.

3 Covering bowlers' run-up
Whenever possible, the bowlers' run-up shall be covered but the covers so used shall not extend further than 4 ft (1.22 m) in front of the popping crease.

Notes
(a) Removal of covers
The covers should be removed as promptly as possible whenever the weather permits.

LAW 11
The complete covering of pitches is the usual practice in most countries and is governed by specific regulations.

LAW 12 INNINGS
1 Number of innings
A match shall be of one or two innings of each side according to agreement reached before the start of play.

2 Alternate innings
In a two-innings match each side shall take their innings alternately except in the case provided for in Law 13 (The follow-on).

LAW 12
If the start of play is delayed, the toss and the winner's declaration of an intention to bat or field may be delayed. The time stipulations of the law must be observed in relation to the adjusted starting time.

3 The toss
The captains shall toss for the choice of innings on the field of play not later than 15 minutes before the time scheduled for the match to start, or before the time agreed upon for play to start.

4 Choice of innings
The winner of the toss shall notify his decision to bat or to field to the opposing captain not later than 10 minutes before the time scheduled for the match to start, or before the time agreed upon for play to start. The decision shall not thereafter be altered.

5 Continuation after one innings of each side
Despite the terms of 1 above, in a one-innings match, when a result has been reached on the first innings the captains may agree to the continuation of play if, in their opinion, there is a prospect of carrying the game to a further issue in the time left (see Law 21 (Result)).

Notes
(a) Limited innings: one-innings match
In a one-innings match, each innings may, by agreement, be limited by a number of overs or by a period of time.
(b) Limited innings: two-innings match
In a two-innings match, the first innings of each side may, by agreement, be limited to a number of overs or by a period of time.

LAW 13 THE FOLLOW-ON
1 Lead on first innings
In a two-innings match the side which bats first and leads by 200 runs in a match of five days or more, by 150 runs in a three-day or four-day match, by 100 runs in a two-day match, or by 75 runs in a one-day match, shall have the option of requiring the other side to follow their innings.

2 Day's play lost
If no play takes place on the first day of a match of two or more days' duration, 1 above shall apply in accordance with the number of days' play remaining from the actual start of the match.

LAW 13
The side enforcing the follow-on retains its right to a second innings.

LAW 14 DECLARATIONS
1 Time of declaration
The captain of the batting side may declare an innings closed at any time during a match irrespective of its duration.

2 Forfeiture of second innings
A captain may forfeit his second innings, provided his decision to do so is notified to the opposing captain and umpires in sufficient time to allow 7 minutes' rolling of the pitch. See Law 10 (Rolling, sweeping, mowing, watering the pitch and re-marking of creases). The normal 10-minute interval between innings shall be applied.

LAW 14
If a team forfeits its second innings, the captain of the opposing side and the umpires must be notified of the forfeiture within 3 minutes of the start of the interval between innings. The umpires shall not allow any forfeiture which is notified after this time.

LAW 15 START OF PLAY
1 Call of play
At the start of each innings and of each day's play and on the resumption of play after any interval or interruption the umpire at the bowler's end shall call 'play'.
2 Practice on the field
At no time on any day of the match shall there be any bowling or batting practice on the pitch.

No practice may take place on the field if, in the opinion of the umpires, it could result in a waste of time.
3 Trial run-up
No bowler shall have a trial run-up after 'play' has been called in any session of play, except at the fall of a wicket when an umpire may allow such a trial run-up if he is satisfied that it will not cause any waste of time.

LAW 16 INTERVALS
1 Length
The umpire shall allow such intervals as have been agreed upon for meals, and 10 minutes between each innings.
2 Luncheon interval: innings ending or stoppage within 10 minutes of interval
If an innings ends or there is a stoppage caused by weather or bad light within 10 minutes of the agreed time for the luncheon interval, the interval shall be taken immediately.

The time remaining in the session of play shall be added to the agreed length of the interval but no extra allowance shall be made for the 10 minutes interval between innings.
3 Tea interval: innings ending or stoppage within 30 minutes of interval
If an innings ends or there is a stoppage caused by weather or bad light within 30 minutes of the agreed time for the tea interval, the interval shall be taken immediately.

The interval shall be of the agreed length and, if applicable, shall include the 10 minute interval between innings.
4 Tea interval: continuation of play
If at the agreed time for the tea interval, nine wickets are down, play shall continue for a period not exceeding 30 minutes or until the innings is concluded.
5 Tea interval: agreement to forego
At any time during the match, the captains may agree to forego a tea interval.
6 Intervals for drinks
If both captains agree before the start of a match that intervals for drinks may be taken, the option to take such intervals shall be available to either side. These intervals shall be restricted to one per

LAW 15
Once 'play' has been called, any violation of this law may bring a caution from the umpires under Law 42.10 for time wasting.

LAW 16
The provisions for flexible intervals are designed to avoid the wastage of playing time and unreasonably short passages of play.

Drink intervals are determined by agreement before the start of the match and neither side can control the taking of drinks outside that agreement or the Law.

session, shall be kept as short as possible, shall not be taken in the last hour of the match and in any case shall not exceed 5 minutes.

The agreed times for these intervals shall be strictly adhered to except that if a wicket falls within 5 minutes of the agreed time then drinks shall be taken out immediately.

If an innings ends or there is a stoppage caused by weather or bad light within 30 minutes of the agreed time for a drinks interval, there will be no interval for drinks in that session.

At any time during the match the captains may agree to forego any such drinks interval.

Notes
(a) Tea interval: one-day match
In a one-day match, a specific time for the tea interval need not necessarily be arranged, and it may be agreed to take this interval between the innings of a one-innings match.
(b) Changing the agreed time of intervals
In the event of the ground, weather or light conditions causing a suspension of play, the umpires, after consultation with the captains, may decide in the interests of time saving to bring forward the time of the luncheon or tea interval.

LAW 17 CESSATION OF PLAY
1 Call of time
The umpire at the bowler's end shall call 'time' on the cessation of play before any interval or interruption of play, at the end of each day's play, and at the conclusion of the match. See Law 27 (Appeals).
2 Removal of bails
After the call of 'time', the umpires shall remove the bails from both wickets.
3 Starting a last over
The last over before an interval or the close of play shall be started provided the umpire, after walking at his normal pace, has arrived at his position behind the stumps at the bowler's end before time has been reached.
4 Completion of the last over of a session
The last over before an interval or the close of play shall be completed unless a batsman is out or retires during that over within 2 minutes of the interval or the close of play or unless the players have occasion to leave the field.
5 Completion of the last over of a match
An over in progress at the close of play on the final day of a match shall be completed at the request of either captain even if a wicket falls after time has been reached.

If during the last over the players have occasion to leave the field the umpires shall call 'time' and there shall be no resumption of play and the match shall be at an end.

LAW 17
The cessation of play, indicated by the call of 'time', is often implied rather than spoken, e.g. at drink intervals and when rain suddenly stops play. In such cases the ball shall be deemed 'dead' for all purposes of the Laws.

The provisions for a minimum number of overs to be bowled from the beginning of the last hour of a match apply in a limited degree to the more junior levels of cricket.

The periods of lost time to be taken into account in calculating reductions in the minimum number of overs to be bowled in the last hour of a match must fall within – or be part of – that last hour. An interruption occurring after or extending past the expiry of the last hour of play should be treated under Law 17.5 and the match would be over.

6 Last hour of match: number of overs
The umpires shall indicate when one hour of playing time of the match remains according to the agreed hours of play. The next over after that moment shall be the first of a minimum of 20 six-ball overs (15 eight-ball overs), provided a result is not reached earlier or there is no interval or interruption of play.

7 Last hour of match: intervals between innings and interruptions of play
If, at the commencement of the last hour of the match, an interval or interruption of play is in progress or if, during the last hour there is an interval between innings or an interruption of play, the minimum number of overs to be bowled on the resumption of play shall be reduced in proportion to the duration, within the last hour of the match, of any such interval or interruption.

The minimum number of overs to be bowled after a resumption of play shall be calculated as follows:

(a) In the case of an interval or interruption of play being in progress at the commencement of the last hour of the match, or in the case of a first interval or interruption a deduction shall be made from the minimum of 20 six-ball overs (or 15 eight-ball overs).

(b) If there is a later interval or interruption a further deduction shall be made from the minimum number of overs which should have been bowled following the last resumption of play.

(c) These deductions shall be based on the following factors:

   (i) the number of overs already bowled in the last hour of the match or, in the case of a later interval or interruption, in the last session of play.
   (ii) the number of overs lost as a result of the interval or interruption allowing one six-ball over for every full 3 minutes (or one eight-ball over for every full 4 minutes) of interval or interruption.
   (iii) any over left uncompleted at the end of an innings to be excluded from these calculations.
   (iv) any over left uncompleted at the start of an interruption of play to be completed when play is resumed and to count as one over bowled.
   (v) an interval to start with the end of an innings and to end 10 minutes later; an interruption to start on the call of 'time' and to end on the call of 'play'.

(d) In the event of an innings being completed and a new innings commencing during the last hour of the match, the number of overs to be bowled in the new innings shall be calculated on the basis of one six-ball over for every 3 minutes or part thereof remaining for play (or one eight-ball over for every 4 minutes or part thereof remaining for play); or alternatively on the basis that sufficient overs be bowled to enable the full minimum quota of overs to be completed under circumstances governed by (a), (b) and (c) above. In all such cases the alternative which allows the greater number of overs shall be employed.

8 Bowler unable to complete an over during last hour of match

If, for any reason, a bowler is unable to complete an over during the period of play referred to in 6 above, Law 22.7 (Bowler incapacitated or suspended during an over) shall apply.

LAW 18 SCORING
1 A run

The score shall be reckoned by runs. A run is scored:

(a) So often as the batsmen, after a hit or at any time while the ball is in play, shall have crossed and made good their ground from end to end.
(b) When a boundary is scored. See Law 19 (Boundaries).
(c) When penalty runs are awarded. See 6 below.

2 Short runs

(a) If either batsman runs a short run, the umpire shall call and signal 'one short' as soon as the ball becomes dead and that run shall not be scored.
A run is short if a batsman fails to make good his ground on turning for a further run.
(b) Although a short run shortens the succeeding one, the latter, if completed, shall count.
(c) If either or both batsmen deliberately run short the umpire shall, as soon as he sees that the fielding side have no chance of dismissing either batsman, call and signal 'dead ball' and disallow any runs attempted or previously scored. The batsmen shall return to their original ends.
(d) If both batsmen run short in one and the same run, only one run shall be deducted.
(e) Only if three or more runs are attempted can more than one be short and then, subject to (c) and (d) above, all runs so called shall be disallowed. If there has been more than one short run the umpires shall instruct the scorers as to the number of runs disallowed.

3 Striker caught

If the striker is caught, no run shall be scored.

4 Batsman run out

If a batsman is run out, only that run which was being attempted shall not be scored. If, however, an injured striker himself is run out no runs shall be scored. See Law 2.7 (Transgression of the Laws by an injured batsman or runner.)

5 Batsman obstructing the field

If a batsman is out obstructing the field, any runs completed before the obstruction occurs shall be scored unless such obstruction prevents a catch being made in which case no runs shall be scored.

LAW 18

A run is deemed to be short, only if the batters cross in the succeeding run. A deliberately taken short run is unfair and all runs made from the delivery off which the short run is attempted shall be disallowed.

6 Runs scored for penalties
Runs shall be scored for penalties under Laws 20 (Lost ball), 24 (No ball), 25 (Wide ball), 41.1 (Fielding the ball), and for boundary allowances under Law 19 (Boundaries).

7 Batsman returning to wicket he has left
If, while the ball is in play, the batsmen have crossed in running, neither shall return to the wicket he has left even though a short run has been called or no run has been scored as in the case of a catch. Batsmen, however, shall return to the wickets they originally left in the cases of a boundary and of any disallowance of runs and of an injured batsman being, himself, run out. See Law 2.7 (Transgression of the Laws by an injured batsman or runner).

Notes
(a) Short run
A striker taking stance in front of his popping crease may run from that point without penalty.

LAW 19 BOUNDARIES
1 The boundary of the playing area
Before the toss for innings, the umpires shall agree with both captains on the boundary of the playing area. The boundary shall, if possible, be marked by a white line, a rope laid on the ground, or a fence. If flags or posts only are used to mark a boundary, the imaginary line joining such points shall be regarded as the boundary. An obstacle, or person, within the playing area shall not be regarded as a boundary unless so decided by the umpires before the toss for innings. Sightscreens within, or partially within, the playing area shall be regarded as the boundary and when the ball strikes or passes within or under or directly over any part of the screen, a boundary shall be scored.

2 Runs scored for boundaries
Before the toss for innings, the umpires shall agree with both captains the runs to be allowed for boundaries, and in deciding the allowance for them, the umpires and captains shall be guided by the prevailing custom of the ground. The allowance for a boundary shall normally be 4 runs, and 6 runs for all hits pitching over and clear of the boundary line or fence, even though the ball has been previously touched by a fieldsman. Six runs shall also be scored if a fieldsman, after catching a ball, carries it over the boundary. See Law 32 (Caught, Note (a)). Six runs shall not be scored when a ball struck by the striker hits a sightscreen full pitch if the screen is within, or partially within, the playing area, but if the ball is struck directly over a sightscreen so situated, 6 runs shall be scored.

LAW 19
Boundary conditions are arranged by agreement between the sides and the umpires before the game and it is best to follow local practices. Allowances for boundaries may be lesser or greater than the normal 4 and 6 runs, if the distances between the pitch and the boundaries are shorter or longer than usual.

Markings for the boundary lines may vary – even around the same playing area. Where the boundary marking is a fence and a gutter or kerb runs inside and near the base of the fence, the fence line shall be fixed as the boundary and a ball which rolls into the gutter or kerb shall be deemed to have reached the boundary. The gutter or kerb will not be the boundary line. This interpretation of the Law will avoid any confusion which might arise when a ball is fielded or a catch is taken with the fielder grounding his or her person on the gutter or kerb, but not beyond the fence line.

Large obstacles within the playing area, e.g. sightscreens or the curator's roller, shall be

3 A boundary
A boundary shall be scored and signalled by the umpire at the bowler's end whenever, in his opinion:
(a) A ball in play touches or crosses the boundary, however marked.
(b) A fieldsman with ball in hand touches or grounds any part of his person on or over a boundary line.
(c) A fieldsman with ball in hand grounds any part of his person over a boundary fence or board. This allows the fieldsman to touch or lean on or over a boundary fence or board in preventing a boundary.

4 Runs exceeding boundary allowance
The runs completed at the instant the ball reaches the boundary shall count if they exceed the boundary allowance.

5 Overthrows or wilful act of a fieldsman
If the boundary results from an overthrow or from the wilful act of a fieldsman, any runs already completed and the allowance shall be added to the score. The run in progress shall count provided that the batsmen have crossed at the instant of the throw or act.

Notes
(a) Position of sightscreens
Sightscreens should, if possible, be positioned wholly outside the playing area, as near as possible to the boundary line.

regarded as part of the boundary line. Thus a fielder who passes with ball in hand behind such objects will be crossing the boundary line and a boundary shall be awarded.

If an intruder on to the field intercepts the ball before it reaches the boundary, the umpire has the discretion to award a boundary or not. He or she may also call 'dead ball' if a batter is likely to be run out if the ball is returned to the keeper or bowler by the intruder.

Should an overthrow or wilful act by a fielder force the ball over the boundary, the runs completed at the instant of that throw or act *plus* the boundary allowance are scored. A run which is in progress is treated as a completed run if the batters have crossed prior to the fielder's action. Runs made after the fielder's action and before the ball reaches the boundary do not count. If the ball reaches the boundary – other than by an overthrow or the wilful act of a fielder – and more runs than the boundary allowance have been fully completed before it does so, those runs are scored and the boundary allowance is not.

LAW 20 LOST BALL
1 Runs scored
If a ball in play cannot be found or recovered any fieldsman may call 'lost ball' when 6 runs shall be added to the score; but if more than 6 have been run before 'lost ball' is called, as many runs as have been completed shall be scored. The run in progress shall count provided that the batsmen have crossed at the instant of the call of 'lost ball'.

2 How scored
The runs shall be added to the score of the striker if the ball has been struck, but otherwise to the score of byes, leg-byes, no-balls or wides as the case may be.

LAW 20
A ball which becomes temporarily unavailable to the fielding side may be called 'lost ball', thus conceding a minimum of six runs to the batter (e.g. a dog may seize and retain the ball on the field of play).

LAW 21 THE RESULT
1 A win: two-innings matches
The side which has scored a total of runs in excess

LAW 21
The unauthorised departure from the field of either side

of that scored by the opposing side in its two completed innings shall be the winners.

2 A win: one-innings matches
(a) One-innings matches, unless played out as in 1 above, shall be decided on the first innings, but see Law 12.5 (Continuation after one innings of each side).
(b) If the captains agree to continue play after the completion of one innings of each side in accordance with Law 12.5 (Continuation after one innings of each side) and a result is not achieved on the second innings, the first innings result shall stand.

3 Umpires awarding a match
(a) A match shall be lost by a side which, during the match,
   (i) refuses to play, or
   (ii) concedes defeat,
and the umpires shall award the match to the other side.
(b) Should both batsmen at the wickets or the fielding side leave the field at any time without the agreement of the umpires, this shall constitute a refusal to play and, on appeal, the umpires shall award the match to the other side in accordance with (a) above.

4 A tie
The result of a match shall be a tie when the scores are equal at the conclusion of play, but only if the side batting last has completed its innings.

If the scores of the completed first innings of a one-day match are equal, it shall be a tie but only if the match has not been played out to a further conclusion.

5 A draw
A match not determined in any of the ways as in 1, 2, 3 and 4 above shall count as a draw.

6 Correctness of result
Any decision as to the correctness of the scores shall be the responsibility of the umpires. See Law 3.14 (Correctness of scores).

If, after the umpires and players have left the field, in the belief that the match has been concluded, the umpires decide that a mistake in scoring has occurred, which affects the result, and provided time has not been reached, they shall order play to resume and to continue until the agreed finishing time unless a result is reached earlier.

If the umpires decide that a mistake has occurred and time has been reached, the umpires shall immediately inform both captains of the necessary corrections to the scores and, if applicable, to the result.

7 Acceptance of result
In accepting the scores as notified by the scorers and agreed by the umpires, the captains of both sides thereby accept the result.

shall be sufficient for the umpires to award the game to the opposing side – *provided that an appeal is made.*

In other circumstances the umpires may act without the lodging of an appeal and award a match against a side refusing to play or conceding defeat.

When the scores are found to be incorrect, the umpires must ensure that the appropriate adjustments are made to the scores and that the proper situation is notified to the respective captains. If a result has not been reached and there is time or a minimum number of overs still to be bowled, the match shall resume until there is a result or a fulfilment of the agreed finishing conditions.

As soon as the winning run is made the game is over and no further events or runs are recorded – unless the runs come from a boundary allowance.

Notes
(a) Statement of results
The result of a finished match is stated as a win by runs, except in the case of a win by the side batting last when it is by the number of wickets still then to fall.
(b) Winning hit or extras
As soon as the side has won (see 1 and 2 above) the umpire shall call 'time', the match is finished, and nothing that happens thereafter other than as a result of a mistake in scoring (see 6 above) shall be regarded as part of the match.

However, if a boundary constitutes the winning hit – or extras – and the boundary allowance exceeds the number of runs required to win the match, such runs scored shall be credited to the side's total and, in the case of a hit, to the striker's score.

LAW 22 THE OVER
1 Number of balls
The ball shall be bowled from each wicket alternately in overs of either six or eight balls according to agreement before the match.
2 Call of 'over'
When the agreed number of balls has been bowled, and as the ball becomes dead or when it becomes clear to the umpire at the bowler's end that both the fielding side and the batsmen at the wicket have ceased to regard the ball as in play, the umpire shall call 'over' before leaving the wicket.
3 No-ball or wide ball
Neither a no-ball nor a wide ball shall be reckoned as one of the over.
4 Umpire miscounting
If an umpire miscounts the number of balls, the over as counted by the umpire shall stand.
5 Bowler changing ends
A bowler shall be allowed to change ends as often as desired provided only that he does not bowl two overs consecutively in an innings.
6 The bowler finishing an over
A bowler shall finish an over in progress unless he be incapacitated or be suspended under Law 42.8 (The bowling of fast short-pitched balls), 42.9 (The bowling of fast high full pitches), 42.10 (Time wasting) and 42.11 (Players damaging the pitch). If an over is left incomplete for any reason at the start of an interval or interruption of play, it shall be finished on the resumption of play.
7 Bowler incapacitated or suspended during an over
If, for any reason, a bowler is incapacitated while running up to bowl the first ball of an over, or is incapacitated or suspended during an over, the umpire shall call and signal 'dead ball' and another bowler shall be allowed to bowl or complete the

LAW 22
Having started his or her run-up for the first delivery of an over, a bowler must complete that over, unless subsequently incapacitated or suspended – in which case the over shall be completed by another player who shall not have bowled any part of the previous over and shall not be allowed to bowl any part of the next.

over from the same end, provided only that he shall not bowl two overs, or part thereof, consecutively in one innings.

8 Position of non-striker
The batsman at the bowler's end shall normally stand on the opposite side of the wicket to that from which the ball is being delivered, unless a request to do otherwise is granted by the umpire.

LAW 23 DEAD BALL
1 The ball becomes dead, when:
(a) It is finally settled in the hands of the wicketkeeper or the bowler.
(b) It reaches or pitches over the boundary.
(c) A batsman is out.
(d) Whether played or not, it lodges in the clothing or equipment of a batsman or the clothing of an umpire.
(e) A ball lodges in a protective helmet worn by a member of the fielding side.
(f) A penalty is awarded under Law 20 (Lost ball) or Law 41.1 (Fielding the ball).
(g) The umpire calls 'over' or 'time'.

2 Either umpire shall call and signal 'dead ball', when:
(a) He intervenes in a case of unfair play.
(b) A serious injury to a player or umpire occurs.
(c) He is satisfied that, for an adequate reason, the striker is not ready to receive the ball and makes no attempt to play it.
(d) The bowler drops the ball accidentally before delivery, or the ball does not leave his hand for any reason.
(e) One or both bails fall from the striker's wicket before he receives delivery.
(f) He leaves his normal position for consultation.
(g) He is required to do so under Laws 26.3 (Disallowance of leg byes), etc.

3 The ball ceases to be dead, when:
(a) The bowler starts his run-up or bowling action.

4 The ball is not dead, when:
(a) It strikes an umpire (unless it lodges in his dress).
(b) The wicket is broken or struck down (unless a batsman is out thereby).
(c) An unsuccessful appeal is made.
(d) The wicket is broken accidentally either by the bowler during his delivery or by a batsman in running.
(e) The umpire has called 'no ball' or 'wide'.

Notes
(a) Ball finally settled
Whether the ball is finally settled or not – see 1 (a) above – must be a question for the umpires alone to decide.

LAW 23
Because the bowler or wicketkeeper has possession of the ball, players must not presume that it has 'finally settled'. The umpires should not decide that a ball has 'finally settled' whilst either batter is out of his or her ground and there is a chance of his or her being put out – unless the fielding side clearly shows no interest.

When the bowler starts his or her run-up the ball comes into play, permitting him or her to deliver it to the striker or attempt to run out either batter, if the opportunity arises. If the bowler drops or retains the ball instead of delivering it, the umpire shall call 'dead ball'.

A fielder's helmet provides little or no advantage other than protection for the head – see also Law 32.2 (e).

The words 'lodges in the clothing or equipment of . . .' should be taken to include the settlement of the ball on or about the person or between items of apparel.

(b) Action on call of 'dead ball'
(i) If 'dead ball' is called prior to the striker receiving a delivery the bowler shall be allowed an additional ball.
(ii) If 'dead ball' is called after the striker receives a delivery the bowler shall not be allowed an additional ball, unless a 'no ball' or 'wide' has been called.

LAW 24 NO BALL
1 Mode of delivery
The umpire shall indicate to the striker whether the bowler intends to bowl over or round the wicket, overarm or underarm, or right or left-handed. Failure on the part of the bowler to indicate in advance a change in his mode of delivery is unfair and the umpire shall call and signal 'no ball'.

2 Fair delivery: the arm
For a delivery to be fair the ball must be bowled not thrown. See Note (a) below. If either umpire is not entirely satisfied with the absolute fairness of a delivery in this respect he shall call and signal 'no ball' instantly upon delivery.

3 Fair delivery: the feet
The umpire at the bowler's wicket shall call and signal 'no ball' if he is not satisfied that in the delivery stride:
(a) the bowler's back foot has landed within and not touching the return crease or its forward extension
or
(b) some part of the front foot whether grounded or raised was behind the popping crease.

4 Bowler throwing at striker's wicket before delivery
If the bowler, before delivering the ball, throws it at the striker's wicket in an attempt to run him out, the umpire shall call and signal 'no ball'. See Law 42.12 (Batsman unfairly stealing a run) and Law 38 (Run out).

5 Bowler attempting to run out non-striker before delivery
If the bowler, before delivering the ball, attempts to run out the non-striker, any runs which result shall be allowed and shall be scored as no-balls. Such an attempt shall not count as a ball in the over. The umpire shall not call 'no ball'. See Law 42.12 (Batsman unfairly stealing a run).

6 Infringement of laws by a wicketkeeper or a fieldsman
The umpire shall call and signal 'no ball' in the event of the wicketkeeper infringing Law 40.1 (Position of wicketkeeper) or a fieldsman infringing Law 41.2 (Limitation of on-side fieldsmen) or Law 41.3 (Position of fieldsmen).

LAW 24
Whilst the underarm ball is listed as a type of delivery, its use, except in very junior cricket, is regarded nowadays as both unnecessary and unacceptable.

Whilst there is a definition of what constitutes a throw, a bowler is not entitled to the benefit of the doubt surrounding his or her action. The slightest doubt about whether a delivery was bowled properly justifies a call of 'no ball'.

The delivery stride begins with the landing of the bowler's back foot, which should be within and not touching the return crease, and ends with the landing of the front foot, some part of which must be behind the batting crease. Note that the front foot may touch or be outside the line of the return crease and its forward extension.

The laws allow for either batter to be run out if there is an attempt to run during the bowler's run-up. If the striker stands out of his or her ground to receive the ball and the bowler throws it at the striker's wicket in an attempt to run him or her out, the batter is protected by a call of 'no ball' (for throwing) from being adjudged out 'obstructing the field' if he or she hits the ball, being stumped or run out. If the striker attempts to run, he or she may be out, according to the circumstances, in any of the four prescribed legitimate

7 Revoking a call
An umpire shall revoke the call 'no ball' if the ball does not leave the bowler's hand for any reason. See Law 23.2 (Either umpire shall call and signal 'dead ball').

8 Penalty
A penalty of one run for a no-ball shall be scored if no runs are made otherwise.

9 Runs from a no-ball
The striker may hit a no-ball and whatever runs result shall be added to his score. Runs made otherwise from a no-ball shall be scored no-balls.

10 Out from a no-ball
The striker shall be out from a no-ball if he breaks Law 34 (Hit the ball twice) and either batsman may be run out or shall be given out if either breaks Law 33 (Handled the ball) or Law 37 (Obstructing the field).

11 Batsman given out off a no-ball
Should a batsman be given out off a no-ball the penalty for bowling it shall stand unless runs are otherwise scored.

Notes
(a) Definition of a throw
A ball shall be deemed to have been thrown if, in the opinion of either umpire, the process of straightening the bowling arm, whether it be partial or complete, takes place during that part of the delivery swing which directly precedes the ball leaving the hand. This definition shall not debar a bowler from the use of the wrist in the delivery swing.
(b) No-ball not counting in over
A no-ball shall not be reckoned as one of the over. See Law 22.3 (No-ball or wide ball).

ways. If the non-striker is out of his or her ground during the bowler's run-up – whether he or she is attempting to run or not – he or she may be run out by the bowler, using any of the methods outlined in Law 28.

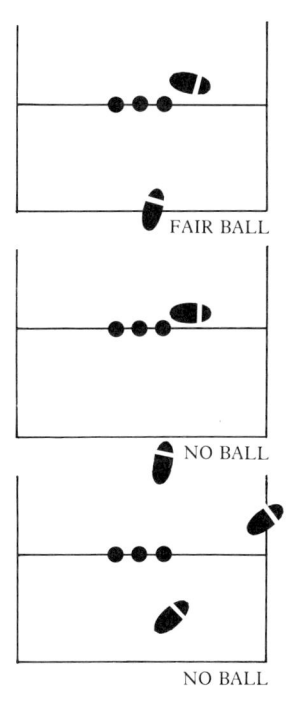

FAIR BALL

NO BALL

NO BALL

LAW 25 WIDE BALL
1 Judging a wide
If the bowler bowls the ball so high over or so wide of the wicket that, in the opinion of the umpire it passes out of reach of the striker, standing in a normal guard position, the umpire shall call and signal 'wide ball' as soon as it has passed the line of the striker's wicket.

The umpire shall not adjudge a ball as being wide if:
(a) The striker, by moving from his guard position, causes the ball to pass out of his reach.
(b) The striker moves and thus brings the ball within his reach.

2 Penalty
A penalty of one run for a wide shall be scored if no runs are made otherwise.

3 Ball coming to rest in front of the striker
If a ball which the umpire considers to have been delivered comes to rest in front of the line of the striker's wicket, 'wide' shall not be called. The

LAW 25
It is unfair to deny the striker a reasonable opportunity to hit the ball whilst playing a normal stroke. If a wide ball is delivered and the striker attempts to play a stroke with his or her arms and bat extended in an abnormal manner, it should not be regarded as being 'within the reach' of the batter and thus a legitimate delivery. The striker cannot make a 'wide' by moving away from or ducking under the path of a ball delivered fairly within his or her reach.

In determining a course of action when a ball comes to rest forward of the striker's

striker has a right, without interference from the fielding side, to make one attempt to hit the ball. If the fielding side interfere, the umpire shall replace the ball where it came to rest and shall order the fieldsmen to resume the places they occupied in the field before the ball was delivered.

The umpire shall call and signal 'dead ball' as soon as it is clear that the striker does not intend to hit the ball, or after the striker has made one unsuccessful attempt to hit the ball.

4 Revoking a call
The umpire shall revoke the call if the striker hits a ball which has been called 'wide'.

5 Ball not dead
The ball does not become dead on the call of 'wide ball'. See Law 23.4 (The ball is not dead).

6 Runs resulting from a wide
All runs which are run or result from a wide ball which is not a no ball shall be scored wide balls, or if no runs are made one shall be scored.

7 Out from a wide
The striker shall be out from a wide ball if he breaks Law 35 (Hit wicket) or Law 39 (Stumped). Either batsman may be run out and shall be out if he breaks Law 33 (Handled the ball) or Law 37 (Obstructing the field).

8 Batsman given out off a wide
Should a batsman be given out off a wide, the penalty for bowling it shall stand unless runs are otherwise made.

Notes
(a) Wide ball not counting in over
A wide ball shall not be reckoned as one of the over. See Law 22.3 (No-ball or wide ball).

LAW 26 BYE AND LEG BYE
1 Byes
If the ball, not having been called 'wide' or 'no ball', passes the striker without touching his bat or person, and any runs are obtained, the umpire shall signal 'bye' and the run or runs shall be credited as such to the batting side.

2 Leg byes
If the ball, not having been called 'wide' or 'no ball', is unintentionally deflected by the striker's dress or person except a hand holding the bat, and any runs are obtained the umpire shall signal 'leg bye' and the run or runs so scored shall be credited as such to the batting side.

Such leg byes shall only be scored if, in the opinion of the umpire, the striker has:
(a) Attempted to play the ball with his bat, or
(b) Tried to avoid being hit by the ball.

3 Disallowance of leg byes
In the case of a deflection by the striker's person, other than in 2(a) and (b) above, the umpire shall call and signal 'dead ball' as soon as one run has

wicket, the umpire must be satisfied that the ball has 'been delivered'. Law 23.2(d) allows for a call of 'dead ball' if the bowler drops the ball accidentally. This clause may be interpreted broadly as encompassing any loss of grip or control which prevents the ball being propelled directly from the hand and in a general forward direction. If the ball is ruled to have been delivered, no runs may be scored, neither batter may be dismissed under any law and no fielder may move from his or her assigned position, until the striker, from one attempt only, hits the ball with the bat.

LAW 26
Any runs made by the batter by running from a wide ball, a no-ball which has not touched the striker's bat or person, or a delivery which has been unintentionally deflected by the striker's person, are recorded as wides or no-balls, not as byes or leg byes.

When the striker deflects the ball intentionally with his body – whether the delivery be fair or a no-ball – the resultant runs made by the batters (including a boundary from an overthrow or a wilful act, or a penalty for an illegal fielding act) shall not be scored except for the penalty allowance if the delivery is a no-ball.

been completed or when it is clear that a run is not being attempted or the ball has reached the boundary.

On the call and signal of 'dead ball' the batsmen shall return to their original ends and no runs shall be allowed.

LAW 27 APPEALS
1 Time of appeals
The umpires shall not give a batsman out unless appealed to by the other side which shall be done prior to the bowler beginning his run-up or bowling action to deliver the next ball. Under Law 23.1(g) (The ball becomes dead) the ball is dead on 'over' being called; this does not, however, invalidate an appeal made prior to the first ball of the following over provided 'time' has not been called. See Law 17.1 (Call of time).
2 An appeal 'how's that?'
An appeal 'how's that?' shall cover all ways of being out.
3 Answering appeals
The umpire at the bowler's wicket shall answer appeals before the other umpire in all cases except those arising out of Law 35 (Hit wicket) or Law 39 (Stumped) or Law 38 (Run out) when this occurs at the striker's wicket.

When either umpire has given a batsman not out, the other umpire shall, within his jurisdiction, answer the appeal or a further appeal, provided it is made in time in accordance with 1 above (Time of appeals).
4 Consultation by umpires
An umpire may consult with the other umpire on a point of fact which the latter may have been in a better position to see and shall then give his decision. If, after consultation, there is still doubt remaining, the decision shall be in favour of the batsman.
5 Batsman leaving his wicket under a misapprehension
The umpires shall intervene if satisfied that a batsman, not having been given out, has left his wicket under a misapprehension that he has been dismissed.
6 Umpire's decision
The umpire's decision is final. He may alter his decision, provided that such alteration is made promptly.
7 Withdrawal of an appeal
In exceptional circumstances the captain of the fielding side may seek permission of the umpire to withdraw an appeal providing the outgoing batsman has not left the playing area. If this is allowed, the umpire shall cancel his decision.

LAW 27
The appeal 'how's that?', or its commonly accepted equivalent, is a request for an opinion from the umpires on whether a batter is out *in any way or not* and it authorises either umpire, acting within the jurisdiction and priority provision, to give the batter out – if the appeal is received within the allowed time.

A captain may not change an umpire's decision, whatever the circumstances. If a fielding captain does not wish to take advantage of a situation in which a batter has been, or is likely to be, given out for a technical breach of the Law, he or she may ask for permission to withdraw an appeal. If the umpire is satisfied that the request would be in keeping with the spirit and the best interests of the game, he or she may grant it and cancel or withhold his or her decision.

LAW 28 THE WICKET IS DOWN
1 Wicket down
The wicket is down if:
(a) Either the ball or the striker's bat or person completely removes either bail from the top of the stumps. A disturbance of a bail, whether temporary or not, shall not constitute a complete removal, but the wicket is down if a bail in falling lodges between two of the stumps.
(b) Any player completely removes with his hand or arm a bail from the top of the stumps, providing that the ball is held in that hand or in the hand of the arm so used.
(c) When both bails are off, a stump is struck out of the ground by the ball, or a player strikes or pulls a stump out of the ground, providing that the ball is held in the hand(s) or in the hand of the arm so used.

2 One bail off
If one bail is off, it shall be sufficient for the purpose of putting the wicket down to remove the remaining bail, or to strike or pull any of the three stumps out of the ground in any of the ways stated in 1 above.

3 All the stumps out of the ground
If all the stumps are out of the ground, the fielding side shall be allowed to put back one or more stumps in order to have an opportunity of putting the wicket down.

4 Dispensing with bails
If, owing to the strength of the wind, it has been agreed to dispense with the bails in accordance with Law 8, Note (a) (Dispensing with bails) the decision as to when the wicket is down is one for the umpires to decide on the facts before them. In such circumstances and if the umpires so decide the wicket shall be held to be down even though a stump has not been struck out of the ground.

Notes
(a) Remaking the wicket
If the wicket is broken while the ball is in play, it is not the umpire's duty to remake the wicket until the ball has become dead. See Law 23 (Dead ball). A member of the fielding side, however, may remake the wicket in such circumstances.

LAW 29 BATSMAN OUT OF HIS GROUND
1 When out of his ground
A batsman shall be considered to be out of his ground unless some part of his bat in his hand or of his person is grounded behind the line of the popping crease.

LAW 28
A wicket may be put down legally by removing completely:
- one or both bails
- the other bail if one is already off
- one stump from the ground if both bails are off
- one stump after having replaced it in a stump hole.

The removal must be done by:
- a ball thrown by a member of the fielding side
- a hand holding the ball
- an arm with the ball being in the hand of that arm.

If the ball is held in both hands, either hand or arm may be used to put down the wicket.

When the umpires decide to dispense with bails, they may accept contact with the stump in lieu of removal from the ground to constitute a wicket being down, provided that the contact is made in the manner prescribed for the removal of the bails from the wicket and the stumps from the ground.

The wicket is down

LAW 29
For the batter to be in his or her ground, part of the bat or person must be touching the ground behind the back edge of the batting crease. In using just the bat to make good his or her ground, the batter must have it in his or her hand.

LAW 30 BOWLED
1 Out bowled
The striker shall be out bowled if:
(a) His wicket is bowled down, even if the ball first touches his bat or person.
(b) He breaks his wicket by hitting or kicking the ball onto it before the completion of a stroke, or as a result of attempting to guard his wicket. See Law 34.1 (Out hit the ball twice).

Notes
(a) Out bowled, not l.b.w.
The striker is out bowled if the ball is deflected onto his wicket even though a decision against him would be justified under Law 36 (Leg before wicket).

LAW 31 TIMED OUT
1 Out timed out
An incoming batsman shall be out timed out if he wilfully takes more than 2 minutes to come in – the 2 minutes being timed from the moment a wicket falls until the new batsman steps onto the field of play.

If this is not complied with and if the umpire is satisfied that the delay was wilful and if an appeal is made, the new batsman shall be given out by the umpire at the bowler's end.

2 Time to be added
The time taken by the umpires to investigate the cause of the delay shall be added at the normal close of play.

Notes
(a) Entry in score book
The correct entry in the score book when a batsman is given out under this Law is 'timed out', and the bowler does not get credit for the wicket.
(b) Batsmen crossing on the field of play
It is an essential duty of the captains to ensure that the ingoing batsman passes the outgoing one before the latter leaves the field of play.

LAW 32 CAUGHT
1 Out caught
The striker shall be out caught if the ball touches his bat or if it touches below the wrist his hand or glove, holding the bat, and is subsequently held by a fieldsman before it touches the ground.

2 A fair catch
A catch shall be considered to have been fairly made if:
(a) The fieldsman is within the field of play throughout the act of making the catch.
  (i) The act of making the catch shall start from the time when the fieldsman first handles the ball

LAW 30
The striker may be out bowled if, in playing at the ball or trying to keep it away from his or her wicket, after having already played at it once, the ball is deflected from his or her bat or person onto the stumps. If a batter knocks the ball onto his or her wicket whilst running or if the ball rebounds from the other wicket, the non-striking batter, or any other player or umpire back onto his or her stumps, the striker shall not be out bowled.

LAW 31
An incoming batter shall be inside the boundary line within 2 minutes of the previous batter being out or retiring. If this time limit is exceeded, without there being a justifiable cause, the umpire, on appeal, shall declare the incoming batter out. The time spent establishing the cause of any batter's delayed entry shall be added to the day's playing time.

LAW 32
For a catch to be valid, a fielder must hold it in such a way that he or she is able to control his or her next action with the ball completely. A fielder's hold on the ball need only be extremely brief, provided control over it and the next action is absolute.

A catch is not good if:
- a fielder in making it – or immediately after making it –

193

and shall end when he both retains complete control over the further disposal of the ball and remains within the field of play.
(ii) In order to be within the field of play, the fieldsman may not touch or ground any part of his person on or over a boundary line. When the boundary is marked by a fence or board the fieldsman may not ground any part of his person over the boundary fence or board, but may touch or lean over the boundary fence or board in completing the catch.
(b) The ball is hugged to the body of the catcher or accidentally lodges in his dress or, in the case of the wicketkeeper, in his pads. However, a striker may not be caught if a ball lodges in a protective helmet worn by a fieldsman, in which case the umpire shall call and signal 'dead ball'. See Law 23 (Dead ball).
(c) The ball does not touch the ground even though a hand holding it does so in effecting the catch.
(d) A fieldsman catches the ball, after it has been lawfully played a second time by the striker, but only if the ball has not touched the ground since being first struck.
(e) A fieldsman catches the ball after it has touched an umpire, another fieldsman or the other batsman. However a striker may not be caught if a ball has touched a protective helmet worn by a fieldsman.
(f) The ball is caught off an obstruction within the boundary provided it has not previously been agreed to regard the obstruction as a boundary.

3 Scoring of runs
If a striker is caught, no runs shall be scored.

Notes
(a) Scoring from an attempted catch
When a fieldsman carrying the ball touches or grounds any part of his person on or over a boundary marked by a line, 6 runs shall be scored.
(b) Ball still in play
If a fieldsman releases the ball before he crosses the boundary, the ball will be considered to be still in play and it may be caught by another fieldsman. However, if the original fieldsman returns to the field of play and handles the ball, a catch may not be made.

LAW 33 HANDLED THE BALL
1 Out handled the ball
Either batsman on appeal shall be out handled the ball if he wilfully touches the ball while in play with the hand not holding the bat unless he does so with the consent of the opposite side.

Notes
(a) Entry in score book
The correct entry in the score book when a batsman is given out under this Law is 'handled the ball', and the bowler does not get credit for the wicket.

grounds any part of his or her body on or over the boundary line
• a fielder catches but then releases the ball before touching or crossing the boundary line – unless the catch is then completed by a fielder other than the original catcher of the ball.

A valid catch may be taken from a rebound off the stumps, an umpire or any player; but if the rebound is from a fielder's protective helmet, the striker is not out and the ball remains in play.

LAW 33
Batters should not handle the ball, even as an act of goodwill to the fielding team, unless there is a clear-spoken or implied expression of consent from a member of the other side. If a batter, in an act of involuntary self-protection, touches the ball with a hand which is not on the bat, he or she shall not be regarded as having wilfully handled the ball.

LAW 34 HIT THE BALL TWICE
1 Out hit the ball twice
The striker, on appeal, shall be out hit the ball twice if, after the ball is struck or is stopped by any part of his person, he wilfully strikes it again with his bat or person except for the sole purpose of guarding his wicket: this he may do with his bat or any part of his person other than his hands, but see Law 37.2 (Obstructing a ball from being caught).

For the purpose of this Law, a hand holding the bat shall be regarded as part of the bat.

2 Returning the ball to a fieldsman
The striker, on appeal, shall be out under this Law, if, without the consent of the opposite side, he uses his bat or person to return the ball to any of the fielding side.

3 Runs from ball lawfully struck twice
No runs except those which result from an overthrow or penalty, see Law 41 (The fieldsman), shall be scored from a ball lawfully struck twice.

Notes
(a) *Entry in score book*
The correct entry in the score book when the striker is given out under this Law is 'hit the ball twice', and the bowler does not get credit for the wicket.
(b) *Runs credited to the batsman*
Any runs awarded under 3 above as a result of an overthrow or penalty shall be credited to the striker, provided the ball in the first instance has touched the bat, or, if otherwise, as extras.

LAW 35 HIT WICKET
1 Out hit wicket
The striker shall be out hit wicket if, while the ball is in play:
(a) His wicket is broken with any part of his person, dress, or equipment as a result of any action taken by him in preparing to receive or in receiving a delivery, or in setting off for his first run, immediately after playing, or playing at, the ball.
(b) He hits down his wicket whilst lawfully making a second stroke for the purpose of guarding his wicket within the provisions of Law 34.1 (Out hit the ball twice).

Notes
(a) *Not out hit wicket*
A batsman is not out under this law should his wicket be broken in any of the ways referred to in 1(a) above if: (i) It occurs while he is in the act of running, other than in setting off for his first run immediately after playing at the ball, or while he is avoiding being run out or stumped.
(ii) The bowler after starting his run-up or bowling action does not deliver the ball; in which case the umpire shall immediately call and signal 'dead ball'.
(iii) It occurs whilst he is avoiding a throw-in at any time.

LAW 34
If the ball hits the striker's bat or body and the striker then hits it again with bat or body, he or she shall be regarded as having hit the ball twice. This may be done legally – but only to avoid being out bowled. If, in attempting to protect the wicket, the striker plays at the ball a second time, and in doing so, prevents a fielder taking a catch, he or she becomes subject to Law 37 (Obstructing the field).

As in Law 33 (Handling the ball), the striker should avoid hitting the ball twice in order to assist the fielding side to retrieve the ball – unless given the clear consent of at least one member of the fielding team and it is impossible to misconstrue the action and intention.

LAW 35
The striker may be out if he or she breaks the wicket during any action related to receiving or playing a fair delivery. This law applies to preparatory and evasive actions taken by the batter and to the start of a run immediately after playing at the ball. It does not apply to a batter who breaks his or her wicket after commencing a run. The words 'immediately after' in the Law should be interpreted as a very brief period of time between the completion of the action of playing at the ball and setting off for a run. If there is an obvious pause or hesitation after the stroke – as the striker assesses the possibilities of a run or a misfield occurs – then the subsequent breaking of the wicket would not be relevant to this Law.

LAW 36 LEG BEFORE WICKET
1 Out l.b.w.
The striker shall be out l.b.w. in the circumstances set out below:

(a) **Striker attempting to play the ball**
The striker shall be out l.b.w. if he first intercepts with any part of his person, dress or equipment a fair ball which would have hit the wicket and which has not previously touched his bat or a hand holding the bat, provided that:
  (i) The ball pitched, in a straight line between wicket and wicket or on the off side of the striker's wicker, or in the case of a ball intercepted full pitch would have pitched in a straight line between wicket and wicket, and
  (ii) the point of impact is in a straight line between wicket and wicket, even if above the level of the bails.

(b) **Striker making no attempt to play the ball**
The striker shall be out l.b.w. even if the ball is intercepted outside the line of the off stump, if, in the opinion of the umpire, he has made no genuine attempt to play the ball with his bat, but has intercepted the ball with some part of his person and if the circumstances set out in (a) above apply.

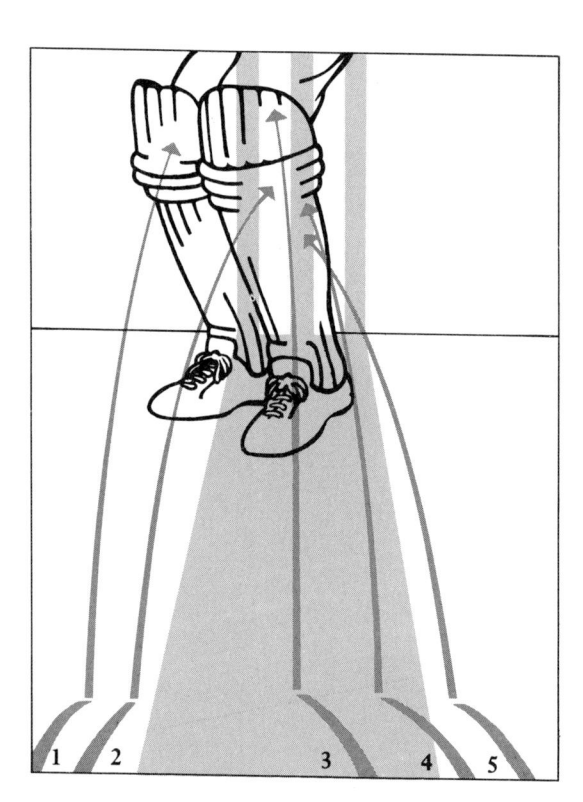

LAW 36
To justify a decision of out l.b.w. from a fair delivery an umpire must be satisfied that:
- the ball landed on the off side of the striker's wicket or in line from wicket to wicket or (if intercepted by the batter's person before landing) would have landed in line with the stumps
- the ball's first contact was with part of the striker's person and not the bat or the hand holding it
- the point of contact with the striker's person was in line from one wicket to the other, or (if there was no genuine attempt to hit the ball with the bat) was outside the off stump
- the ball would have bowled the wicket down.

If there is any reasonable doubt on any of the above points, the umpire's decision is: 'not out'.

Leg before wicket
1 Not out, unless the umpire considers that the striker made no genuine attempt to hit the ball with bat.
2 Probably out but the umpire may rule not out if he feels the ball was turning sharply enough to have missed the stumps altogether.
3 Probably out, but the umpire may rule not out if he feels that the ball would have passed over the top of the stumps.
4 Probably out, but the umpire may rule not out if he feels the ball was turning so sharply that it would have missed off stump.
5 Not out.

LAW 37 OBSTRUCTING THE FIELD
1 Wilful obstruction
Either batsman, on appeal, shall be out obstructing the field if he wilfully obstructs the opposite side by word or action.
2 Obstructing a ball from being caught
The striker, on appeal, shall be out should wilful obstruction by either batsman prevent a catch being made.

This shall apply even though the striker causes the obstruction in lawfully guarding his wicket under the provisions of Law 34. See Law 34.1 (Out hit the ball twice).

Notes
(a) Accidental obstruction
The umpires must decide whether the obstruction was wilful or not. The accidental interception of a throw-in by a batsman while running does not break this Law.
(b) Entry in score book
The correct entry in the score book when a batsman is given out under this Law is 'obstructing the field', and the bowler does not get credit for the wicket.

LAW 38 RUN OUT
1 Out run out
Either batsman shall be out run out if in running or at any time while the ball is in play - except in the circumstances described in Law 39 (Stumped) - he is out of his ground and his wicket is put down by the opposite side. If, however, a batsman in running makes good his ground he shall not be out run out, if he subsequently leaves his ground, in order to avoid injury, and the wicket is put down.
2 'No ball' called
If a no-ball has been called, the striker shall not be given run out unless he attempts to run.
3 Which batsman is out
If the batsmen have crossed in running, he who runs for the wicket which is put down shall be out; if they have not crossed, he who has left the wicket which is put down shall be out. If a batsman remains in his ground or returns to his ground and the other batsman joins him there, the latter shall be out if his wicket is put down.
4 Scoring of runs
If a batsman is run out, only that run which is being attempted shall not be scored. If however an injured striker himself is run out, no runs shall be scored. See Law 2.7 (Transgression of the Laws by an injured batsman or runner).

LAW 37
A striker is entitled to take every legitimate action to avoid being bowled. If, in avoiding dismissal, the striker causes a catch to be dropped he or she shall be given out 'obstructing the field'.

If either batter deliberately impedes or distracts an opposition fielder, he or she shall be given out 'obstructing the field'. Note that if the non-striker prevents the taking of a possible catch, it is the striker who shall be given out 'obstructing the field'.

LAW 38
Either batter may be run out if out of his or her ground in any situation whilst the ball is in play *except*:
- when the striker is receiving a delivery
- when the striker's bat or person is not grounded after making good his or her ground, as required by Law 29, because of the necessity to take evasive action whilst running to avoid being hurt by the ball or a collision.

In the case of the striker receiving a fair delivery and not attempting to run, he or she may not be run out by the wicketkeeper unless another fielder handles the ball first. The striker may only be run out off a no-ball if he or she attempts a run. If the batters are running, the one nearer to the wicket which is put down at the time shall be out. If both are in the same ground when the wicket is put down at the other end, the one who arrived second in the crease shall be out.

Notes
(a) Ball played on to opposite wicket
If the ball is played on to the opposite wicket neither batsman is liable to be run out unless the ball has been touched by a fieldsman before the wicket is broken.
(b) Entry in score book
The correct entry in the score book when the striker is given out under this Law is 'run out', and the bowler does not get credit for the wicket.

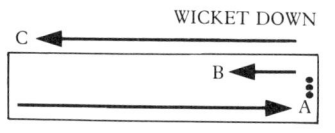

Injured batter B out even though runner C has made ground.

BATTER B OUT

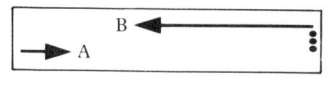

BATTER A OUT

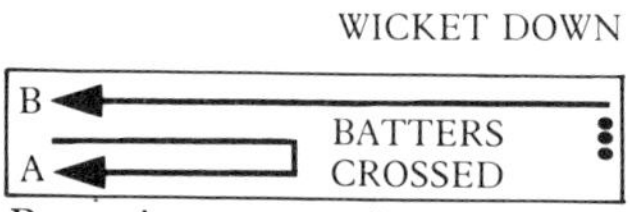

Batter A returns to the crease after B has made ground, therefore batter A out.

BATTER A OUT

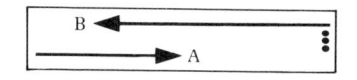

LAW 39 STUMPED
1 Out stumped
The striker shall be out stumped if, in receiving a ball, not being a no-ball, he is out of his ground otherwise than in attempting a run and the wicket is put down by the wicketkeeper without the intervention of another fieldsman.
2 Action by the wicketkeeper
The wicketkeeper may take the ball in front of the wicket in an attempt to stump the striker only if the ball has touched the bat or person of the striker.

Notes
(a) Ball rebounding from wicketkeeper's person
The striker may be out stumped if in the circumstances stated in 1 above, the wicket is broken by a ball rebounding from the wicketkeeper's person or equipment or is kicked or thrown by the wicketkeeper onto the wicket.

LAW 39
If the striker touches the ball with bat or person, the wicketkeeper may come in front of the wicket to stump the batter. This does not allow the wicketkeeper to impede the striker, who is trying to keep the ball out of his or her stumps – except when the wicketkeeper is trying to take a catch (see Law 37).

LAW 40 THE WICKETKEEPER
1 Position of wicketkeeper
The wicketkeeper shall remain wholly behind the wicket until a ball delivered by the bowler touches the bat or person of the striker, or passes the wicket, or until the striker attempts a run.

In the event of the wicketkeeper contravening this Law, the umpire at the striker's end shall call and signal 'no ball' at the instant of delivery or as soon as possible thereafter.

2 Restriction on actions of the wicketkeeper
If the wicketkeeper interferes with the striker's right to play the ball and to guard his wicket, the striker shall not be out, except under Laws 33 (Handled the ball), 34 (Hit the ball twice), 37 (Obstructing the field) and 38 (Run out).

3 Interference with the wicketkeeper by the striker
If in the legitimate defence of his wicket, the striker interferes with the wicketkeeper, he shall not be out, except as provided for in Law 37.2 (Obstructing a ball from being caught).

LAW 41 THE FIELDSMAN
1 Fielding the ball
The fieldsman may stop the ball with any part of his person but if he wilfully stops it otherwise, 5 runs shall be added to the run or runs already scored; if no run has been scored, 5 penalty runs shall be awarded. The run in progress shall count provided that the batsmen have crossed at the instant of the act. If the ball has been struck, the penalty shall be added to the score of the striker, but otherwise to the score of byes, leg byes, no-balls or wides as the case may be.

2 Limitation of on side fieldsmen
The number of on side fieldsmen behind the popping crease at the instant of the bowler's delivery shall not exceed two. In the event of infringement by the fielding side the umpire at the striker's end shall call and signal 'no ball' at the instant of delivery or as soon as possible thereafter.

3 Position of fieldsmen
Whilst the ball is in play and until the ball has made contact with the bat or the striker's person or has passed his bat, no fieldsman, other than the bowler, may stand on or have any part of his person extended over the pitch (measuring 22 yards (20.12 m × 10 ft (3.05 m)). In the event of a fieldsman contravening this Law, the umpire at the bowler's end shall call and signal 'no ball' at the instant of delivery or as soon as possible thereafter. See Law 40.1 (Position of wicketkeeper).

Notes
(a) Batsmen changing ends
The 5 runs referred to in 1 above are a penalty and the batsmen do not change ends solely by reason of this penalty.

LAW 40
The striker has the right to score from a delivery and to protect his or her wicket, without interference from the fielding side. If the wicketkeeper intrudes into the striker's area too soon, the umpire shall call 'no ball', thus ensuring that the striker shall not be out except by one of the four ways allowable from a no-ball.

LAW 41
This law is infringed if the ball is stopped or diverted by an article which is not part of a fielder's usual dress or equipment. It is also violated if the fielder uses a customary article of dress or equipment for an unconventional fielding purpose, e.g. stopping the ball with a cap or protective helmet not being worn at the time of the act of fielding.

The restrictions on the placement of the field do not extend to the bowler or wicketkeeper. The wicketkeeper's movements are governed by Laws 39 and 40.

The official width of a pitch does not vary but the playing surface widths often differ according to the types of artificial and natural surfaces provided. It is still a contravention of Law 41 if a fielder has any part of his or her body, including extended arms and hands, within 5 ft (1.52 m) of a line joining the centre of the 2 middle stumps.

LAW 42 UNFAIR PLAY
1 Responsibility of captains
The captains are responsible at all times for ensuring that play is conducted within the spirit of the game as well as within the Laws.
2 Responsibility of umpires
The umpires are the sole judges of fair and unfair play.
3 Intervention by the umpire
The umpires shall intervene without appeal by calling and signalling 'dead ball' in the case of unfair play, but should not otherwise interfere with the progress of the game except as required to do so by the Laws.
4 Lifting the seam
A player shall not lift the seam of the ball for any reason. Should this be done, the umpires shall change the ball for one of similar condition to that in use prior to the contravention. See Note (a).
5 Changing the condition of the ball
Any member of the fielding side may polish the ball provided that such polishing wastes no time and that no artificial substance is used. No-one shall rub the ball on the ground or use any artificial substance or take any other action to alter the condition of the ball.

In the event of a contravention of this Law, the umpires, after consultation, shall change the ball for one of similar condition to that in use prior to the contravention.

This Law does not prevent a member of the fielding side from drying a wet ball, or removing mud from the ball. See Note (b).
6 Incommoding the striker
An umpire is justified in intervening under this Law and shall call and signal 'dead ball' if, in his opinion, any player of the fielding side incommodes the striker by any noise or action while he is receiving a ball.
7 Obstruction of a batsman in running
It shall be considered unfair if any fieldsman wilfully obstructs a batsman in running. In these circumstances the umpire shall call and signal 'dead ball' and allow any completed runs and the run in progress or alternatively any boundary scored.
8 The bowling of fast short-pitched balls
The bowling of fast short-pitched balls is unfair if, in the opinion of the umpire at the bowler's end, it constitutes an attempt to intimidate the striker. See Note (d).

Umpires shall consider intimidation to be the deliberate bowling of fast short-pitched balls which by their length, height and direction are intended or likely to inflict physical injury on the striker. The relative skill of the striker shall also be taken into consideration.

In the event of such unfair bowling, the umpire

LAW 42
The captains have an obligation to see that their players observe the Laws and conduct themselves in a proper manner. Umpires do not have to wait for an objection before taking action against unfair play or misconduct. A series of steps to be taken by the umpires in specific circumstances are set out in the Law. In the case of players' misconduct there are usually special regulations in domestic rules of most controlling bodies.

Any noise or action likely to disadvantage the striker, or actually doing so, and any deliberate hindering of a batter in running is not permissible. In such instances the umpire shall call 'dead ball' to protect the batters from being out and, in the case of the hindered run, the batters – whether they have crossed or not – are allowed to complete that run.

The procedure for dealing with a bowler who takes an unnecessarily long time to bowl an over or who causes damage to the pitch is the same as that for intimidatory bowling, except for the call of 'no ball'. Umpires may apply the cautionary procedures for time wasting to players other than bowlers.

at the bowler's end shall adopt the following procedure:

(a) In the first instance the umpire shall call and signal 'no ball', caution the bowler and inform the other umpire, the captain of the fielding side and the batsmen of what has occurred.

(b) If this caution is ineffective, he shall repeat the above procedure and indicate to the bowler that this is a final warning.

(c) Both the above caution and final warning shall continue to apply even though the bowler may later change ends.

(d) Should the above warnings prove ineffective the umpire at the bowler's end shall:

> (i) At the first repetition call and signal 'no ball' and when the ball is dead direct the captain to take the bowler off forthwith and to complete the over with another bowler, provided that the bowler does not bowl two overs or part thereof consecutively. See Law 22.7 (Bowler incapacitated or suspended during an over).
>
> (ii) Not allow the bowler, thus taken off, to bowl again in the same innings.
>
> (iii) Report the occurrence to the captain of the batting side as soon as the players leave the field for an interval.
>
> (iv) Report the occurrence to the executive of the fielding side and to any governing body responsible for the match who shall take any further action which is considered to be appropriate against the bowler concerned.

9 The bowling of fast high full pitches

The bowling of fast high full pitches is unfair. See Note (e). In the event of such unfair bowling the umpire at the bowler's end shall adopt the procedures of caution, final warning, action against the bowler and reporting as set out in 8 above.

10 Time wasting

Any form of time wasting is unfair.

(a) In the event of the captain of the fielding side wasting time or allowing any member of his side to waste time, the umpire at the bowler's end shall adopt the following procedure:

> (i) In the first instance he shall caution the captain of the fielding side and inform the other umpire of what has occurred.
>
> (ii) If this caution is ineffective he shall repeat the above procedure and indicate to the captain that this is a final warning.
>
> (iii) The umpire shall report the occurrence to the captain of the batting side as soon as the players leave the field for an interval.
>
> (iv) Should the above procedure prove ineffective the umpire shall report the occurrence to the executive of the fielding side and to any governing body responsible for that match who shall take appropriate action against the captain and the players concerned.

(b) In the event of a bowler taking unnecessarily long to bowl an over the umpire at the bowler's end shall adopt the procedures, other than the calling of 'no ball', of caution, final warning, action against the bowler and reporting.

(c) In the event of a batsman wasting time (see Note (f)) other than in the manner described in Law 31 (Timed out), the umpire at the bowler's end shall adopt the following procedure:

(i) In the first instance he shall caution the batsman and inform the other umpire at once, and the captain of the batting side, as soon as the players leave the field for an interval, of what has occurred.

(ii) If this proves ineffective, he shall repeat the caution, indicate to the batsman that this is a final warning and inform the other umpire.

(iii) The umpire shall report the occurrence to both captains as soon as the players leave the field for an interval.

(iv) Should the above procedure prove ineffective, the umpire shall report the occurrence to the executive of the batting side and to any governing body responsible for that match who shall take appropriate action against the player concerned.

11 Players damaging the pitch

The umpires shall intervene and prevent players from causing damage to the pitch which may assist the bowlers of either side. See Note (c).

(a) In the event of any member of the fielding side damaging the pitch the umpire shall follow the procedure of caution, final warning and reporting as set out in 10(a) above.

(b) In the event of a bowler contravening this Law by running down the pitch after delivering the ball, the umpire at the bowler's end shall first caution the bowler. If this caution is ineffective the umpire shall adopt the procedures, other than the calling of 'no ball', of final warning, action against the bowler and reporting.

(c) In the event of a batsman damaging the pitch the umpire at the bowler's end shall follow the procedures of caution, final warning and reporting as set out in 10(c) above.

12 Batsman unfairly stealing a run

Any attempt by the batsman to steal a run during the bowler's run-up is unfair. Unless the bowler attempts to run out either batsman – see Law 24.4 (Bowler throwing at striker's wicket before delivery) and Law 24.5 (Bowler attempting to run out non-striker before delivery) – the umpire shall call and signal 'dead ball' as soon as the batsmen cross in any such attempt to run. The batsmen shall then return to their original wickets.

13 Players' conduct

In the event of a player failing to comply with the

instructions of an umpire, criticising his decisions by word or action, or showing dissent, or generally behaving in a manner which might bring the game into disrepute, the umpire concerned shall, in the first place report the matter to the other umpire and to the player's captain requesting the latter to take action. If this proves ineffective, the umpire shall report the incident as soon as possible to the executive of the player's team and to any governing body responsible for the match, who shall take any further action which is considered appropriate against the player or players concerned.

Notes
(a) The condition of the ball
Umpires shall make frequent and irregular inspections of the condition of the ball.
(b) Drying of a wet ball
A wet ball may be dried on a towel or with sawdust.
(c) Danger area
The danger area on the pitch, which must be protected from damage by a bowler, shall be regarded by the umpires as the area contained by an imaginary line 4 ft/1.22 m from the popping crease, and parallel to it, and within two imaginary and parallel lines drawn down the pitch from points on that line 1 ft/30.48 cm on either side of the middle stump.
(d) Fast short pitched balls
As a guide, a fast short pitched ball is one which pitches short and passes, or would have passed, above the shoulder height of the striker standing in a normal batting stance at the crease.
(e) The bowling of fast full pitches
The bowling of one fast, high full pitch shall be considered to be unfair if, in the opinion of the umpire, it is deliberate, bowled at the striker, and if it passes or would have passed above the shoulder height of the striker when standing in a normal batting stance at the crease.
(f) Time wasting by batsmen
Other than in exceptional circumstances, the batsman should always be ready to take strike when the bowler is ready to start his run-up.

Experimental Laws and Conditions 1985

Following discussions at the Cricket Council earlier in the year, the following Experimental Laws were agreed at the International Cricket Conference Meeting in July. The NCA Executive Committee at their Old Trafford meeting on 23rd October 1984 agreed to adopt the Experimental Laws for the 1985 cricket season, as set out on the enclosed paper considered by the Executive.

LAW 2.1 SUBSTITUTES
In normal circumstances, a substitute shall be allowed to field only for a player who satisfies the umpire that he has been injured or become ill during the match. However, in very exceptional circumstances, the umpires may use their discretion to allow a substitute for a player who has to leave the field or does not take the field for other wholly acceptable reasons, subject to consent being given by the opposing captain. If a player wishes to change his shirt, boots, etc. he may leave the field to do so (no changing on the field) but no substitute will be allowed.

LAW 2.6 RUNNER'S EQUIPMENT
Delete existing words and insert the following:
The player acting as runner for an injured batsman shall wear the same external clothing and external protective equipment as the injured batsman.

LAW 41.4 FIELDSMEN'S PROTECTIVE HELMETS
Protective helmets, when not in use by members of the fielding side, shall only be placed, if above the surface, on the ground behind the wicketkeeper; in the event of the ball striking the helmet whilst in this position, whether played or not, five penalty runs shall be awarded as laid down in Law 41.1 and note (a) of that Law.

The International Cricket Conference has agreed that this experimental law should be incorporated in the full Laws in 1985 but that will be subject to the approval of MCC at its Annual General Meeting. It is therefore accepted that subject to the acceptance of NCA this will be an experimental law in all cricket in the UK represented by NCA.

RECORDING OF NO BALLS AND WIDES
The International Cricket Conference has agreed that no balls and wides should be recorded against the bowler and the Secretary of the ICC is investigating a suitable method of recording this in the score book. Whilst this brings about a change in the method of scoring, it does not require an amendment to the Laws.

LAW 2.1
This experimental law is not as precise as the existing law in its wording but, in general, carries the same intention except that in no circumstance may a substitute be allowed for a player who, not being permitted to change his or her apparel on the field, leaves it for that purpose.

LAW 2.6
The runner need not wear similar apparel and protective equipment to that which is under the incapacitated batter's outer clothing or equipment. At some levels of cricket a protective helmet may not be available as well as the batter's. In such a case, the injured batter must not be forced to forego his or her protective equipment.

LAW 41.4
Usually only one protective fielding helmet is involved and, if not being worn, must be carried to a position behind the wicketkeeper at the change of ends. Helmets not being used for lengthy periods should be removed from the field. Immediately a ball in play makes contact with a helmet placed above ground, law 41.1 operates for the award of penalty runs as for a fielder wilfully stopping the ball other than with his or her person.

Index

action, bowling, 75-8, 104-6
action, bowling, inswinger, 94-6
appeals, Laws, 191
approach, bowling, 72-4
arm ball (drifting delivery off spinner), 87-8
attacking strokes, 66

back-foot movement, fault correction, 55-6, 58-9, 61-2
back-foot strokes, 38-65
   defensive shot, 43-4
   fault correction, 55-65
   leg glance, 45-6
backhand flip, 121
backing-up, batting, 68
backing-up, fielding, 125, 128, 130
backlift, fault correction, 30
bails, Laws, 174-5, 192
ball, size and condition of, Laws, 173, 200, 203
ball, stopping, 6, 7, 8, 125, 127, 130, 133
ball release, bowling, 80, 83, 86, 90, 95, 98
bats, size of, Laws, 174
batswing, fault correction, 33-4
batter's ground, Laws, 192
batting, attacking strokes, 66
   fault correction, 28-37, 55-65
   preparation for, 10-13
   running between wickets, 67-70
body position, bowling, 72-4, 76, 95, 104-5
body position, throwing, 117-18
'bosie', 92-3
boundaries, Laws, 183-4
'bowled', Laws, 193
bowling, basic action, 75-8, 104-6
   body position, see body position
   fault correction, 102-6
   unfair, Laws, 200-1
bowling crease, 100
bowling crease, Laws, 175

calling, batting, 67
captaincy, field setting, 159-62
   qualities and responsibilities, 157-8
   qualities and responsibilities, Laws, 200

catching, 6-7, 8
   close-to-the-wicket, 130
   fault correction, 133-4
   outfield, 125-6
'caught', Laws, 193-4
cessation of play, Laws, 180-2
children, cricket for, see juniors, cricket for
close-to-the-wicket field positions, 129
close-to-the-wicket fielding, 129-31
coaching, aims and functions, 1-5
   basis of leadership, 3
   communication, 2
   demonstrating skills, 3-4
   encouragement and punishment, 2, 4
   relationship with players, 1-2
   teaching styles, 1
communication, 2-3, 157
conduct of players, Laws, 202-3
Continuous cricket (game), 164-5
cover drive, back-foot, 40
cover drive, front-foot, 17
creases, Laws, 175-7
cross-bat strokes, back-foot, 47-54, 58-65
cross-bat strokes, front-foot, 26-7, 35-7
cross-over step, 116
crow hop, 117
cut, fault correction, 58-61
   late, 49-50
   square, 47-8

dead ball, Laws, 180, 187-8
declaration, Laws, 178
defensive shot, back-foot, 43-4
defensive shot, forward, 22-3
delivery, bowling, 72-4, 100
Diamond cricket (game), 165
drifting delivery, 87-8
driving, back-foot, 38-42, 55-7
driving, front-foot, 14-21, 29-34
drop step, 117
dry wicket, see pitch, condition of

equipment, batting, 10
   fielding, Laws, 204
   runners, Laws, 169, 204
   wicketkeeping, 108
exercise, see physical fitness

205

fault correction, back-foot strokes, 55-65
   bowling, 102-6
   catching, 133-4
   front-foot strokes, 28-37
   run-up, 102-3
   stopping, 133
   throwing, 132-3
field placements, 123, 159-62
fielding, fault correction, 132-4
   faults, 132
   Laws, 199
   steps, 116-17
   turns, 117-18
fitness, see physical fitness
flight, ball, 100-1
flipper, 93
follow-on, Laws, 178
follow-through, bowling, 73-4, 96, 106
follow-through, fault correction, 34
forward defensive shot, 22-3
front-foot drive, cover, 17
   off, 14-16
   on, 18-19
   straight, 18
front-foot movement, fault correction, 31, 35
front-foot strokes, 14-37
   fault correction, 28-37
   forward defensive shot, 22-3
full toss balls, 14, 17, 18, 26

games, for juniors, 163-6
good-length balls, 20, 22, 24, 101
'googly', 92-3
grip, batting, 11-12, 13, 29
   bowling, 79, 83, 86, 87, 90, 94, 97
   fault correction, 29
   throwing, 119
ground, condition of, 82, 84, 89, 93, 97, 157-8
ground, condition of, Laws, 170
group activities, check list, 8
guard, taking, 11

half-pitcher, 51
'handled the ball', Laws, 194
head and eyes position, fault correction, 32
'hit ball twice', Laws, 195
'hit wicket', Laws, 195
hitting, 6, 7, 8
hooking, 53-4
hooking, fault correction, 61-5

in-fielding, see close-to-the-wicket fielding
indoor cricket, 163

innings, Laws, 169, 177-8
inswinger, 94-6
intervals, Laws, 179-80
intimidation, Laws, 200-1

jump turn, 118
juniors, cricket for, 163-6

l.b.w., 100
l.b.w., Laws, 196
late cut, 49-50
leg byes, Laws, 190-1
leg cutter, 97-9
leg glance, back-foot, 45-6
leg glance, front-foot, 24-5
leg spinner, 77
   left-handed, 87
   right-handed, 89-91
length, bowling, 101
light, unfit, Laws, 170, 179
line, bowling, 101
long hop balls, 51
lost ball, Laws, 184

match results, Laws, 184-6
motivation, players, 1-2
movement, fielding, 116-17, 125, 127
movement, wicketkeeping, 109-12
moving out to drive, 20-1
muscular endurance and flexibility, 137, 139, 142-56

no ball, Laws, 187, 188-9, 204

'obstructing the field', Laws, 197
off cutter, 77, 82-3
off drive, back-foot, 38-9
off drive, front-foot, 14-16
off spinner, 77, 84-8
   drifting delivery, 87-8
   left-handed, 86
   overspun, 89
   undercut, 88
on drive, back-foot, 41-2
on drive, front-foot, 18-19
'out of ground', Laws, 192
outfield positions, 124
outfielding, attacking, 124-6
outfielding, defending, 127-8
outswinger, 77, 79-81
overhand throw, 119-20
overpitched balls, 14, 17, 18, 24, 26
overs, Laws, 180-1, 186-7

pace, 72, 82, 100
Pairs cricket (game), 166

physical fitness, 136-56
  standards, 141
  testing, 138-41
  training programmes, 141-56
pitch, condition of, 82, 84, 89, 93, 97, 157-8
  condition of, Laws, 170, 176-7, 203
  damaging the, Laws, 202
  Laws, 174
pivot turn, 117
play, cessation of, Laws, 180-2
  start of, Laws, 179
  unfair, Laws, 200-3
players' conduct, Laws, 202-3
poor light, Laws, 170, 179
protective equipment, Laws, 204
pull, 51-2
pull, fault correction, 61-5

release, bowling, 80, 83, 86, 90, 95, 98
retiring, Laws, 169
reverse turn, 117
'run out', Laws, 197-8
running between wickets, 67-70
running endurance, 139-40
run-up, 72-4, 102-3

scoring, Laws, 172-3, 182-3
short arm throw, 120
short-pitched balls, 38, 40, 41, 43, 45, 47, 49, 51, 101
shoulder and arm movement, fault correction, 32-3
side-arm throw, 120
skills, 6-8
  checklist, 7-8
  demonstrating, 4
slip fielding, 129, 159
speed endurance, 136-7, 142
speed of movement, 137, 139, 141
spin bowling, 84-93
square cut, 47-8
stance, batting, 12, 13, 29
  fault correction, 29-30
  fielding, 124, 127, 129
  wicketkeeping, 108-9
start of play, Laws, 179
stealing runs, Laws, 202
stopping, ball, 6, 7, 8, 125, 127, 130, 133
straight drive, back-foot, 40-1
straight drive, front-foot, 18
straight-bat strokes, back-foot, 38-46, 55-7
straight-bat strokes, front-foot, 14-23, 29-34
stride, bowling, 75-6, 94
'stumped', Laws, 198

stumping, 113
stumps, Laws, 174
substitutes, Laws, 168-9, 204
suspension of play, Laws, 170-1
sweep, 26-7, 35-7

tactics, bowling, 100-1
  captaincy, 157-60
  on winning the toss, 157-8
throwing, 7, 8, 119-22, 125, 128, 130, 132-3
throwing, body position, *see* body position
throws, direction of, 122
time wasting, Laws, 201-2, 203
'timed out', Laws, 193
top spinner (overspun off spinner), 88
top spinner, wrist spun, 93

umpires, Laws, 170-2, 200
underhand throw, 121
unfair bowling, Laws, 200-1
unfair play, Laws, 200-3

weather conditions, 157-8
weather conditions, Laws, 170-1, 179
wet wicket, *see* pitch, condition of
wicket, 'down', Laws, 192
wicketkeeper, Laws, 199
wicketkeeping, 108-14
wickets, Laws, 174, 192
wickets, running between, 67-70
wide balls, 40, 47, 49
wide balls, Laws, 187, 189-90, 204
wind direction, 84, 87, 89, 93, 94, 97
winning the toss, 157-8
winning the toss, Laws, 178
wrist-spun bowling, 89-93
wrist-spun top spinner, 93
'wrong 'un', 92-3